The Cuban Economy

Pitt Latin American Series

George Reid Andrews, General Editor

THE CUBAN ECONOMY

Edited by Archibald R. M. Ritter

University of Pittsburgh Press

Published by the University of Pittsburgh Press, Pittsburgh, Pa., 15260

Manufactured in the United States of America

Printed on acid-free paper

10 9 8 7 6 5 4 3 2 1

LIBRARY OF CONGRESS CATALOGING-IN-PUBLICATION DATA

Ritter, Archibald R. M.

The Cuban economy / Archibald R.M. Ritter.

p. cm. — (Pitt Latin American series)

Includes bibliographical references and index.

ISBN 0-8229-4218-6 (Cloth : alk. paper)

1. Cuba—Economic conditions—1990– I. Title. II. Series.

HC152.5.R57 2004

330.97291—dc22

2003021092

This book is dedicated to all those responsible for the Cuban economy, that they may succeed in achieving sustained prosperity for their country with both equity and liberty.

Contents

Figures

Tables

Acknowledgments

The idea for this book arose in September 1999, at a conference at Carleton University in Ottawa, Canada. The conference brought together a wide range of experts on the Cuban economy, including Cuban scholars from the University of Havana, as well as those residing in Chile, Canada, Venezuela, and elsewhere. Scholars from the United Nations, and universities in the United States, Canada, and Britain also participated. The presentations at that conference, and the lively discussion they generated, formed the seeds for the essays in this volume. I only regret that not all participants could be represented here.

I would like to express my gratitude to a number of organizations that supported the work that generated this book. The Canadian International Development Agency financed a five-year collaborative program between the University of Havana and Carleton University and was a major supporter of the 1999 conference. The Ford Foundation also provided valuable financial support for the conference. The Canadian Foundation for the Americas (FOCAL) also provided support in kind, as well as a subsidy for the publication of this book, for which we are especially grateful. Finally, I wish to thank Carleton University and the University of Havana for their support.

PART I

Economic Performance and the Process of Reform

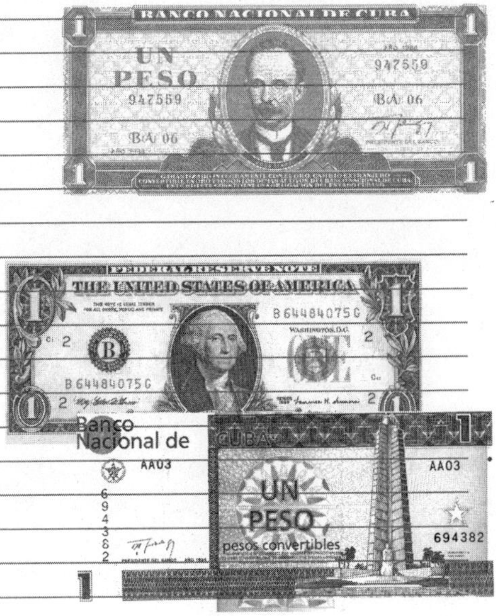

CHAPTER 1

The Cuban Economy in the Twenty-first Century
Recuperation or Relapse?

Archibald R. M. Ritter

Facing a deep economic crisis of meltdown dimension in the first half of the 1990s, Cuba's leadership modified its basic development strategy with a variety of institutional and policy innovations. By 1995 the Cuban economy had begun to recover, although by 2003 it still had not achieved the precrisis levels of 1990 or 1985. The economy was also hurt by the impact of the international economic slowdown of 2001–2, which was even further intensified by the aftermath of the 11 September 2001 terrorist attack in New York.

Since 1994 Cuba's economic performance has been mixed, with some positive results and some continuing problems. Certain policy and institutional innovations seemed to be functioning well at this time, while others did not. Key elements of the crisis have been resolved effectively, notably the fiscal crisis and the suppressed inflation that resulted from the "monetizing" of the fiscal deficit from 1990 to 1993. Sectors of the economy have performed admirably, notably tourism, nickel, petroleum extraction, and electricity generation. Food production and availability and levels of investment have improved somewhat, but further significant improvement is possible and desirable. However, there are important economic problems that have not been handled effectively: the dual monetary and exchange rate system; the failure to diversify and expand merchandise exports; the inability to revive the sugar sector, leading to the shock therapy of August 2002; the mismanagement of the policy environment for the microenterprise sector; the reduction in the real value of budgetary revenues devoted to education, health, and public services, generally leading to major reductions in real income levels for people working in these sectors; and the inability to significantly recover the material standard of living that existed prior to 1985.

Are Cuba's economic policy initiatives of the 1990s functioning effectively now in the 2000s in order to achieve an enduring recovery while maintaining previous advances in social areas? Has a solid foundation for sustainable recovery with equity for the coming decade now been established in Cuba? Are further types of policy innovations or changes necessary in Cuba to achieve sustainable growth with equity?

Cuba's Economic Crisis and Policy Response in the 1990s

The origins and nature of Cuba's economic crisis and its response to the crisis are well known. The most important cause of the crisis was the decline in foreign exchange receipts—by around 75 percent from 1990 to 1993—resulting from the termination of the hidden subsidization inherent in the special trade and aid relationship with the former Soviet Union and the countries of Eastern Europe. However, the impact of the Soviet Union's collapse and the end of the special relationship with the Soviet bloc actually followed a five-year period of worsening economic difficulties from about 1985 to 1990.

The generosity of the former Soviet Union toward Cuba in the 1970s and 1980s has seldom been paralleled in history. The assistance was obscured from general public view and was not acknowledged by the Cuban government. Cuban officials and analysts argued that the special arrangements with the Soviet Union constituted not aid but the fair exchange of commodities (Rodriguez 1990). The hidden subsidization of the Cuban economy occurred in part through the pricing of merchandise imports and exports. The USSR paid a ruble price for its sugar and nickel imports from Cuba that was a multiple of the prevailing world price at official exchange rates for many years. At the same time, Cuba paid a price that was well below the prevailing market price for its petroleum imports from the USSR. Furthermore, Cuba engaged in the re-export of both sugar and petroleum in its trade with the USSR, capturing significant middleman profits for some years. (Cuba purchased sugar from other countries at the low world price and resold it to the USSR at a higher price. Cuba also purchased petroleum from the USSR at a lower price and re-exported it to other countries in the region at the prevailing higher world price.) How significant was this type of subsidization? Quantitative estimates place it at 23–36 percent of national income in the 1980–87 period (Ritter 1990).

On top of the subsidization through the pricing of traded goods was the buildup of a bilateral debt to the USSR amounting to about U.S.$23.5 billion by 1990 (Ritter 1990). This debt reflected the recurring trade deficits of Cuba with the USSR as well as the capital account credits provided by the USSR. This debt apparently will never be repaid. There were also additional bilateral debts with some of Cuba's Eastern European trading partners. Furthermore, there were military credits of an indeterminate magnitude as well as the rental payments for military facilities such as the Lourdes radar base, plus the expenditures of USSR military procurement and personnel in Cuba.

Cuba's ostensible prosperity of 1975–85 was therefore due in part to Soviet subsidization and was unsustainable. As soon as the Soviet Union indicated that it was going to move toward a market determination of its exchange rate and market determined prices for its trade, it was clear the subsidization would end. This would be reflected immediately in a large reduction in the purchasing power for Cuba's exports. The consequent reduction of imports of intermediate products, energy, raw materials, foodstuffs, replacement parts, machinery, and equipment would then produce a major economic contraction. This is in fact what happened from 1989 to 1994.

Four additional factors contributed to the crisis. First was the fragility of Cuba's economic structure and its lack of export diversification. Cuba's export structure had evolved little in the years since 1959, but it was still dependent on a few primary commodities, including sugar, nickel, tobacco, and other agricultural products.

Second was Cuba's lack of access to credits from foreign sources at reasonable cost. In the 1980s Cuba built up a significant convertible currency debt. Cuba's ratio of debt to exports (of goods and services) was close to double that for Latin America as a whole. The debt service burden (interest as a percentage of exports of goods and services) was 27.1 percent, close to the 28.0 percent level for all of Latin America in 1988 (Ritter 1990, 134). When Cuba declared a moratorium on interest and principal payments, many foreign lenders halted new lending. Nor was Cuba a member of some of the major international institutions such as the International Monetary Fund, World Bank, Inter-American Development Bank, or Caribbean Development Bank that could have provided financial support.

Third was the central planning system, which continued to be problematic. Cuba's economic management was characterized by general demarketization (though with a very small self-employment sector and larger underground economy), bureaucratization, and excessive centralization. These characteristics resulted in pervasive micro-irrationalities, the absence of a rational structure of prices such that meaningful cost accounting could exist, general economic paralysis, and the suppression of entrepreneurship. Efforts such as the Rectification Process adopted in 1986 were not successful in improving the planning system. Related to this were a variety of continuing policy pathologies such as the absence of a meaningful and unified exchange rate and extreme trade protectionism through bureaucratic control of imports.

Fourth was a hardening of the U.S. trade embargo with the imposition of the "Toricelli" bill in 1992, which further strengthened obstacles to Cuban exports.

These four factors contributed to a multidimensional set of crises rooted in the reduction of the available foreign exchange and the capacity to purchase imports. The economy went into a process of contraction from 1989 to 1993. The asphyxiation from reduced foreign exchange for the purchase of imported energy, raw materials, intermediate products, capital goods, and foodstuffs generated a macroeconomic crisis, with an approximate 40 percent decline in output per person by 1993. It also produced an energy crisis, with petroleum imports declining from 13 million metric tons in 1989 to 5.8 million in 1992 (EIU 1992, 23.) Because imports accounted for 93 percent of total petroleum supplies in 1990, the result was a severe reduction in transportation services and the generation of electricity, with consequent power blackouts and shutdowns of industry. Third was a food crisis, with reduced domestic food production resulting from reduced fertilizer, energy, and replacement part imports, as well as reduced food imports. Limited availability of food led to inadequate nutrition by 1992, as reflected in the incidence of neuropathy leading to blindness—temporary, thankfully—of some twenty-five thousand to forty thousand persons.

There was also a collapse of savings, which reached a low of 2.6 percent of gross domestic product (GDP) in 1993, and gross investment, which also hit a low of 5.2 percent in 1994. The limited replacement investment and postponed maintenance and repairs together with cannibalization of equipment in some sectors all contributed to an accelerated deterioration of the entire capital stock. Levels of net investment were likely negative—that is, the capital stock was likely deteriorating more rapidly than it could be replaced.

The contraction of economic activity led to reduced tax revenues, rising fiscal deficits, accelerated money creation, and an escalation of inflationary pressures. The result was a monetary crisis in which the real purchasing power of the Cuban peso declined precipitously, leading to a burgeoning demand for U.S. dollars (for store-of-value and medium-of-exchange purposes) and a subsequent process of dollarization of the economy. The rapid real inflation resulted in large reductions in the real purchasing power of budgets of the education, public health, and public sector generally as well as in the peso incomes of employees in these activities. In consequence, there was intense pressure on the provision of social services. Citizens responded to the decline in their standard of living by pursuing self-employment activities, most of which were illegal at the time. They resorted to illegal or black-market activities and exchanges and to finding all and any means to acquiring the U.S. dollars vital for survival.

In the face of this crisis and the need for foreign exchange, Cuba's leadership announced the "Special Period in Time of Peace," an era that lasted from 1990 to 2003, in which tough policies were necessary to deal with difficult circumstances. The leadership modified the development strategy with a number of innovations designed for the new international context within which Cuba had to survive. Between 1993 and 1996, the government of Cuba implemented a variety of institutional reforms, including legalizing the holding of U.S. currency; liberalizing remittance payments from relatives abroad; legalizing self-employment in some low-technology areas; reestablishing agricultural markets; liberalizing the foreign investment law; converting state farms to quasi-cooperatives; establishing four export processing zones; reinvigorating small-holder farming; and reorganizing the state enterprise system and ministries as well as some banking reforms.

The policy reforms also included a reestablishment of a reasonable fiscal balance, with consequent reductions in money creation and inflationary pressures, reduced subsidies to enterprises, changes in the structure of the taxation system, and reductions in military expenditures. By 1996 most of the economic reforms were in place. A few additional reforms were introduced after 1998, such as administrative reforms for state enterprises, but the principal priority seemed to be assimilating the changes already in place.

In his challenging essay on long-term reform processes in Cuba (in this volume), Carmelo Mesa-Lago presents evidence supporting the hypothesis that the introduction of reforms slowed down in about 1996. This was in part because the good results of the 1993–95 reforms led the revolutionary leadership to conclude that additional reforms were unnecessary and could in fact be destabilizing for the regime.

Economic Performance during the Special Period: The External Sector

The various reforms adopted in the 1993–96 period arrested Cuba's economic meltdown. Many of Cuba's key economic indicators began to improve after 1994. This was true for foreign exchange earnings, output levels, petroleum extraction and energy availability, food production and availability, tax revenues and the fiscal balance, monetary indicators, and labor force utilization. The central constraint on economic performance, however, continued to be the availability of foreign exchange for purchasing imported capital goods, petroleum, intermediate inputs, and consumer products, especially food. Indeed, the acquisition of foreign exchange is of such overriding importance that a redesign of Cuba's basic development strategy was necessary in the new context of the "Special Period."

Merchandise exports were basically stagnant in the 1990s. The volume of Cuban exports in 2000 was 68.6 percent of the 1989 level, and the purchasing power of those exports dropped to 34.2 percent of the 1989 level (Naciones Unidas 2001b, 27). The deficit in merchandise trade expanded, reaching U.S.$3.2 billion by 2000 (see table

1.1). Sugar exports have been particularly disappointing. The cause seems to be intractable production problems in agricultural and milling processes, as explained by Brian Pollitt in this volume. The harvests of 2001 and 2002 totaled 3.5 and 3.2 million tons, among the lowest yields of the past decade—indeed, of the past fifty years. The policy response of the Cuban government to this situation in mid-2002 was a form of shock therapy applied yet again to the sector, namely the shutdown of 70 of 156 sugar mills, a culmination of the long-term failure to manage the sector effectively. In effect, Cuba's main cash cow generating the necessary foreign exchange for the country had been starved to death slowly through underinvestment.

On the other hand, exports of nickel have increased, reaching over 27 percent of total exports in 1999. This is due in large part to production-enhancing investments in a joint venture with Canadian enterprise Sherritt International. Cigar exports also expanded prior to 2000, accounting for 11.8 percent of total exports in 1999. On the other hand, despite high initial expectations, biotechnological exports did not perform well and accounted for only 1.8 percent of total merchandise exports in 1999 (Naciones Unidas 2001b, 28).

Cuba's most noteworthy success in its international economic interaction has been the expansion of international tourism. Recent estimates of gross tourism revenues for 2000 are U.S.$1.9 billion. Family remittances from the Cuban diaspora are also a

Table 1.1 Balance of Payments, 1991–2001
(in Millions of U.S. Dollars)

	1991	1992	1993	1994	1995	1996	1997	1998	1999	2000	2001
Exports											
Total	3,563	2,522	1,968	2,542	2,926	3,707	3,873	4,085	4,288	4,807	4,893
Goods	2,980	1,779	1,137	1,381	1,507	1,866	1,819	1,512	1,456	1,692	
Services	584	742	832	1,160	1,419	1,841	2,054	2,572	2,832	3,115	
Imports											
Total	4,702	2,737	2,339	2,849	3,565	4,125	4,619	4,841	5,003	5,587	5,651
Goods	4,234	2,315	1,984	2,353	2,883	3,569	3,987	4,181	4,323	4,816	
Services	468	422	355	497	683	556	632	660	680	771	
Commercial balance	–1,138	–215	–371	–308	–639	–419	–746	–757	–715	–780	–758
Current transfers											
Total	18	43	263	470	646	744	792	813	828	850	750
Remittances					537	630	670	690	700	720	
Factor services, net	–334	–248	–264	–423	–525	–493	–483	–449	–569	–670	–750
Capital account											
Total	1,421	419	356	262	596	174	457	409	486	640	770
of which, foreign investment			54	563	5	82	442	207	205		

Sources: Naciones Unidas (2001b, 27, 35; 2001c).

significant source of foreign exchange. While it is difficult to accurately calculate remittances, they were estimated to be U.S.$720 million in 2000.

Cuba established four export processing zones in 1997 as a mechanism for expanding exports. So far their role has not been particularly prominent and they have almost dropped from view. Larry Willmore's analysis in this volume of Cuba's export processing zones concludes that despite generous tax incentives and a well-educated labor force, the zones will likely continue to be of limited significance in expanding exports due to high labor and production costs in real terms relative to other locations.

Foreign Direct Investment (FDI) in the form of joint ventures with state enterprises has been of major importance to Cuba. There is some ambiguity about the value of FDI inflows, and Jorge Pérez-López cites a variety of estimates. One of the more reliable estimates of the FDI inflow is that of the United Nations Economic Commission for Latin America and the Caribbean, which has placed it at U.S.$1.6 billion from 1993 to 1999. The principal sources and sectors for foreign investment include Canada in nickel, petroleum extraction, electricity generation, brewing, and paper; Spain in tourism and cigars; Chile in citric fruit; and Italy in telephone communications.

While foreign investment may not seem large in terms of overall volume, it has been the vehicle for valuable transfers of technology. In some cases, these have been environmentally friendly and energy efficient, particularly in comparison to vintage Soviet technology. For example, new technologies introduced by foreign partners—mainly Sherritt International—have dramatically increased petroleum extraction. Sherritt also introduced technologies for generating electricity using the natural gas previously flared, or wasted, and has invested in a gas pipeline from Varadero to Havana. Foreign enterprises have also introduced the latest management systems, notably in the tourism sector. Finally, foreign enterprises in joint venture arrangements often have the marketing expertise, networks, and muscle to facilitate market access for Cuban products. In the tourism sector, for example, foreign hotel chains and tour operators promote Cuban destinations. Habanos S.A., a cigar marketing joint venture that is 50 percent owned by Altidis, a Spanish-French firm that has a near-monopoly of cigar sales in Europe, is an instance in which Cuba is relying on a foreign firm's marketing strength to expand revenues from exports.

Unfortunately, outflows of profits and interest payments on debt have reached high levels. These outflows made up a large proportion of the U.S.$670 million deficit in factor service payments in 2000 (table 1.1). Cuba may have entered a situation in which profit remittances by foreign firms continually exceed new direct foreign investment. From 1994 to 1999, for example, the burden of interest payments plus profit repatriation of U.S.$2,942 million (the major components of the factor service deficit) exceeded the accumulated investment inflow of U.S.$1,504 million (table 1.1).

Due to the moratorium on debt servicing declared in 1985, Cuba has had to endure its economic crisis of the 1990s without significant access to the major sources of international credit. Cuba is not a member of the international financial institutions such as the International Monetary Fund, the World Bank, and the Inter-American Development Bank. However, when it rejoins these it will have significant volumes of credit available at zero conditionality—that is, with no external conditions for its use. Additional credit then would also be available from these institutions, but levels of conditionality would come into operation. Cuba also has had some limited access to other sources of credit, such as commercial banks, suppliers, and official lending agencies. But it has also found it necessary to borrow short term to finance export activities such as sugar as well as to purchase imports with high-interest loans from lenders such as Sherritt International.

The relative lack of access to international credit allowed for only a limited cushioning of the shortage of foreign exchange in the 1992–98 period. There was no possibility of jump-starting the economy with external financial support for the importation of the necessary inputs and capital goods to permit a more rapid macroeconomic turnaround in the style of the Czech Republic, Poland, Slovakia, Slovenia, Estonia, or Hungary. Cuba has had to implement a harsh process of structural adjustment that has led to serious reductions of real living standards, particularly for people in the peso economy, such as pensioners, employees in state enterprises, and workers in education, medicine, and the public service.

These problems are exacerbated by Cuba's debt service problem. Cuba's total convertible currency debt (excluding debt to successor states of the former Soviet Union) stood at U.S.$11 billion in 2000 (Naciones Unidas 2001b, 36). Its debt-to-export ratio continued to be higher than the Latin American average. In 1998 this ratio was 289 percent compared to 224 percent for the region (UNECLAC 2000, 107). Unfortunately, despite years of discussions with the Paris Club (an association of its governmental creditors) Cuba has not yet resolved this impasse. The debt to Russia is also significant, amounting perhaps to U.S.$27 billion. However, the estimation of the value of the debt is contentious. Russia is a member of the Ad Hoc Group of Creditor Countries in the Paris Club regarding Cuba's debt. Russia expects to receive some partial payment from Cuba for its large bilateral debt. On the other hand, it appears that Cuba considers this debt to now be zero.[1]

Table 1.2 Principal Economic Indicators, 1990–2001

	1990	1991	1992	1993	1994	1995	1996	1997	1998	1999	2000	2001
GDP per capita (1989 = 100.0)	96.0	86.1	77.1	66.1	66.4	67.9	72.8	74.3	75.0	79.3	83.3	85.6
GDP per capita growth rate (%)	–4.0	–10.3	–10.5	–14.2	+0.4	2.2	7.3	2.1	0.9	5.8	5.1	2.7
Gross investment as % of GDP	24.8	14.0	6.5	6.4	5.2	7.0	7.1	7.7	7.9	7.9	7.7	7.5
National savings as % of GDP	12.7	5.4	2.8	2.6	4.6	5.6	6.3	5.6	6.4			
Unemployment	7.3	7.7	6.1	6.2	6.7	7.9	7.6	7.0	6.6	6.0	5.8	4.5
Underemployment	10.3	19.0	24.2	34.0	32.5	32.1	26.6	25.7	25.1			
Sugar harvest (million tons)	8.4	7.2	7.2	4.2	4.0	3.3	4.3	4.1	3.2	3.7	3.9	3.5
Gross external debt												
U.S. dollars (billions)	7.0	8.0	10.0	8.8	9.1	10.5	10.5	10.1	11.2	11.1	11.0	11.1
% of total exports	118	225	397	492	358	360	295	267	289	259	229	
Exchange rate (pesos/U.S. dollars)												
Official	1.0	1.0	1.0	1.0	1.0	1.0	1.0	1.0	1.0	1.0	1.0	1.0
Quasi–official	7.0	20.0	35.0	78.0	95.0	32.1	19.2	23.0	21.0	20.0	21.0	22.0

Sources: Naciones Unidas (2000a, 253; 2001a, 288–91; 2001b, 13, 44; 2001c).

Economic Performance: The Domestic Economy

During the 1995–2000 period, the improvement in the foreign exchange earnings and receipts from tourism, family remittances, and direct foreign investment ignited economic growth. As a result, Cuba's growth was positive in the 1996–2000 period, averaging 3.9 percent in per capita terms (see table 1.2). By 2000, GDP per capita had recovered significantly, although it was still about 17 percent below the 1989 level. To the casual observer, there were a variety of signs of economic recovery by 2001, such as fewer electrical blackouts, increased public and automotive traffic, fewer bicycles on the street, a major expansion of dollar store retailing, and the accelerated restoration of Old Havana.

Real Levels of Income

It is difficult to estimate accurately the real incomes of Cuban citizens during the 1990s. This is because there is no reasonable measure of true inflation—that is, an accurate and transparent consumer price index that allows for the changing mix of consumer purchases from the rationing system, the dollar stores, the agricultural markets, and the self-employment sector, not to mention the pervasive underground economy. The quantity of goods and services available through the low-priced rationing system has declined sharply. Products that were previously rationed are now often available only for U.S. dollars in dollar stores, where prices are at world levels plus a 140 percent markup (an implicit sales tax). As people spend a growing proportion of their income in dollar stores, the authentic purchasing power of regular incomes has diminished.

Despite the measurement difficulties, ECLAC analysts estimated that the average monthly salary in *real* terms in 1998 was 54.8 percent of the level in 1989, a decline of over 45 percent. However, this reduction occurred in three stages: first a 75 percent reduction from 1989 to 1993, then a significant recovery in 1995–96, followed by stability from 1996 to 1998. Those without access to U.S. dollars have experienced a drastic decline in real income. For this reason, professionals such as doctors, public officials, state employees, and pensioners are desperate to earn additional income by driving their family cars as taxis, becoming self-employed, or finding income supplements. The broad range of income supplements includes theft and/or the illegal sale of all varieties of products within the state sector but under the control of individuals in strategic positions; gratuities, fees, or income supplements for service providers within the state sector, such as manicurists, estheticians, and doctors; reselling of various products purchased for pesos in order to acquire dollars, such as selling the newspaper *Granma* for U.S. dollars; selling one's services in the underground economy rather than through official channels—for example, private teachers, plumbers, electricians, carpenters, construction workers, auto mechanics, taxi drivers, etc.; illegal activities such as *jineterismo,* or quasi-prostitution, such as occurred during the early 1990s. Sharing dollar earnings or remittance receipts regularly occurs within families as well. The multigenerational family undoubtedly plays an important role in ensuring that those with access to dollars share them with others, especially with retired persons receiving pensions of approximately 90 to 120 pesos per month. Without income sharing and extralegal sources of income such as those mentioned above, many people would be destitute.

Education and Social Services

Despite reductions in per capita income, Cuba has done a good job of maintaining the levels of education and social services reached in the relatively prosperous 1970s and 1980s. Most major indicators of health and educational coverage have improved or at least have not deteriorated. The exception is higher education, where enrollment declined from 242,400 in 1990/91 to 102,600 in 1998/99 (Naciones Unidas 2000a, table A62). This was partly because of a decision to adjust for a previous oversupply of some types of professionals and partly because of the reduced incentive for young people to prepare themselves for low-paying peso-sector professional careers.

Official budgetary figures for health and education suggest that spending in pesos has been more or less maintained in these areas. However, these figures do not take into consideration the real level of inflation, which has reduced the actual value of peso budgetary allotments to these sectors. As a result, the real incomes of teachers, professors, doctors, nurses, and other health and education workers, as well as maintenance of schools and hospitals, and the availability of supplies have been seriously reduced. Anecdotal evidence suggests that the quality of education and health services has suffered in consequence.

Petroleum Extraction and Food Production

Perhaps the most successful areas of the domestic economy have been petroleum extraction and food production, the latter outlined by William Messina Jr. in this volume. Although there has not been a full recuperation to previous levels of food availability, food production has benefited from institutional changes, particularly the establishment of agricultural markets.

As mentioned, the increase in petroleum production is principally a result of the joint venture with Sherritt International. Domestic petroleum extraction now generates about 70 percent of Cuba's electricity, assisted by previously flared natural gas in the Varadero area.

Taxation and Fiscal Policy

Another successful area of reform has been in taxation, which has restored the fiscal foundation for social programs and the functioning of the state apparatus. The fiscal situation in the early 1990s was in crisis, as the deficit escalated to 36 percent of GDP in 1993. This deficit was largely financed by money creation, leading to rapid though suppressed inflation. The result was a devaluation of the peso in the parallel market to about 150 pesos per U.S. dollar in 1994 and a flight to the U.S. dollar as a haven for savings. A series of difficult tax reforms involving a number of tax increases reduced the deficit to about 2 percent of GDP by 1998 and to a degree restored the value of the peso and confidence in it. The peso has not returned to the parallel market value it maintained during the 1980s, but it remained at 20 to 22 pesos per U.S. dollar until late 2001, when it declined in value to 26 pesos per U.S. dollar.

Continuing Economic Challenges

Increasing Investment and Domestic Savings

Cuba continues to face a number of ongoing challenges that will require appropriate reforms in order to construct a foundation for an enduring economic recovery.

One of the more pressing challenges is to raise levels of domestic savings and investment. According to the United Nations Economic Commission for Latin America and the Caribbean (UNECLAC), gross investment levels collapsed by 87 percent from 1989 to 1993 (1997, 352). By 1998 Cuba's gross investment as a percentage of GDP was 7.9 percent, compared with 21.1 percent for Latin America and the Caribbean for the same year (Naciones Unidas 2001b, 130, 291). Taking depreciation into account, the real contraction of the capital stock must have been particularly serious in these years due to lack of maintenance, cannibalization of machinery and equipment, and the accelerated decay that accompanies industrial shutdowns and lack of use. A chief source of low investment levels is a low level of national saving. In 1998 national savings amounted to only 6.4 percent of GDP, compared to 20.2 percent for all of Latin America and the Caribbean (83, 291).

Investment has recovered somewhat since 1994, but the recovery has been slow and is concentrated in certain sectors, notably tourism. The magnitude of the task of renovation, reconstruction, and re-equipment in areas such as housing, urban infrastructure, public buildings, and the stock of vehicles is apparent even to the casual observer. Moreover, much of the old equipment from the Soviet bloc is obsolete, prodigious in its use of resources, environmentally unfriendly, and internationally uncompetitive. Eventually Cuba's investment effort will have to increase so that economic growth can become sustained, broad-based, and environmentally sound, and so that real incomes and social programs can recover.

Institutional Reform

A second challenge is Cuba's need to improve the structure and functioning of economic institutions. One part of this is to reform its state enterprise sector to make the institutions more effective and efficient. In a major study of the Cuban economy published in 1997, United Nations analysts concluded that, "Like other socialist countries of Eastern Europe, the Cuban development model was already becoming inoperative prior to the 1989 collapse" (UNECLAC 1997, 120). Cuba is currently trying to overcome weaknesses in its centralized system of economic management by decentralizing enterprise financing, decision making, and responsibility. Whether it will succeed this time, after disappointing results with earlier attempts, remains to be seen.

A further challenge is how to manage micro- and small-scale enterprise. Self-employment in nonprofessional activities was legalized in September 1993. It has been valuable for Cuba, generating employment, raising tax revenues, providing valuable goods and services, utilizing domestic resources, contributing to foreign exchange earnings, and furthering domestic entrepreneurship. However, higher incomes in some areas of the self-employment sector and ideological objections to such small-scale "capitalism" have led the government to introduce a tough regulatory environment and an onerous tax regime, both designed to reduce incomes and restrict growth in the microenterprise sector.

Perhaps the simplest but most lethal type of control placed on microenterprise is the refusal to grant permits to enterprises so that the sector is placed in a situation of steady contraction. Moreover, the taxation regime for microenterprise can lead to marginal tax rates in excess of 100 percent in some circumstances. It also is a good deal more burdensome than the tax regime for foreign enterprises operating in Cuba as joint ventures with state enterprises, as argued by Archibald Ritter in this volume. Many of the self-employed view these policy measures as an attempt to not contain but asphyxiate them.

The tax and regulatory measures have had negative consequences for Cuba, such as the promotion of the underground economy and theft from the state sector. An appropriate regulatory environment for small enterprise could increase the benefits and reduce the negative effects in this sector. Opening self-employment to all who wish to enter would increase competition and increase supplies of goods and services, thereby lowering prices and normalizing incomes.

Perhaps the most serious weakness of the existing microenterprise regulatory and tax regimen arises from the prohibition of professional self-employment in micro-, small-, and medium-scale enterprises. The absence of small-scale enterprise in professional areas, business services, scientific and engineering services, computer services, management and consulting services, and some more innovative high-tech manufacturing areas is a severe liability for the Cuban economy. These activities have expanded rapidly in other countries. They employ large numbers of productive and highly remunerated employers and workers. They provide vital specialized services mainly to other private and public enterprises in the economy and to public, nongovernmental and private institutions of all types. They operate efficiently in that they provide their specialized services to many clients in contrast to comparable in-house specialists who provide services only to their specific employers. Expanding networks of specialist professional firms and larger enterprises also facilitate the diffusion of new technologies and have contributed to general productivity improvement. They permit rapid and flexible responses to new production possibilities and dislocations, as anyone with a perception of a problem and a business opportunity can move immediately into a new area without painful and time-consuming bureaucratic authorizations.

The absence of small- and medium-scale professional enterprises in Cuba means that many of the above-mentioned advantages they can impart to the economy are lost. While there has been an attempt in Cuba to establish state enterprises in some of these professional service areas, such state enterprises are generally bureaucratic, cumbersome, excessively large, and subject to uninformed external authority. All of this damages their agility, their motivation to take risks and to strive mightily, and their capability to move innovatively.

A further challenge of an institutional and macroeconomic or financial character is the maintenance of Cuba's social security system, as analyzed by María Cristina Sabourin Jovel in this volume. In view of the general aging of the population of Cuba—similar to many high-income countries—novel approaches may be necessary in order to ensure the long-term financial viability of the system.

"Dollarization" and "De-Dollarization"

A third challenge for Cuba is addressing the semi-official dollarization and the monetary/institutional dualism that currently shape Cuban society and the economy. The place of the U.S. dollar has steadily strengthened and expanded since its legalization in 1993. The Cuban economy relies heavily on inflows of U.S. dollars from family remittances (mainly from the United States), tourism, and tourist spending. The government acquires U.S. currency through the dollar stores, often called "stores for the collection of foreign exchange." It also requires citizens to pay taxes and fees for some public services, such as passports, exit visas, and airfares for Cubana de Aviación, in U.S. dollars, thereby granting the U.S. dollar an official status. There are two exchange rates for the Cuban peso. The first is the official parity rate of 1 U.S. dollar = 1 peso, used for much international trade and internal public accounts. The second is a quasi-official rate that has varied from twenty-one to twenty-six pesos per dollar from 1998 to 2003. This latter rate is the relevant exchange rate for citizens when they are buying or selling pesos and dollars for everyday use.

The coexistence of peso and dollar currencies and economies in Cuba, together with the dual exchange rate system, generate a variety of problems. The basic reason for this is that the average wage and income are somewhere between U.S.$9 and U.S.$17 per month at the quasi-official exchange rate. (The average wage in Cuba was estimated at 232 pesos and the average income from all sources at 359 pesos in 2000 [CEEC 2001, 8].) This means that those Cubans with access to U.S. dollars from remittances, foreign travel, or tips and gratuities from tourism, for example, generally have higher real incomes than those without such access. Moreover, as noted earlier, ever-increasing proportions of goods and services are available for dollars in dollar stores and not for pesos. The result is that everyone has been chasing dollars since the early

1990s. In other words, there has been a strong incentive for people to leave or reduce those economic activities that earn pesos and enter or expand those that earn dollars. The result is that the general structure of material rewards in Cuban society bears little relationship to the true social value of the employment generating the incomes.

The Cuban government also loses *seigniorage* from the use of the U.S. dollar. U.S. dollars in circulation in Cuba must be earned (except for those received as remittances), so that the seigniorage is captured in large part by the U.S. Federal Reserve and ultimately the U.S. government.

From an economic perspective, it would be desirable to unify the exchange rates and the peso and dollar economies within Cuba, as analyzed in this volume by Nicholas Rowe and Ana Julia Yanes. It would also be of major benefit to restore the peso as a strong convertible currency that citizens and others would be anxious to utilize for normal monetary purposes. A possible switch from the U.S. dollar to the euro of the European Union makes little sense for Cuba, especially in the longer term when normalization with the United States is bound to occur. (However, permitting the use of the euro in tourist areas dominated by European tourists is reasonable.)

The probable types of policies necessary for monetary unification will involve a devaluation of the current official peso/dollar parity exchange rate and a realignment of the general structure of prices and salary/wages. This will not be easy, of course, and Cuba does not yet seem ready to deal with this issue head-on.

Expanding and Diversifying Exports

A fourth challenge is to expand and diversify merchandise exports. With the exception of nickel and tobacco, Cuba's exports have not been dynamic. Indeed, the structure of Cuba's merchandise exports as of 2002 was surprisingly similar to what it was in 1960, but with sugar eclipsed while some other traditional exports have expanded.

Ultimately, Cuba will need to diversify as well as expand its exports if it is to achieve a sustainable economic recovery. This will require a variety of policy changes. Unification of the exchange rate and the peso and dollar economies is particularly important. At present, enterprises in the peso economy such as those in the sugar sector receive only one peso for every dollar of foreign exchange earned through exports. Obviously this reduces or destroys both the incentive and the real capability to export. Export diversification is also hindered by the inability of state enterprises to adapt quickly to the character of foreign demand. Liberalizing the rules of operation for small- and medium-scale enterprise would therefore be especially helpful. Finally, normalizing relations with the United States would open a vast and geo-economically sensible export market, not to mention a new source of tourists.

One sector of the economy that could have significant export potential in the long term is the informatics software industry. This activity has evolved encouragingly so far under difficult circumstances, as argued by Luis Casacó in this volume. Within an appropriate policy environment, this sector could utilize Cuba's highly skilled labor force for an activity of increasing significance. However, there are still a number of obstacles facing this sector, including lack of public access to personal computers, which poses a major obstacle to rapid and broad-based popular learning in this area.

Shock Therapy for the Sugar Economy

Cuba's sugar agro-industrial complex has been the foundation of Cuba's economy since early colonial times. However, shortly after 1959 the Castro government viewed it as one medium through which Cuba was made dependent on the United States. As a result, the first development strategy of the Castro regime called for a de-emphasis on sugar, its replacement in part with other crops, and a process of instant industrialization. The dismal and rapid failure of this strategy then induced the government to reverse the strategy in 1964. The new strategy re-emphasized sugar, establishing a production target of ten million tons to be produced in 1970, triple the harvest of 1963. This larger crop was to be sold at a subsidized price to the Soviet Union. Under this strategy, the economy was turned upside down as investment, labor, transport, and national attention all turned to the sugar sector, leaving the rest of the economy bereft of resources and in crisis. Not surprisingly, this strategy was also abandoned in 1970.

A more balanced approach to sugar and the rest of the economy commenced in 1971. With this approach, the sector functioned reasonably well into the 1980s. However, it came to be characterized by steady disinvestment as maintenance and replacement investment were postponed and ignored. Then with the end of the special relationship with the Soviet Union around 1990, Cuba had to sell sugar at lower prevailing world prices. With reduced revenues and new priorities in tourism and biotechnology, investment in the sugar sector continued to be postponed. As a result, most sugar mills resemble technological museums, with machinery and equipment often dating back to the turn of the previous century and the 1920s.

The sugar sector continued to perform poorly through the 1990s despite efforts to improve it. With sugar prices declining to around U.S.$0.08 per pound in 2002, the government decided to restructure the industry, permanently shutting down some 70 of 156 sugar mills around the island, with another fourteen producing molasses and a few becoming museums. This restructuring constituted major shock therapy reminiscent of the on-again, off-again approaches of the 1960s. As Brian Pollitt points out, however, some mills had not operated in the 2000/2001 and 2001/2002 harvests, however, although this was in the expectation that in time they would be improved and reopened. The main activities to replace cane in agriculture will be forestry and pasture for cattle as well as some food products.

The implications of mill shutdowns for regional and local development will be severe. The closing of a mill involves the shutting of the economic engine of the sugar town in which it is located. It also implies a shutdown of numerous related economic activities servicing the needs of the mills and the sugar agro-industrial workers. Moreover, the mills provide electricity for the mill towns, so that the production of electricity will be decreased as well. To deal with the displacement of perhaps one hundred thousand workers from the cane fields, the mills, the transportation of the cane, etc., the Cuban government will provide education programs in new agricultural and industrial skills. It will try to switch a proportion of the cane lands to fruit such as mangoes and citrus, and it will try to develop new industrial activities.

Although the sugar sector restructuring is to occur within a two-year period, this is a rapid pace for such a complex process. Indeed, it represents one of the problems with the old style of central planning where decisions affecting large parts of the economy are taken rather than gradual, decentralized, trial-and-error, and piece-meal changes that normally occur under a market mechanism. Indeed, the massive changes forced on the sugar economy during the "sucro-phobic" and "sucro-philiac" phases of the development strategies of the 1960s led to exceedingly negative results. The principal lesson from this earlier era would be to proceed cautiously and gradually instead of adopting an extremist shock therapy approach.

There are a number of doubts that can be raised concerning the wisdom of the new sugar strategy. First, is the sugar sector inherently inefficient or is its ostensible inefficiency due to other factors? For example, the sector has served as a cash cow that has been steadily milked to death, with insufficient reinvestment back into the sector. Second, has the exchange rate regime under which the sector operates systematically penalized it? Third, has the central planning system effectively blocked a normal process of gradual and decentralized diversification in those areas where sugar is least appropriate? Fourth, to what extent will forestry and cattle operations as well as food cultivation absorb much of the labor displaced from cane cultivation, milling transportation, and all the ancillary activities? Fifth, by how much will the total volume of the sugar harvest decline over a transitional period due to cane transportation disruption and coordination problems and to a reduction in cane acreage—even if the ostensibly lower yielding lands are taken out of cane? Sixth, by what criteria are mills being shut down and lands shifted out of sugar cane absolute advantage or comparative advantage? Presumably some of the best cane lands in terms of soil fertility and location should be shifted to food production, not the worst lands. Will this be the case? And, finally, will the sugar town communities affected by the shutdowns and the switch to forestry and cattle rearing (which use relatively little labor) be sustainable when their current major labor intensive activity disappears?

Allowing for Independent Analysis and the Diffusion of Information

Another challenge for the economy concerns the quantity and quality of information and independent analysis. The transfer of knowledge and the ability to communicate freely are indispensable in any economy and society. Open analysis and criticism provide a mechanism for self-correction, exposing flawed policies and errors, bringing illicit actions to light, and suggesting alternate courses of action. These interactions can occur through the media, specialized and professional publications, professional associations, educational institutions and programs, nongovernmental organizations, and informal communication. This happens to some degree in Cuba. However, official secrecy limits the availability of information on many aspects of the economy. Moreover, information diffusion operates with a good-news-only bias or on a public's-need-to-know basis.

Equally damaging, economic analysts or writers are required to play a public relations role for official public policy decisions rather than to be independent critics.[2] From the perspective of society, this is a serious disadvantage, first, because everybody makes mistakes; second, because people, managers, enterprises, and governments are imperfect; and, third, because policies are often ill-designed or badly implemented. The early exposure of such imperfection, flaw, and error is obviously preferable to long delay and cover-up by public relations personnel and cheerleaders posing as analysts.

Controlling Corruption

An additional challenge is corruption, analyzed in this volume by Jorge Pérez-López. Corruption of some sort has long existed in Cuba, but it has emerged in the 2000s as an area of significant government concern. Corruption manifests itself in a number of different ways. First, supplies such as agricultural products often "leak" from the state sector at the production, transportation, or wholesale-retail levels for illegal exchange on the black market and even for house-to-house delivery. For instance, tobacco and cigars leak from the state sector to supply the ubiquitous market for counterfeit cigars of varying quality in the dollar market. Second, some people who have access to public goods use public property, such as cars and their drivers, for private purposes. Third, those who control access to scarce consumer goods and services—such as retailers or store clerks—often provide the scarce rationed products outside the rationing system or under the counter for higher prices that include a cut for the perpetrator. The importance of this issue for Cuba's leadership is apparent from the large police presence on the streets of Havana, which is oriented partly to stopping the illegal circulation of products as well as theft. The establishment in June 2001 of the Ministerio de Auditoria y Control, aimed at curbing corruption, particularly within the state sector of the economy, is a further indicator of the significance of this issue.

A further dimension of corruption is the pervasive party patronage phenomenon. It should be noted that this phenomenon is viewed as being normal and proper in Cuba and few question its validity or ethics. However, outside of Cuba it is considered to be a serious form of corruption. The acquisition of preferred employment positions, especially at higher levels (including economic institutions), and various types of material reward (such as housing, foreign travel, television sets, and automobiles) are normally based more on party linkages and certification and less on relevant qualifications. This cannot help but impair the effective functioning of the economy

Immediate Economic Challenges

The policy and institutional challenges described above will have to be addressed in the context of recent world and local events that have had important impacts on central features of the Cuban economy. First and foremost is the international economic contraction, which was already under way in early 2001 and intensified after the 11 September terrorist attacks. Air travel to many destinations, including tourist destinations, diminished. Employment cuts then spread through the airline industry and tourist destinations throughout the world. Levels of business investment in general have also declined significantly. However, it is also possible that an upturn in both the tourist economy and the international macroeconomy may occur rather quickly.

The Cuban economy could not avoid the effect of the international economic slowdown. Tourism is the most vulnerable sector. According to a speech by Fidel Castro on 2 November 2001, tourist arrivals to Cuba declined by about 10 percent in September and 14 percent in October. However, this may be short-lived if confidence in the security of air travel is quickly reestablished. It is of interest to note that President Castro spoke strongly against terrorism from any source following 11 September. Even more significant, Cuba finally agreed to sign all twelve United Nations accords against terrorism. These actions were aimed at maintaining a reputation for security, one of Cuba's key tourism assets.

The cigar industry is another vulnerable sector. In view of their high price, cigars are considered luxury items and an international economic downturn may reduce their market significantly. Nickel export volumes and earnings have also declined. In addition, damage to export sugar and citrus crops as well as sugar mills in the Matanzas area from Hurricane Michelle, which struck 4 November 2001, will likely contribute to a short-term reduction in exports. The storm also damaged electrical and communications systems and up to ten thousand homes (Snow 2001).

Cuba's foreign exchange earnings will be affected by the closure of Russia's radar facility, or "spy base," at Lourdes, announced in October 2001 by President Vladimir Putin—without consultation with Cuba. Military rental payments and military procurement from Cuban sources will be lost, as well as consumer purchases and housing rentals by the two thousand Russian citizens who staffed the base. The total reduction of foreign exchange accruing to Cuba from the base has been estimated at U.S.$200 million. Moreover, it can be expected that exports of sugar will also decline significantly in view of the shutdown of much of the sugar production capacity.

These factors have led to a reduction of foreign exchange available to Cuba in the immediate and short term. Even before 11 September 2001, Cuba was facing difficulties in repaying the short-term trade credits it had obtained from Spain, France, and suppliers in Chile, Panama, and South Africa (*Cuba Business* 2001, 3). The official shortage of foreign exchange led the Cuban government to increase its purchases of dollars in the official exchange houses (*casas de cambio* or *cadecas*) within Cuba. The government appears to be purchasing unlimited volumes of U.S. dollars while limiting U.S. dollar sales. By October 2001 this action had pushed the quasi-official exchange rate to twenty-six pesos per dollar from the twenty to twenty-two pesos per dollar rate that had been maintained for some years.

The economic deterioration was so serious that on 2 November 2001 President Castro made a number of assurances to the Cuban people in a speech meant to maintain public confidence. He stated that the *cadecas* would not close, that all bank accounts in pesos, dollars, and convertible pesos would be honored, that state dollar stores and agricultural markets would be maintained, and that prices in state peso and dollar stores would not be raised.

A further result of the reduction in foreign exchange earnings has been that Cuba is now in arrears in its payments to a number of major creditor countries, including Mexico, Japan, Spain, Canada, and apparently Argentina and France (Frank 2002). But Cuba has been able to make increasingly large cash purchases from the United States for foodstuffs. The purchase of needed products for popular consumption at the best price takes precedence over servicing past debts. Purchases from the United States also strengthen the anti-embargo forces in that country.

Cuba's Economic Prospects

Cuba has been gradually emerging from its crisis of the 1990s. Policy modifications and institutional reforms made in the 1993 to 1996 period yielded important positive results, although their effects are incomplete. At the 4.2 percent average rate of per capita economic growth for 1996 to 2000, Cuba should recover its 1990 level of income by about 2005. However, some of the current sources of economic growth, namely family remittances and tourism, are vulnerable. Sugar exports will likely continue to shrink. But, on the other hand, improvements in oil extraction and nickel mining appear to be sustainable and may be strengthened further.

Although in the short term the Cuban economy cannot avoid being affected by the international slowdown and the effects of 11 September, in the long term Cuba's economic performance will also depend on a variety of other factors. Among the positive factors are basic levels of human development, well-developed institutions in parts of society, a backlog of innovations in the outside world awaiting implementation in Cuba, tourism potential, and a large U.S. market.

Improved economic performance will require that Cuba address a number of daunting challenges, such as expanding and diversifying exports, increasing investment levels, terminating monetary and institutional dualism, creating an appropriate environment for self-employment and small- and medium-scale enterprise, and addressing other institutional and policy problems and information control. Cuba's relationship with the United States, which appears to be frozen at least until the end of the presidency of George W. Bush, will also have an important bearing on Cuba's economy. Interestingly enough, even without full normalization, the actual liberalization of trade in food and medicines is a significant benefit to Cuba, as would be the possible liberalization of travel by U.S. citizens to the country.

In some senses it might be said that Cuba is in a pretransition phase, similar to the situation in Hungary and Poland prior to their departure from central planning and one-party rule in the late 1980s. Cuba still has its major process of economic reform, not to mention political reform, ahead of it. Castro will die at some time. Cuban economic policy as well as the institutional structure will likely remain paralyzed until then.

In response to the current economic slowdown and reduction in foreign exchange earnings, President Castro has assured Cuban citizens that some specific liberalizing reforms of the 1993–95 period will not be reversed. But does this mean that the reforms he did not mention could be reversed? It also seems improbable that new liberalizing reforms could be introduced, although conceivably economic realities might force some such changes. More likely, Cuba will proceed on its current course. It will probably continue to go it alone and ride out the current economic difficulties, awaiting a balmier international macroeconomic environment.

Notes

1. The official documents of the Central Bank of Cuba, such as the Economic Report for 1999, make no mention whatsoever of the debt to the former Soviet Union or Russia in any context.

2. The blocked access in Cuba to the Instituto Cubano de Economistas Independientes's Web site was a recent example of the imperative of the Cuban government to control access to information and analysis. An example of the Cuban government's reluctance to permit analyses it is unable to control is its withdrawal from participation in the *Human Development Report 2001* of the United Nations Development Program (UNDP). One suspects that the reason for this is official dissatisfaction with the *Human Development Report 2000,* in which Cuba ranked thirteenth in Latin America and the Caribbean for the human development index and third for the human poverty index.

References

Banco Central de Cuba. 2000. *1999 Economic Report*. Havana, Cuba.

Castro, President Fidel. 2001. Speech of November 2. *Granma,* 20 November, at www.granma. cubaweb.cu.

Cawthorn, Andrew. 1999. "Euro Countdown in Fidel Castro's Cuba," 4 May, at www.cubanet.org/CNews/y99/may99/05e10.htm.

Centro de Estudios de la Economía Cubana (CEEC). 2001. *La economía Cubana en el 2000.* Havana, Cuba: CEEC.

Comité Ejecutivo del Consejo de Ministros. 1998. *Bases generales del perfeccionamiento empresarial*. Havana, Cuba.

Cuba Business. 2001. Vol. 15, no. 7 (September).

Economist Intelligence Unit. 1992. *Economic Review of Cuba*.

Frank, Marc. 2002. "Cuba Said to Miss Japan Mexico Debt Repayments," Reuters News Service, 10 October.

Lee, Susanna. 2001. "Tenemos el inexcusable deber de aplastar todas las manifesraciones de corrupción," *Granma,* 3 June, at www.granma.cubaweb.cu/2002/06/03.

Naciones Unidas. 2000a. *La Economia Cubana: Reformas estructurales y desempeño en los noventa.* Santiago, Chile.

______. 2000b. *Estudio económico de America Latina y el Caribe.* Santiago, Chile.

______. 2001a. *Anuario estadístico para America Latina y el Caribe 200.,* Santiago, Chile

______. 2001b. *Cuba: Evolución económica durante 2000.* Mexico, D.F.

______. 2001c. *Balance preliminar de las economías de America Latina y el Caribe,* Santiago, Chile.

Ritter, Archibald R. M. 1990. "The Cuban Economy in the 1990s: External Challenges and Policy Imperatives." *Journal of Interamerican and World Affairs* 32, no. 3 (1990): 117–50.

Rodriquez, Carlos Rafael. 1990. Interview with the author, 12 July 1990.

Snow, Anita. 2001. "Thousands of Cuban Homes Destroyed." Associated Press, 6 November, at www.cubanet.org/Cnews/y01/nov01/07e4.htm.

Togores, V. 1999. "Cuba: Efectos sociales de la crisis y el ajuste de los 90's." Unpublished paper.

UN Development Program. 2001. *Human Development Report 2001.* New York: Oxford University Press.

UN Economic Commission for Latin America and the Caribbean (UNECLAC). 1997. "The Cuban Economy in the 1990s: Structural Reform and Economic Performance." Unpublished manuscript. Santiago, Chile.

______. 2000. *Preliminary Overview of the Economies of Latin America and the Caribbean.* Santiago, Chile.

CHAPTER 2

Economic and Ideological Cycles in Cuba
Policy and Performance, 1959–2002

Carmelo Mesa-Lago

The socialist economic system was introduced to Cuba in 1961 and continues today, albeit transformed, though economic organization policies have changed five or six times under the revolution following a vicious cycle tendency. These cycles have been connected with ideological shifts of divergent degree and length that have alternately moved the economy away from the market and toward the market, with opposite outcomes. To identify these cycles in a simple manner, in some of my previous works I have labeled the movements away from the market as *idealists* and movements toward the market as *pragmatists*. The basis for this labeling and also for my argument is an article published twenty-nine years ago in which I designed a continuum model to compare socialist systems (Cuba was one among five of those systems). I placed the cycles between two poles, representing antagonistic (pure or abstract) economic systems: one mainly but not exclusively characterized by antimarket tendencies and emphasis on ideological development, and the other by market-oriented policies and a pragmatic emphasis on economic development (Mesa-Lago 1973; for an analysis of economic cycles in socialist economies, see Kornai 1992). The article was mainly theoretical, based on limited evidence and covering only ten years; however, this essay expands and refines my hypotheses and tests them with statistics (taken from Mesa-Lago 2003 and recent Cuban data) during a much longer period of observation.

Features of the Cycles

In idealistic cycles, leaders set unrealistic targets (for example, ten million tons of sugar, forging a "New Man," egalitarianism, and self-sufficiency in food) that eventually fail and provoke adverse economic and social effects, hence raising a threat (real or perceived) of regime instability. Facing that situation the political leadership shifts course toward the market in order to strengthen/save the system and keep its power.

Pragmatist cycles (market-oriented policies) lead to moderate improvements in the economy and living standards, but they also generate some adverse social effects such as inequality and unemployment. When the political leadership feels the regime is strong enough, a new idealistic cycle is launched.

The economic logic suggests that if pragmatist cycles bring about overall positive outcomes, such policies should be continued and strengthened. And yet, a move to the market involves delegation of economic power, decentralization, the surge of independent economic agents, and, hence, a loss of economic and political control by the government. The political logic (maintaining politico-economic power), therefore, runs against the economic logic and may explain the shift back to an idealistic cycle. Furthermore, a move toward the market generates inequality, unemployment, and other effects deemed socially unacceptable by the leadership.

Most cycles last from five to seven years, creating instability and confusion and harming economic performance in the long run because policies are not given enough time for proper implementation and results. In early pragmatist cycles, market reforms are introduced in a cautious, timid manner, but they become bolder and more difficult to reverse in later pragmatist cycles, although their negative social effects worsen. Conversely, idealistic cycles become weaker over time and very difficult to reinstate. Policies occasionally reach a peak in a cycle and decline in importance in subsequent cycles.

The role of the maximum leader (Fidel Castro) is crucial in the generation of cycles. Despite many changes over the past forty-three years and some degree of politico-economic institutionalization, Castro still concentrates considerable political power and makes the most important policy decisions. His customary preference for centralized decision making, collectivization of the means of production, egalitarianism, and mobilization make him favor antimarket policies, but he has taken a pragmatist stand and reversed those preferences every time it has been necessary to save his regime.

External factors, positive or negative, may help to launch, sustain, or terminate a cycle, among them Soviet aid and the U.S. embargo. The Cuban leadership's fear that domestic political destabilization would open the door to U.S. intervention can play a role in the gestation of a cycle.

Methodology

Stages

The period to be covered is the first forty-three years of the revolution (1959–2001), within which six stages are identified: (1) Market Erosion, Soviet Orthodox

Table 2.1 Cycles in Cuba's Economic Policies, Outcomes, and External Factors, 1959–2001

Cycles	1959–63/64–66	1966–70	1971–85	1986–90	1991–93/94–96	1997–2001
Policies						
Agricultural free markets	≈≈≈	↓E	ΔR	↓E		RΔ ≈
Self-employment	≈	↓E	ΔR	↓E	RΔ	↓
Voluntary labor, mobilization	BΔ	Δ	↓	Δ	↓	≈
Foreign investment	↓	↓E	Δ*	↓	ΔP	≈
State budget	≈	↓E	ΔR	↓	ΔP	≈
Collectivization	Δ	Δ	≈↓	ΔP	↓	≈
Centralized decision making	Δ	Δ	↓	Δ	↓	≈
Rationing over prices	BΔ	ΔP	↓	Δ	↓	↓
Egalitarianism	Δ	ΔP	↓	Δ	↓	↓
Moral over material incentives	≈	ΔP	↓	Δ	↓	↓
Free social services	Δ	ΔP	↓	Δ	↓	≈
Outcomes						
Economic growth	Δ↓Δ	↓	ΔP	↓	↓	Δ ↓Δ↓
Liquidity (monetary surplus)	Δ	Δ	↓	Δ	ΔP	↓ ↓
Inflation	Δ↓	?Δ	Δ↓	Δ?	ΔP	↓ Δ↓
Fiscal deficit	≈	?	↓	Δ	ΔP	↓ ≈
Trade deficit	Δ	Δ	≈Δ	Δ	↓	Δ ΔP
Open unemployment	Δ↓	↓	Δ	Δ	ΔP	↓
External Factors						
Soviet aid, price subsidies	BΔ	Δ	ΔP	≈	↓E	
U.S. embargo	B		Ford, Carter relaxation	Reagan, Bush	Torricelli and Helms-Burton	≈
Others	OAS embargo imposed	Soviet invasion of Czechoslovakia	OAS embargo lifted, Club of Paris loans	Payment of foreign loans suspended	Foreign investment starts and grows	Slowdown in foreign investment

Key: Δ Increase; ↓ Decline; ≈ No change; B Begins; E Eliminated; P Peak; R Reestablished.
*Authorized under tight restrictions.
Sources: Based on statistics for 1959–95 (Mesa-Lago 2000) and 1996–2001 (ONE 1998–2001; BCC 1999–2002; and Mesa-Lago 2003).

Model, and Socialist Debate, 1959–66, which is further divided into three substages (although difficult to characterize, this cycle was away from the market); (2) Adoption and Radicalization of Guevarism, 1966–70 (idealist); (3) Soviet Model (pre-Gorbachev) of Timid Economic Reform, 1971–85 (pragmatist); (4) Rectification Process (idealist), 1986–90; (5) Special Period and Market Oriented Reform, 1991–96 (pragmatist); and (6) Halting or Slowdown of the Reform, 1997–2001. These six stages/cycles are shown in the two segments in table 2.1: the upper segment deals with policies, and the lower segment deals with outcomes of such policies and external factors that may influence a cycle.

Policies

Changes in eleven policy features in each of the stages or cycles are shown in the upper segment of the table: (a) agricultural free markets, (b) self-employment, (c) voluntary (unpaid) work and labor mobilization; (d) foreign investment; (e) state budget; (f) collectivization; (g) centralized decision making; (h) rationing over prices; (i) egalitarianism; (j) moral over material incentives; and (k) free social services. Some of these policies are typically associated with an idealistic cycle (move away from the market)—for instance, collectivization, centralized decision making, voluntary labor and mobilization, rationing over prices, egalitarianism, moral incentives, and free social services. Other policies are connected with a pragmatist cycle (move toward the market), such as agricultural free markets, self-employment, opening to foreign investment, decentralization in decision making, use of the state budget to control fiscal balance, market prices over rationing, material incentives, and charging for some public services. Changes in those policies are denoted with the following signs: increase Δ; decrease ↓; and unchanged ≈. In addition, when a policy begins, it is denoted with a *B;* when it reaches a peak, with a *P;* when it is eliminated, with an *E;* and when it is reestablished, with an *R.*

Outcomes

The lower segment of the table selects six key outcomes and exhibits their changes in each of the stages or cycles: economic growth, liquidity (excess money in circulation or monetary overhang), inflation, fiscal deficit, merchandise trade deficit, and open unemployment. An important outcome that cannot be measured is income distribution because official statistics have never been published on it; however, it will be qualitatively assessed based on rough foreign estimates and scattered domestic information. Other indicators cannot be calculated due to lack of data. The same symbols for change of policy are used in the outcomes. Within some of the stages an outcome may exhibit variation; hence, more than a symbol is used. For example, in the three substages of 1959–66, economic growth first increases, then declines, and then increases.

Domestic and External Factors Influencing Cycles

It is assumed herein that the key domestic factor in economic policy changes is Castro's decision. Pérez-Stable has argued that Cuban cycles cannot be exclusively explained by the conventional tension between central planning and the market but, most important, by the tension between political institutionalization and mobilizational authoritarianism. She has added that Castro's impact on how Cuba is governed, as well as Castro's charismatic leadership and revolutionary ideology, have prevented developmental logic from normalizing state socialism and implementing comprehensive market reforms (Pérez-Stable 1999, 63–69). In the 1990s there were minor political changes in Cuba, such as relatively more space for private and public life autonomous from government control. And yet Castro still holds the most important political jobs: chief of state, president of the council of state, president of the council of ministers and its executive committee, first secretary of the Cuban Communist Party and head of its political bureau, and commander in chief of the armed forces. As president of the council of state he nominates the Supreme Court president, and that institution is subordinated to the council of state. The only institution he does not preside over is the national assembly, but it has little power, meets only twice annually for two or three days, and during the rest of the year the council of state governs by decree. Finally, the constitution empowers Castro to declare a state of emergency and to modify the exercise of rights and obligations embedded in it.[1]

A remarkable similarity is observed in Cuba under Castro and China under Mao, where the two powerful revolutionary leaders shaped cyclical economic policies; it was only after Mao's death that the market-oriented reform in China was consolidated and dramatically deepened and expanded. In the 1990s there was a moderate process of economic decentralization and rise in the economic technocracy in the island. Furthermore, in a few instances Castro had to publicly explain and justify unpopular economic policies, and, in a couple of cases, he had to agree on an economic measure he initially opposed (for example, the reintroduction of free agricultural markets and the imposition of wages taxes, albeit postponed). But Castro has rejected any possibility of implementing a Chinese-style market-oriented reform in Cuba, and he still makes the crucial economic decisions. It could be argued, nevertheless, that his powers to fully reverse policy (launch an idealistic cycle) have considerably eroded since he introduced economic reforms in 1993 because he lacks policy alternatives and external sources of support (the USSR and CMEA have disappeared). And yet the halting or slowing down in the economic reform since 1996 suggests that at least he is still able to determine the speed of the process.

The main external factors (positive and negative) that may have influenced cycles are presented at the bottom of the second part of table 2.1; the two most important are the former USSR and the United States; a third factor ("others") involves additional foreign actors. For instance, the initiation of Cuban trade with the Soviet Union in 1960 and the latter's supply of oil and granting of economic aid to Cuba facilitated the inception of the first cycle, while the increase in Soviet aid, expansion of price subsidies, and oil concessions helped to launch the third cycle and sustain it. Conversely, the disappearance of the USSR and termination of its aid and price subsidies, as well as sharp reduction of its trade and supply of oil at preferential prices, led to the termination of the fourth cycle and the launching of the fifth. The imposition of the U.S. embargo and its expansion by the Organization of American States (OAS) in the first half of the 1960s isolated Cuba and facilitated the inception of the first cycle; conversely, the lifting of OAS restriction to trade with Cuba in 1975 and President Carter's opening in 1976 helped in the pragmatist third cycle. The presidencies of Reagan and Bush and the halting of hard currency loans from the Club of Paris may have played an adverse role in the inception of the fourth cycle.

Analysis of Policies and Outcomes in the Cycles

Market Erosion, Soviet Orthodox Model, and Socialist Debate, 1959–66

This stage is divided into three substages. The first (Liquidation of Capitalism and Erosion of the Market, 1959–60) led at the end of 1960 to the virtual elimination of the market due to rapid collectivization of the means of production, hence forcing the implementation of a command economy of the conventional Stalinist type in the second substage (Orthodox Soviet Central Planning Model, 1961–63). The imposition of the U.S. embargo (1961) and its extension by the OAS (1964), as well as the declaration that the revolution was socialist in 1961, reinforced Cuba's isolation in the Western Hemisphere and the establishment of the Soviet model with the incentive of significant economic aid and trade from the USSR. There were significant continuities in the first two substages: increasing collectivization of the means of production, virtual elimination of foreign investment, centralization of decision making, and increasing egalitarianism and provision of free social services. In addition, since 1961 rationing had expanded and the role of market prices had gradually decreased. The inward development strategy was based on rapid industrialization (according to Che Guevara, Cuba would lead Latin America in industrial output per capita in 1965) and agricultural diversification.

The Soviet planning model was unsuitable to Cuba because of its sugar-centered economy, the exodus of managers, and a lack of previous planning experience and adequate statistics; to compound the problem, collectivization was very rapid and widespread, and the planning mechanism was hastily implemented. The industrialization plan set too ambitious targets in the short run and needed imported premises that did not arrive on schedule, while agricultural diversification did not bear the expected fruits but led instead to a cut in the sugarcane planted area. As a result, sugar exports declined and provoked a deficit in the trade balance. The double failure (of central planning and industrialization) led to the third substage (Socialist Debate and Experiment with Alternative Models, 1964–66), where two contending ideological groups proposed antagonistic projects: the Guevarists, who, partly influenced by Mao's ideas, advocated an idealist antimarket approach (forging a New Man with moral stimulation, voluntary labor and mobilization, and further collectivization, egalitarianism, and free social services), and the pro-Soviet pragmatist faction, led by Carlos Rafael Rodríguez, who, influenced by Libermanism, favored a timid market-oriented reform (use of selected market tools with more reliance on material incentives, some decentralization in decision making, and a halt in collectivization, egalitarianism, and free social services). The economy was divided between the two groups: the Guevarists controlled two-thirds, and the pro-Soviet controlled the remaining one-third. Such division made it very complex to characterize the third substage, but, in general, its trends were away from the market.

This stage lasted seven and one-half years (divided as follows in the three substages: two, three, and two and one-half years). Performance is difficult to assess because little data are available for 1959–60, and the introduction of the Soviet model in 1962 changed the method of national accounts, thus making it technically impossible to do comparisons with 1959–61. Outcomes were mixed and oscillating: economic growth increased, declined, and partly recovered; inflation rose and decreased; liquidity and the trade deficit steadily expanded; and the fiscal deficit apparently was held under control (but accurate statistics are not available).

Adoption and Radicalization of the Guevarist Model, 1966–70

Castro remained silent during the debate, but by the end of 1965 the leaders of the two contending factions had been removed from the Cuban scenario: Guevara had left to lead the guerrilla movement in South America and Rodríguez had resigned as director of the Institute of Agrarian Reform. In mid-1966 Castro publicly embraced several features of Guevara's model and implemented them during this stage, although in a more idealistic manner and distorted with his own additions (for instance, he dropped the central plan and the budget, strengthened centralization, and exaggerated the use of moral stimulation). He boasted that Cuba was ahead of the USSR in building socialism and communism. Despite his bravado and departure from the Soviet economic model, as well as sponsoring the *guerrilla foco* in Latin America (that undermined the pro-Soviet communist parties), the USSR increased its aid and trade. In 1967, however, the Russians reduced oil supply to the island, to which Castro retorted by processing and condemning the pro-Soviet microfaction. The invasion of Czechoslovakia in 1968, nevertheless, was supported by Castro and eventually led to the continuation of Soviet oil supply and aid. The brief confrontation with the USSR, therefore, reinforced the idealistic cycle but did not provoke adverse economic effects.

The development strategy was shifted from inward (import-substitution industrialization) to outward with the 1965–70 sugar plan, which set a target of ten million tons of sugar. The major effort to achieve that goal took place during this cycle, which peaked with the revolutionary offensive in 1968, the most dramatic movement away from the market under the revolution: a further push in collectivization with the elimination of free peasant markets and family plots in state farms, the nationalization of fifty-eight thousand small businesses, and penalization of self-employment (foreign investment continued to be banned); huge labor mobilizations and voluntary work to help in the sugar harvest and for ideological reasons; expansion of rationing and virtual elimination of scarcity prices as allocating tools; significant emphasis in egalitarianism, such as reduction in wage differentials, gradual substitution of material incentives by moral stimulation, and further expansion of free social services; and more centralized decision making but with a decline in the central plan, substituted by sectorial plans (sugar, cattle) directly controlled by Castro (the state budget disappeared for a decade).

This idealist cycle only lasted four and one-half years. Performance is difficult to measure because of lack of accurate data. However, available information shows that most outcomes were negative: economic growth slowed down and was either stagnant or declined in 1970 (sugar output was 15 percent short of the target, and the record harvest was achieved at the cost of a decrease in the rest of the economy); liquidity reached a record, and excess money in circulation made the currency virtually worthless and prompted a jump in labor absenteeism to 25 percent of the labor force (casting serious doubts on moral stimulation); inflation probably rose and the trade deficit expanded considerably. Information is not available on the fiscal deficit due to the discontinuation of the state budget. On the other hand, open unemployment declined to a record low (but at the cost of an expansion of underemployment and declining labor productivity) and income distribution probably became the most equal under the revolution (as some foreign estimates indicate).

Soviet Model (pre-Gorbachev) of Timid Economic Reform, 1971–85

The double failure in 1970 (of the sugar plan and the shaping of a New Man) combined with significant economic deterioration left Cuba in limbo, provoked a dangerous crisis, and prompted a timid policy reversal toward the market starting in 1971. Nixon was the U.S. president, and the only alternative for external trade and aid available to Cuba was the Soviet Union. Castro qualified endorsement of the Soviet invasion of Czechoslovakia in 1968, as well as the failure of guerrilla warfare in South America with Guevara's death in 1967, paved the way to a reconciliation with Cuba's socialist partner. Soviet trade and aid peaked in this stage, particularly nonrepayable price subsidies to the island exports and imports, and Cuba entered the Council for Mutual Economic Assistance (CMEA), all of them positive external factors that contributed to implement and expand policies during this cycle. Under President Ford, secret negotiations with Cuba began and the OAS lifted its sanctions in 1975, while Carter's presidency relaxed tensions with Cuba further (interest section offices were established). These positive external factors probably helped to sustain this cycle. The arrival of Reagan to the presidency in the 1980s, however, provoked new tensions (Cuba created territorial militias), but there was a compensatory factor: the granting of hard-currency loans by the Club of Paris.

In this pragmatist cycle, the leadership virtually reversed all its previous policies in a timid move toward the market. Although gradual reduction in private farms and expansion of state-controlled cooperatives continued in this stage, there were some measures contrary to collectivization: the reintroduction of free peasant markets, family plots in state farms, and self-employment; the granting of permission to private farmers to hire workers; the authorization to the population for private home construction and swaps; and the enactment of a law allowing foreign investment (although with almost nil results due to its restrictions). The previous emphasis on egalitarianism, moral incentives, and labor mobilization were criticized as ineffective "idealistic errors," hence wage differentials were defended and material incentives reinstated and expanded; voluntary labor was drastically curtailed as it was labeled inefficient; a parallel market was created in which supply and demand determined the price of goods; and charges were imposed on some public utilities and other services. At the same time, the central planning apparatus was reinforced, although with some decentralization measures (for example, more decision-making power at the enterprise level), and the state budget reestablished as key tools for a command economy, although with very limited use of selected market tools. A process of economic and political institutionalization took place in this cycle. It should be noted, nevertheless, that the new planning technocracy faced serious resistance from the Old Guard to implement these policies; some of them were criticized by Castro (for example, free peasant markets and self-employment) and others were not fully implemented (for example, workers' profit sharing and self-financing of state enterprises).

This cycle is so far the longest under the revolution (fifteen years), and statistics to measure performance, considerably better in quantity and quality, show a significant improvement: economic growth reached the highest rates under the revolution (particularly in 1971–75, when growth was aided by record sugar prices; sugar crops averaged more than seven million tons in 1976–85 and most nonsugar output recovered and surpassed previous levels); liquidity decreased dramatically until 1980; fiscal surpluses were generated from 1978 (when the state budget was reintroduced) until 1985, except for one year; there was either low inflation or deflation except for a significant jump in 1981 due to price increases (prices had been frozen since 1961); and the trade deficit was either stagnant or declined in the 1970s (because of generous Soviet price subsidies) but rose again in the first half of the 1980s (as some of those subsidies were curtailed). Conversely, open unemployment pockets appeared for the first time since the early 1960s (due to the emphasis on labor productivity, the slowdown in job creation, and the entrance in the labor market of the baby boom engendered in 1959–65), and inequalities probably rose (although hard data are not available).

The Rectification Process, 1986–90

The significant economic recovery in the previous pragmatist cycle solved the crisis of 1970 and led to a noticeable improvement in living conditions on the island, and yet both domestic and external forces conspired against the continuation and strengthening of market-oriented policies. Castro and the Old Guard resented the growing economic power of the planning technocracy, its elimination of some dear revolutionary institutions (such as voluntary labor), the growing inequality and inception of a tiny, wealthy new class of peasants, middlemen in the free peasant markets, self-employed, and housing traders. Castro's criticism of these groups in 1982, the imposition or threat of taxes on them, and the accusations of greed and corruption were a preamble of the reversal in policy. Externally, Gorbachev took over power in the USSR in 1985 and launched perestroika and glasnost; as a result, internal pressure in the USSR began to mount on Cuba to reduce the trade deficit and better use Soviet economic aid (trade and aid were stagnant and price subsidies were reduced). In view of both domestic economic improvement and the external pressures explained, one should have expected that Cuba would swim on the new wave rising in the USSR and Eastern Europe, but the leadership was afraid that such a move would threaten the revolutionary spirit, provoke social tensions, lead to destabilization of the regime, and erode their grip on power. To compound the situation, due to the heavy burden of the debt service in hard currency, Cuba in 1986 suspended payment of the foreign debt with the Club of Paris, and the latter responded by halting all fresh credit until the payment of such debt was renegotiated, an impasse that continues today. In the United States, the Reagan and Bush presidencies relentlessly continued the embargo on Cuba, giving an excuse to the Cuban leadership to tighten control as a defense against imperialism and capitalism.

A new idealistic cycle, the Rectification of Errors and Negative Tendencies, was launched by Castro in mid-1986 and lasted until 1990. It was expected to find an optimal middle point between the idealistic errors of 1966–70 and the economic mistakes of 1971–85 (the head of the planning agency was fired and put on trial, accused of mechanically copying a model not suitable for Cuba). In practice, most of the rectification policies resembled the antimarket bias of the previous idealistic cycle, although without reaching its extremes: the process of elimination of private farms was accelerated, free peasant markets and self-employment were abolished and their functions expected to be performed by the state, and private housing construction and swaps were considerably restricted; voluntary labor was reintroduced with the creation of military-style construction brigades and massive use of labor mobilization in agriculture; material incentives were sharply reduced and moral incentives reinstated; the emphasis on egalitarianism and free social services came back (there was a resurrection of the Guevarist ideals); rationing expanded again and the parallel market was eliminated; and decentralization measures were halted and decision making retaken by the political leadership but with a decline in planning and lack of an integrated model of organization to substitute both the central plan and the market. A new development strategy was based on a food program with unrealistic targets that optimistically foresaw that in five years the island would be self-sufficient in food and generate a surplus for export. In fact, biotechnology was promoted as a source of exports that would make Cuba a world power in that field. The only sensible development strategy, however, was the expansion of foreign tourism in enclaves.

This idealistic cycle lasted about four and one-half years, and, although Cuba's statistical yearbook suspended publication with the 1989 edition, still there are enough data (expanded since 1996) to show that this cycle provoked a recession and virtually all indicators of performance deteriorated: the rate of economic growth was negative, liquidity expanded significantly, the fiscal surplus turned into a growing deficit, the trade deficit reached a historical record, and open unemployment continued increasing (a significant departure from the decline in unemployment in 1966–70). Data on inflation is incomplete (statistics stopped in 1988) and impedes an assessment; the same is true of inequality, but it might have decreased. The recession in this stage put Cuba in a more vulnerable economic situation to confront the end of the Soviet camp. If market-oriented policies had continued, the transition probably would have been easier in the 1990s.

The Special Period in Time of Peace and the Market-Oriented Reform, 1991–96

At the end of the 1980s, the unrealistic policies of rectification (for example, the food program) were clearly unsuccessful and, at the start of the 1990s, the disappearance of the USSR and the CMEA, as well as the demise of socialism in Eastern Europe, shut down Cuba's vital pipeline. Cuban-Russian trade dropped dramatically and became restricted to a barter of oil for sugar at world market prices (all price subsidies ended); Russia ceased to buy key Cuban products such as nickel and citrus and to export consumer, intermediate, and capital goods; Soviet soft loans and credits (donations in practice) decreased from about five to six billion U.S. dollars annually to a few million sporadically; Soviet investment in hundreds of projects ceased and Russian technicians returned; oil supply sank and transfers in hard currency for Soviet oil committed for export but not consumed by Cuba were terminated. Virtually all trade with and all economic aid from Eastern European nations came to an end. In addition, the U.S. embargo was tightened somewhat by the Torricelli Act of 1992, although this was not as important as other U.S. measures introduced later. As in 1964 and 1970, Cuba faced in 1991 another double failure, and the devastating losses provoked the worst crisis under the revolution and the ending of rectification. This time there was no foreign power capable and willing to help; hence, the only alternative open to Cuba was to integrate into the world capitalist market. A new, pragmatist cycle was launched and labeled the Special Period in Time of Peace, a euphemism for an emergency structural adjustment program to save the economy and the regime.

The Cuban leadership first unsuccessfully tried to cope with the unexpected catastrophe and urgent need of hard currency relying on external policies only, such as carefully controlled foreign investment and tourism, but these did not stop the economic decline. The desperate situation in the summer of 1993 forced the introduction of domestic market reforms, albeit modest and partial, which were reluctantly implemented in piecemeal fashion, lacking an integrated and cohesive long-run plan, with occasional setbacks and a halt or slowdown since 1996. The trend toward the market was the strongest under the revolution, and the previous steady process of collectivization was reversed for the first time. A constitutional amendment allowed private and mixed property of the means of production, and a new foreign investment law granted greater incentives than its predecessor in 1982, although authorization of central ministries and even the Executive Committee of the Council of Ministries is usually required. State farms were transformed into cooperatives, and land parcels were granted to families; agricultural free markets, as well as artisan markets and self-employment, were reauthorized, and the informal sector of the economy grew considerably. There was a process of decentralization in decision making, first in the foreign sector and later in the domestic sector, where quasi-private enterprises were created; the state budget became a key tool in fiscal policy and tough measures were enforced to reduce government expenditures (for example, subsidies to consumer prices and state enterprises) and increase revenue (for example, by taxes). Rationing ceased to be the main allocator of food and consumer goods and was largely replaced by market prices, in pesos and dollars (possession and circulation of dollars were permitted and overwhelmingly come from exile remittances); prices were set by supply and demand in new state dollar shops, as well as in agricultural, artisan, and black markets. Voluntary work and labor mobilization, egalitarianism, and moral incentives yielded to the strongest emphasis on material incentives, profit making, and efficiency; and although free social services continued in health care and education, virtually all other services were charged and public utilities rates raised.

This pragmatist cycle lasted six years, which is divided into two substages for the evaluation of performance: the worst crisis under the revolution (1991–93) and a modest recovery (1994–96). In the first substage, all indicators but one deteriorated: there was a huge economic decline (about 35 percent of GDP), while liquidity, inflation, and the fiscal deficit rose to the highest levels under the revolution and open unemployment continued to be high. The trade deficit decreased in spite of the drastic decline in exports because imports sank even more. It is impossible to evaluate the situation of income distribution. In the second substage there was a recovery in the majority of the indicators: economic growth increased, while liquidity, inflation, and the fiscal deficit declined (the last two more than the first). Conversely, unemployment peaked and then decreased somewhat but still remained high (a significant manpower surplus receiving unemployment compensation was reported in the state sector), and the trade deficit expanded significantly. All information available indicates that income inequalities expanded to the highest levels under the revolution because of several causes: the reduction of rationing to guarantee minimum rations to all the population, the rapidly growing role of prices in allocating consumer goods, the sharp devaluation of the peso and the expanding use of the dollar, and the rising income of small farmers, the self-employed, black-market operators, recipients of foreign remittances, and entrepreneurs and workers connected with the dollar economy (Mesa-Lago 1998).

The Halting or Slowdown of the Economic Reform, 1997–2001

Economic cycles are difficult to detect at the beginning because information is insufficient and policy features are unclear. But since 1996 the process of economic reform has been either halted or slowed down. Raúl Castro's speech in March of that year was an indicator of the shift as he strongly criticized the negative effects of all the market policies introduced since 1993; denounced some Cuban academic institutions and scholars favorable to stronger economic reforms as being ideologically penetrated by the enemy; threatened more state regulations, higher taxes, and tougher sanctions on the emerging nonstate sector; and called for an ideological campaign to strengthen the revolutionary spirit. Several of these measures were subsequently implemented and a purge of leading reformists occurred. Both domestic and external causes may explain the inception of this new cycle. Policies of the previous cycle halted the economic decline, promoted a modest recovery, and saved the regime from the crisis of 1993. Castro and the Old Guard, therefore, felt secure and decided to halt the market reform process to avoid further decline in their economic power and a potential destabilization of the regime. Furthermore, the introduction of the "Track II" of the Torricelli Law in 1995 and the enactment of the Helms-Burton Act in 1996 raised new fear of U.S. intervention and strengthened the hard-liners in Cuba.

The hypothesis of a halting or slowdown in the trend toward the market is supported by important evidence. Self-employment has been curtailed by new regulations, fees, and taxes, which has resulted in a decrease in their number. The introduction of several scheduled reform policies has been indefinitely postponed; for instance, the dismissal of 500,000 to 800,000 unneeded workers in the state sector, the authorization to Cuban citizens to manage small businesses, the creation of workers' contributions for social security pensions, a general price reform, and the convertibility of the peso. There have been no further significant advances in agricultural markets, privatization, or decentralization in decision making. Foreign investment only grew by U.S.$400 million in 1997–2001, contrasted with U.S.$2.1 billion in 1991–96. So far there has not been use of voluntary work and massive labor mobilizations (as in the second and fourth cycles), but at the end of the 1990s and in the early 2000s there have been constant and massive public mobilizations against Cuban exiles and U.S. policies. On the other hand there is continuous advancement on the previous cycle trend on prices over rationing, material over moral incentives, and contrariness to egalitarianism.

Official statistics on performance in 1997–2001 mostly show deterioration. The economic growth rate slowed down in 1997–98, increased in 1999–2000, and slowed down again in 2001; GDP in 2001 was still 19 percent below the 1989 level. Monetary liquidity steadily rose in 1998–2001 and reached a record in 2001, 13 percent above the level of 1993, in the midst of the crisis. Inflation increased in 1997–98, but reportedly there was deflation in 1999–2001, in flagrant contradiction with the increase in monetary liquidity and the devaluation of the peso and increase in prices in 2001. The fiscal deficit was stagnant, while the trade deficit steadily grew and peaked in 2000–2001, 18 percent the record level of 1989 (this time without automatic Soviet credits to cover it). Conversely, open unemployment steadily declined, although there are indications of a growing labor surplus (Oficina Nacional de Estadísticas 1998–2001; Banco Central de Cuba 1999–2002; UNECLAC 2000, 2001, 2002; Mesa-Lago 2003). No hard data on income distribution has been published, but more abundant information is available (for example, on concentration of bank accounts, income differentials, and the declining compensatory effect of rationing), and articles by Cuban scholars clearly indicate an increasing trend in inequality (Togores 1999; Mesa-Lago 2002).

Some Cuban scholars acknowledge that the partial and incomplete reform of the economic structure in the 1990s was unable to transform it in the degree required to promote sustained development. One of them sees the slowdown of 1997–98 as an indicator that the recovery was supported by residual factors, hence making difficult in the middle term to return to precrisis levels; another sees that slowdown as an outcome of the relative paralysis of the economic reform. At least one thinks it is unavoidable to have a rigorous debate on the alternatives to cope with the effects of the crisis and to accelerate its solution through a more viable and logical development strategy (Carranza 2001; Monreal 2001; Marquetti 2000; Mesa-Lago 2003).

A Look at the Future

This chapter contributes significant evidence to support the hypothesis of Cuban economic-ideological cycles during the forty-three years of the revolution. The question is whether that type of evolution is likely to continue or not; more precisely, is another idealist cycle and antimarket shift possible? The analysis of the halting or slowdown in the market-oriented reform since 1996 can shed light on this question. Only in the policy of self-employment was there a retrenchment that consisted of imposing restrictions and taxes, but there has not been a virtual banning of self-employment as happened in the two idealist cycles. In eight other policies there has been stagnation but not reversal, while in three policies the move toward the market has continued.

Castro maintains his power to make crucial economic decisions, but, for the first time under the revolution, he has been forced to accept a policy that he publicly repudiated: the reintroduction of free agricultural markets. One of the hypotheses of this chapter is that in recent pragmatist cycles a dramatic reversal of policies has become more difficult. Two limitations faced by the leaders may explain that phenomenon: (1) there are no alternatives available because of the disappearance of a superpower capable of providing an economic pipeline; and (2) the people have become exhausted after more than four decades of experimentations and promises, skeptical of idealistic targets, and more resistant against another cycle of severe deprivation. The most Castro and the Old Guard can do, therefore, is halt or slow down the process, but it will be very difficult to reverse it.

Can those two limitations be overcome? A change in U.S. policy—that is, the lifting of the embargo—could significantly expand Cuban trade, credit, investment, and tourism, but such a change would be inexorably tied with strengthening rather than reversing market-oriented policies, as U.S. relations with China have demonstrated. Furthermore, unless the current Helms-Burton Act is repealed, a political and economic rapprochement between the two countries does not seem possible while Castro continues to rule in Cuba. Can middle-powers help Cuba to open policy space? China is not likely to do so. Actually, Sino-Cuban trade has been stagnant or declining in the past decade, and no significant aid has been provided to Cuba; furthermore, even if the Chinese leaders were willing to help Cuba, they would be interested in seeing their model of market-oriented reform implemented on the island. Some Arab nations such as Libya share Cuba's antagonism with the United States and would not mind an idealistic radicalization process on the island. They actually may supply oil to Cuba, perhaps at preferential prices, but they are not capable of providing a pipeline to sustain that nation's economy. Venezuela under Chavez is in a similar situation, and after the failed coup of 2002, oil supply at low prices has been halted.

Lifting the Cuban people's spirits can only be done in the long run with an improvement of the economic situation and living standards, and this is only feasible with the deepening of market-oriented reforms. Cuban leadership may try to temporarily mobilize the population behind nationalistic banners against the United States and domestic devils, such as the return of Elián González and the referendum sponsored by the dissidents in the Varela Project. But these are short-term mobilizational techniques that have been used many times in the past and largely lost steam. They cannot sustain the interest of the people. They are economically costly and hence detract rather than help to improve living standards.

Castro turned seventy-six in August 2002, but he may live several years more and, together with the Old Guard, hold a grip on crucial economic decisions. Yet his ability to freeze the reform in Cuba for a long time might be improbable, particularly if the economic situation deteriorates further, as the events of 2002 suggest.

Notes

I acknowledge the valuable comments of Jorge Domínguez (Harvard) and Damian Fernández and Marifeli Pérez-Stable (Florida International University) on a preliminary version of this chapter, although I take full responsibility for it.

1. For a full analysis of Cuba's current political structure, see Domínguez (2000). There is a debate on how important political changes have been in Cuba since the 1990s. Pérez-Stable described some minor changes in three areas of the political system but concluded: "Although reluctantly open to partial economic reforms, *the government adamantly resists significant changes in the political system*" (Pérez-Stable 1999, 72). Domínguez (1997) claimed that there has been a change in Cuba's political system, whereas I responded that there have been some changes within the political system rather than a change in the system itself (Mesa-Lago 1997).

References

Banco Central de Cuba. 1999–2002. *Informe económico 1998* to *2001.* Havana, Cuba.

Carranza Valdés, Julio. 2001. "La economía Cubana: Un balance breve de una década crítica." University of London Institute of Latin American Studies, Workshop Facing the Challenges of the Global Economy, January 25–26.

Domínguez, Jorge. 1997. "Comienza una transición hacia el autoritarismo en Cuba." *Encuentro* 6–7 (fall–winter): 7–23.

_______. 2000. "The Cuban Political System in the 1990s." Paper presented at the LASA Congress, Miami, March 16–18.

Kornai, János. 1992. *The Socialist System: The Political Economy of Socialism.* Princeton: Princeton University Press.

Marquetti Nodarse, Hiram. 2000 "Cuba: Reanimación del sector industrial." *Revista bimestre Cubana* 13 (July–December): 5–30.

Mesa-Lago, Carmelo. 1973. "A Continuum Model to Compare Socialist Systems Globally." *Economic Development and Cultural Change* 21, no. 4 (July): 573–90.

_______. 1997. "Cambio de régimen o cambios en el régimen?" *Encuentro* (fall–winter): 36–45.

_______. 1998. "Assessing Economic and Social Performance in the Cuban Transition of the 1990s." *World Development* 26, no. 5 (May): 857–76.

_______. 2000. *Market, Socialist, and Mixed Economies: Comparative Policies and Performance—Chile, Cuba, and Costa Rica.* Baltimore: Johns Hopkins University Press.

_______. 2002. *Growing Economic and Social Disparities in Cuba: Impact and Recommendations for Change.* Miami: University of Miami, Institute for Cuban and Cuban American Studies.

_______. 2003. *The Cuban Economy at the Start of the Twenty-first Century: Evaluation of Performance and Debate on the Future.* Forthcoming.

Monreal, Pedro. 2001. "Export Substitution Industrialization in Cuba." University of London Institute of Latin American Studies, Workshop Facing the Challenges of the Global Economy, January 25–26.

Oficina Nacional de Estadísticas. 1998–2001. *Anuario Estadístico de Cuba 1996* to *2000.* Havana, Cuba.

Pérez-Stable, Marifeli. 1999. "Caught in a Contradiction: Cuban Socialism between Mobilization and Normalization." *Comparative Politics* (October): 63–69.

Togores González, Viviana. 1999. "Cuba: Efectos Sociales de la Crisis y el Ajuste Económico en los 90." In *Balance de la Economía Cubana a Finales del los 90s,* 82–112. Havana, Cuba: CEEC.

United Nations Economic Commission for Latin America and the Caribbean (UNECLAC). 2000. *La economía Cubana: Reformas estructurales y desempeño en los noventa.* Mexico, D.F.: Fondo de Cultura Económica.

_______. 2001–2. *Cuba: Evolución económica durante 2000* and *2001.* Mexico, D.F.

PART II

Central International Issues

CHAPTER 3

Cuban Monetary Policy
Peso, Dollar, or Euro?

Nicholas Rowe and Ana Julia Yanes Faya

Britain debates whether to continue with an independent national currency or to adopt the euro. Canada debates whether to continue with flexible exchange rates or switch to fixed exchange rates, a currency board, or monetary union with the United States. Argentina had a currency board tying the peso to the U.S. dollar, debated whether to adopt full dollarization, and then abandoned the currency board and reverted to (dirty) floating exchange rates. These are just three examples of a worldwide debate about monetary nationalism. This is not a new debate, but it has become much more widespread in the past decade. In this essay we examine the choices currently facing Cuba and try to predict whether Cuba's monetary future will be the peso, the dollar, or the euro.

A Brief History of Monetary Nationalism in Cuba

The debate on monetary nationalism is not a new one in Cuba. The use of foreign currency in Cuba from 1898 onward differs from the recent dollarization processes in Latin America, because Cuba used the U.S. dollar even before having its own currency. The birth of the Cuban peso and the strengthening of the institutions of the Cuban republic took place at the same time. Cuba went from a dollar and then dual currency to a peso regime and has now returned to a dual currency regime. And very recently Cuba has started to introduce a third currency, the euro.

As early as December 1898 the government of the United States stipulated that taxes and tariffs would be paid to the Cuban government in U.S. dollars.[1] The value of the silver Spanish coins in terms of gold was fluctuating with a tendency toward depreciation. This led to the adoption of the U.S. dollar, not only for official but also for commercial purposes, during the first decade of this century. In 1914 the Cuban government passed a law that aimed to eliminate Cuba's absolute dependence on U.S.

currency.[2] This law gave Cuban currency the same value in terms of gold as the U.S. dollar. But the Cuban government issued only coins, not paper money, so people continued to use more convenient U.S. paper money as well.

In 1933 the Cuban government issued paper currency similar to the U.S. dollar.[3] After 1934 both the peso and the dollar enjoyed legal status. From 1934 to 1951 the Cuban peso had become the predominant currency used for domestic transactions, but dollars remained a favorite hoarding medium.[4] The dual monetary system under which the United States and the Cuban peso both enjoyed legal tender status only came to an end under a governmental law of 1948.[5]

After the Cuban revolution the holding of the U.S. dollar by individual Cubans was made illegal, and dollars were rarely seen during the 1970s and 1980s, except in the (very small) foreign tourist sector and its dollar stores (which Cubans were not allowed to enter). But in the 1990s, with the transition of Eastern Europe economies from plan to market, Cuba experienced an economic crisis. The dollar reappeared as the medium of exchange on the black market. The Cuban government introduced economic reforms that led to the development of a dual economy. In 1993 the Cuban government legalized the holding and use of dollars for all Cubans. The growing presence of tourism and foreign investment, the ending of the state monopoly of foreign trade, self-financing of foreign exchange, and other economic and legal reforms have created two sectors—a traditional state sector that uses mainly the domestic currency and the new sector that uses the dollar. Tourism, remittances, and foreign investment became sources of dollars for Cuban citizens. Individuals, foreign firms, and even the state firms chose the dollar, not only as a store of value but also as a medium of exchange. Although the government has initiated a set of reforms to strengthen the peso, with some success, Cubans today continue to use both dollars and pesos.

The latest twist in Cuba's monetary history involves the euro. In 1999 Cuba required the euro to be used for all transactions with euro zone countries. In June 2002 hotels in Varadero, Cuba's most important destination for foreign tourists, began accepting euros as well as dollars. Other tourist resorts soon followed. Cuban government announcements suggest this is a deliberate policy to reduce reliance on the dollar. "The euro will help to free us from the privileges and tyranny of the dollar," Reuters reports President Castro as saying in May 1999.

The Spectrum of Monetary Nationalism/Internationalism

The debate over monetary nationalism is a debate about the degree to which one country's monetary system should be independent of other countries' monetary systems. It is useful to think of a spectrum of different arrangements.

At one extreme end of the spectrum there is a fully independent national monetary policy—for example, Canada's current monetary policy, where the Bank of Canada adopts a single domestic objective—keeping the Canadian inflation rate at 2 percent. This does not mean that the Bank of Canada ignores the exchange rate, but the exchange rate serves only as an indicator to help the bank hit its ultimate inflation target. Nor does it mean that events in the rest of the world have no effect on Canadian monetary policy. If there is a recession in Asia, for example, and the demand for Canadian exports falls, the Bank of Canada will loosen monetary policy to prevent recession and deflation in Canada.

Moving along the spectrum we come to a policy of fixed exchange rates between the domestic currency and some foreign currency (or basket of foreign currencies). Under fixed exchange rates, the exchange rate itself becomes the main target for monetary policy. If the domestic currency seems about to depreciate below the stated target, the central bank tightens monetary policy (by raising interest rates or by selling foreign currency reserves), regardless of the rate of inflation or unemployment in the domestic economy.

There are many varieties of fixed exchange rate systems. The target can be a simple fixed peg or a crawling peg. Responsibility for maintaining the target exchange rate can be the unilateral responsibility of the domestic central bank or the multilateral responsibility of two or more central banks, as it was between France and Germany immediately before the introduction of the euro. The currencies may be freely convertible or, as in Cuba, there may be restrictions on convertibility (in which case a free market exchange rate will differ from the official exchange rate).

Next along the spectrum is the currency board, as in Argentina during the 1990s or in Hong Kong. There is only one difference between a currency board system and a fixed exchange rate system with free convertibility. A currency board adds 100 percent foreign exchange reserves (usually held in the form of short-term government bonds rather than noninterest-bearing currency) against domestic currency. What this means is that the central bank can never be forced to devalue by running out of reserves, since it can never run out of reserves (but it may nevertheless be forced to devalue by other considerations, such as imminent bankruptcy or unwillingness to accept unemployment, deflation, or the high interest rates caused by a self-fulfilling prophecy of devaluation).

At the other extreme of the spectrum is the abandonment of any domestic currency and the adoption of some foreign or international currency as the domestic medium of exchange. This can be a unilateral arrangement, as in Panama, which uses the U.S. dollar but has no say in U.S. monetary policy, or it can be a multilateral arrangement, like the euro. The main difference between a currency board and the adoption of an international currency is that devaluation is now logically impossible, for there is nothing to devalue.

Though useful as a heuristic device, these four different monetary arrangements, as points along the spectrum of monetary nationalism, do not rule out intermediate points, nor different variations within any one of the four points, nor mixtures of different arrangements. In Canada, for example, most transactions use the Canadian dollar, but some are in U.S. dollars. What is special about Cuba, at the present day, is that its monetary system contains elements from all four points along the spectrum. The official exchange rate is fixed at one to one, but the peso is not convertible into dollars at this rate. The peso is freely convertible into dollars on the black market at a varying exchange rate, currently about twenty-eight pesos to the dollar.[6] The peso can also be legally converted at about the same exchange rate into convertible pesos, which can be spent like dollars in the dollar stores.[7] The convertible peso has some elements of a currency board system, but though dollars can usually be converted into convertible pesos, and convertible pesos can be spent like dollars within Cuba, convertible pesos cannot be converted into dollars. The dollar itself circulates and is used as a medium of exchange in some sectors of the economy. And in 2002 the euro began to circulate also.

Government Policy and Market Choices

It is tempting to think of the government deciding which point on the spectrum to choose. But this is misleading. Ultimately, it is the decisions of individuals that determine which currency they will use. Government policy may be an important influence on those decisions, but it can never wholly determine individuals' choices. This is true in Canada, where private transactions may be made in any currency that the parties wish to use, and where some dollarization has occurred without it being part of government policy. And it is also true in Cuba, where some people held and used dollars even when it was a criminal offense to do so.

The positive question "What will Cuba's monetary future actually be?" requires us to forecast Cuban government policy, the actions of individual Cubans, and the interaction between government policy and individual choice. The normative question "What ought Cuba's monetary future be?" requires us to recognize that any government choice is constrained by how individual Cubans will respond to any government policy. This may mean that Cuba's monetary future, just like Cuba's monetary past, may be very different from what the Cuban government wants. This essay is a mixture of both positive and normative questions.

Macroeconomic Stabilization and Flexible Exchange Rates

The standard argument for flexible exchange rates is that they permit the central bank to pursue domestic objectives, such as macroeconomic stabilization, without the additional constraint of maintaining a fixed exchange rate. This argument is at its starkest for a small open economy with perfect capital mobility, as illustrated by the standard Mundell-Fleming macroeconomic model. With fixed exchange rates the domestic rate of interest is also exogenous; therefore, the central bank can influence neither the exchange rate nor the rate of interest and so is unable to influence aggregate demand. Any shocks to aggregate demand or supply, whether originating domestically or from abroad, will cause instability of domestic prices and output, which the bank is powerless to counteract. Under flexible exchange rates however, provided the bank can at least partly forecast the shocks beyond the horizon of the monetary policy lag, it can "lean against the wind" and at least partly mitigate the effect of those shocks on domestic prices and output. A fall in aggregate demand, relative to aggregate supply, would normally cause domestic prices and output to fall. Under flexible exchange rates, this could be counteracted by letting the exchange rate depreciate, to increase the demand for net exports, and by letting the interest rate fall, to increase consumption and investment demand.

Cuba does not currently enjoy perfect capital mobility; indeed, zero capital mobility would be a close approximation to Cuba's present reality. A small open economy with zero capital mobility does have some freedom to pursue an independent interest rate policy, even under fixed exchange rates. A fall in aggregate demand relative to aggregate supply could be counteracted by letting the interest rate fall, to increase consumption and investment demand. The resulting increase in domestic spending would cause net exports to fall, and this would cause a balance of payments deficit and a loss of foreign exchange reserves, which could not be sustained indefinitely without the central bank running out of foreign exchange.

Unfortunately, Cuba does not possess significant foreign exchange reserves. This means that under fixed exchange rates, even with zero capital mobility, and even in the short run, the central bank would be unable to pursue an independent monetary policy. With zero reserves, any attempt to use monetary policy to stimulate domestic demand would cause an immediate devaluation of the peso.

But what makes the standard Mundell-Fleming macroeconomic model so inapplicable to Cuba is not just Cuba's low capital mobility and low foreign exchange reserves, it is that the Cuban economy is a long way from being a free-market economy. Cuban net exports, and Cuban capital markets, are subject to many government controls and regulations. And so net exports, and savings and investments, respond more to government rationing than to the price signals of exchange rates and interest rates. There is a massive excess demand for foreign exchange at the official exchange rate of one peso to one U.S. dollar. Even though individual Cubans can buy U.S. dollars on the free market at about twenty-eight pesos to the dollar, the importation of consumer goods is a government monopoly, and the government can set any markup it chooses on imported goods. Thus the real exchange rate faced by Cubans buying imported goods can be controlled by the Cuban government quite independently of the nominal exchange rate in the free market. Similarly, private capital markets are almost nonexistent, and firms with soft budget constraints have an excess demand for loans at government-controlled rates of interest.

There is no bond market in Cuba, so the central bank cannot perform monetary policy in the traditional sense by buying or selling government bonds. And with almost no foreign exchange reserves, the central bank cannot freely buy or sell foreign exchange either. A simple model of monetary policy in Cuba would instead assume that the central bank passively monetizes government deficits and government loans to enterprises. Monetary policy is subordinate to fiscal policy. The nearest thing to pure monetary policy in Cuba would be changes in the rate of interest paid on savings accounts. An increase in that rate of interest would be the closest thing to a textbook open market sale of bonds, since both withdraw currency from circulation and both increase interest rates and decrease consumption demand. But this policy would have no effect on investment demand in Cuba, since enterprises with soft budget constraints will always want to borrow as much as they are allowed.

What this means is that the standard argument in favor of having a national currency with flexible exchange rates—that it gives the central bank more freedom to use monetary policy for macroeconomic stabilization—is irrelevant for Cuba, since monetary policy is not currently being used to stabilize the economy. The Cuban economy has operated for many years with generalized excess demand for goods, most of which are rationed at fixed peso prices. The Cuban government would like to eliminate this excess demand, by converting the budget deficit into a surplus and thus removing the excess supply of money, but it has been unable to do so.

Only if there were major structural reforms in the Cuban economy, so that it responded more to price signals and less to direct controls, would the standard argument in favor of having a national currency with flexible exchange rates become relevant. These structural reforms would include the elimination of rationing and making the peso fully convertible.

The Benefits of Fixed Exchange Rates

A standard argument in favor of fixed exchange rates is that the constraint they impose on monetary policy can be a good thing if the monetary authorities cannot be trusted to use their power wisely. A constrained optimum is worse than the unconstrained optimum, but may still be better than the realistic alternative. It may be better for Cuban monetary policy to be decided in Washington than in Havana. This argument was accepted in Argentina, given its repeated history of hyperinflation. It is probably valid for Cuba as well, since Cuban inflation, as proxied by the free market exchange rate, has been much worse than U.S. inflation, and the Cuban history of macroeconomic stabilization is equally unimpressive.

But the problem with this argument is that it asks the Cuban government to tie its own hands. Fixed exchange rates can always be unfixed. And a fixed exchange rate for the Cuban peso, given Cuba's lack of foreign exchange reserves and lack of access to international credit markets, would be very vulnerable indeed to speculative attack. In fact, fixed exchange rates are a policy that has been tried and has failed to discipline Cuban monetary policy. Nominally, Cuba has had a fixed official exchange rate against the U.S. dollar since the revolution. But this has not prevented it from printing enough money to cause a 95 percent depreciation of the unofficial exchange rate. Indeed, the official exchange rate is now irrelevant, except as a way to tax exports and subsidize imports for favored enterprises.

Imposing discipline on Cuban monetary policy would take much more than a simple fixed exchange rate. A currency board is no more realistic. First, because Cuba cannot get the foreign exchange needed to have 100 percent reserves. Second, because even if it did somehow find those reserves, Cubans would probably expect the government to be unable to resist the temptation to spend them or to restrict convertibility and would immediately cash in all their pesos for dollars, leading to very rapid dollarization. To be credible, the currency board would need to be under the physical control of some foreign entity, like the Swiss embassy, and even here the Cuban government could presumably restrict convertibility by putting a police cordon around the embassy.[8]

Of the four main points along our spectrum, the two middle ones (fixed exchange rates and a currency board) are simply not realistically feasible. That leaves only the two extremes: flexible exchange rates at one extreme and full dollarization (or perhaps euroization) at the other extreme.

Dollarization

Suppose the Cuban government decided to abandon the peso altogether and allow some foreign currency, such as the U.S. dollar, to become the money generally used in Cuba. Demonetizing the peso should not be especially difficult. The government could simply announce that it would no longer accept pesos after a certain date. Given the large size of government as a share of the Cuban economy, it is unlikely that Cubans would thereafter continue to accept pesos in private transactions, provided any alternative medium of exchange were available, and U.S. dollars are available and are already widely acceptable as a medium of exchange. In addition, ceasing to enforce the laws against producing counterfeit pesos would provide a coup de grâce, if one were needed.

But if the peso were demonetized without compensation, this would amount to a large lump sum tax on the Cuban population, with a very irregular and unfair distribution. And if there were full compensation, so that pesos could be exchanged for U.S. dollars (say at twenty-eight pesos per dollar, this would require the Cuban government to have many millions of U.S. dollars in reserves (about 15 percent of Cuban GDP to replace the currency in circulation and about 20 percent of Cuban GDP if it wanted to replace savings accounts as well). Dollarization with full compensation would require the same level of initial foreign exchange reserves as setting up a currency board. A deliberate government policy of sudden dollarization is not realistic. The Cuban government lacks the foreign currency for any significant compensation, and without compensation the policy would be extremely unpopular and would create sudden terrible hardship for some individuals.

A slower path to dollarization is more feasible. By collecting more payments and taxes in dollars, and by making more payments in dollars, the peso could be slowly discouraged and replaced by the dollar as the sole medium of exchange. The slow route to dollarization does not eliminate the pain of dollarization without compensation, or the cost to the government of dollarization with compensation, but the pain or the cost could be spread out over more years. With full dollarization, the government could not devalue the currency, nor impose exchange controls, nor could it monetize deficits. The discipline on domestic monetary policy would be absolute, because there would be no domestic monetary policy. The Cuban government would be unable to monetize deficits, since it cannot print U.S. dollars. But would the Cuban government be willing to impose this discipline on itself?

The Cuban government would lose all seigniorage revenue under full dollarization, which would instead go to the U.S. government. Annual seigniorage is equal to the value of the money printed each year (minus the costs of printing and replacing worn out notes, which we will ignore). As a percentage of national income this is equal to the growth rate of the nominal money supply divided by the (income) velocity of circulation. To give a rough estimate of the amount of seigniorage, suppose the growth rate of the money supply is 12 percent per annum (which gives a 10 percent inflation rate assuming 2 percent growth in real income) and velocity is six, so that people on average hold on to two month's income in currency. Then seigniorage would be 12 percent divided by six, which equals 2 percent of national income. By abandoning its national money, the Cuban government would then need to increase taxes or cut spending by 2 percent of national income. This is a nontrivial amount, and it is hard to see the Cuban government willingly accepting this, especially when the main beneficiary would be a foreign government (and, a fortiori, the U.S. government).

Now a 12 percent growth rate of the money supply is perhaps a realistic figure for the long term, but during emergencies the Cuban government has increased the money supply by much greater amounts. According to CEPAL estimates, seigniorage went as high as 16 percent of GDP in 1993. All governments want to run deficits in emergencies, when it is very hard to raise taxes or cut spending quickly. Most governments can finance temporary deficits by borrowing, but that is hard or impossible for the Cuban government. Under full dollarization, the Cuban government would face a very tight budget constraint, in the short run as well as in the long run. It is very hard to believe the Cuban government would willingly give up its only way to finance emergency expenditure.

A second major problem of dollarization is the impossibility of a domestic lender of last resort. Under fractional reserve banking, there is always a risk of bank runs and the bank running out of reserves. Normally this problem can be avoided by making the central bank act as the lender of last resort to provide unlimited currency to a commercial bank facing a run on its deposits. But the central bank cannot play the role of lender of last resort if the deposits are in dollars and the central bank cannot print dollars. Banks must therefore either keep 100 percent reserves against dollar deposits or risk bank runs.[9]

Dollar or Euro?

One of the disadvantages of dollarization, in the eyes of the Cuban government, is that the seigniorage would go to its enemy, the U.S. government. For every dollar that goes to Cuba and stays in Cuba, the U.S. Federal Reserve can print one more dollar for domestic circulation, without causing domestic inflation, and so one dollar's worth of goods and services gets transferred from Cuba to the U.S. government. (Unless the dollar originally came to Cuba as a free gift, in which case the transfer of resources is from the individual foreign donor to the U.S. government.) Even if the dollar eventually leaves Cuba and has to be withdrawn from circulation by the Federal Reserve, Cubans have made an interest-free loan to the U.S. government for the whole time the dollar stayed in Cuba. Naturally, this gives a strong reason for the Cuban government to prefer euroization to dollarization, for then the seigniorage would go to Europe rather than Washington. But which would be best for the Cuban economy?

The standard criteria for an optimal currency region include high labor and capital mobility within the region; symmetric rather than asymmetric aggregate demand and supply shocks within the region; and a high amount of interregional trade and finance. On the first criterion (high labor and capital mobility), Cuba is not an optimal currency area with any other country (indeed, on this criterion Cuba itself can hardly be called an optimal currency area). On the second criterion (symmetric shocks), neither the dollar zone nor the euro zone look especially compatible with Cuba. The third criterion (interregional trade and finance) looks more promising. Cuba receives far more European tourists than U.S. tourists. By adopting the euro instead of the U.S. dollar as its currency for the tourist sector, the European tourists would be saved the transaction costs and uncertainties of converting their euros into dollars, and Cuba could raise prices accordingly and earn more tourist revenue. The gain to Cuba could be of the order of a couple of percent of its gross receipts from euro zone tourists.

But Cuba's main source of foreign exchange is not tourism but remittances, and most of those remittances come from the United States.[10] It is hard to predict how the volume of those remittances would be affected if either the donors or the recipients had first to convert their U.S. dollars into euros. But presumably the recipients would bear some of the increased transactions costs, and the net amount of foreign exchange available to be spent in Cuba would fall. Now the welfare of either the donors or the recipients may be of no direct concern to the Cuban government, but the volume of foreign exchange spent in Cuba does matter to the Cuban government, because the Cuban government sells goods in the dollar stores to the recipients. It is exactly as if the U.S. donors themselves went to Cuba as tourists and spent their dollars in the government dollar stores but then handed over the goods to their Cuban relatives. The Cuban government can tax those remittances by raising the prices in the dollar store above world prices.[11] An increase in the transactions costs of remittances, from requiring payment in euros rather than dollars, will reduce the money spent by these virtual U.S. tourists and thereby reduce the Cuban government's tax revenues from the dollar stores. If the foreign currency earned from virtual U.S. tourists exceeds that earned from actual European tourists, then Cuba should prefer dollarization to euroization. But apart from any arguments about optimal currency areas, and whether Cuba does more trade with the dollar zone than with the euro zone, there is the fact that the U.S. dollar has a long history of acceptance in Cuba, while the euro has none.

Money is an asset that yields services to the person who holds it, rather like a consumer durable, such as a refrigerator. But unlike refrigerators, the usefulness of holding any particular brand of money depends on how many of your trading partners also hold and accept that brand of money. There is a network externality in money, as there is in telephones or languages. And where there are network externalities there is path dependence. History matters. Cubans are familiar with the U.S. dollar. They know what it is worth and trust its value. They accept it because they know that other individual Cubans, not just the dollar stores, will in turn accept it from them. Even criminal penalties were insufficient to prevent individual Cubans from holding and accepting U.S. dollars. The mere availability of an alternative foreign currency, the euro, will not necessarily drive the dollar out of circulation. Attempts by the Cuban government to replace the dollar with the euro may merely turn a two-currency economy into a three-currency economy and raise transactions costs still further.[12]

The French can switch from francs to euros by way of a transition period within which the franc and the euro are freely convertible at a fixed exchange rate, but the Cuban government cannot fix the exchange rate between the euro and the dollar. The government of France can abolish the franc, but the Cuban government cannot abolish the dollar. It would be a lot harder for the government of Cuba to get Cubans to switch from dollars to euros than for the government of France to get the French to switch from francs to euros. Switching from dollars to euros may not be feasible.

Reducing Dollarization

If the Cuban government can reduce dollarization, and thereby increase the demand for pesos, it can increase its ability to collect seigniorage. There are various policies the Cuban government could use to reduce the extent of dollarization of the Cuban economy. In 1994, at the height of the economic crisis, almost all goods and services were rationed, and the monthly peso salary of most workers was more than was needed to buy the goods actually available, and so the value of the marginal peso earned by an individual Cuban was almost zero. There was nothing to spend it on. It is not surprising that the black market exchange rate rose to 120 pesos to the dollar, since the marginal dollar could buy extra goods, and the marginal peso could not. Opening the agricultural markets, where Cubans could spend marginal pesos, albeit at high prices, immediately caused the peso to appreciate to about forty pesos per dollar. Allowing the legal exchange of pesos for convertible pesos, which could be spent in the dollar stores at par with the U.S. dollar, increased the demand for pesos even more, and it appreciated further to about twenty pesos per dollar, until the recent depreciation to twenty-eight pesos per dollar. These steps, coupled with attempts to control the budget deficit and reduce the stock of pesos in circulation, helped to prevent the collapse of the peso as a store of value and medium of exchange.

If it wished, the Cuban government could further reverse dollarization by requiring tourist hotels to accept pesos only. If tourists had to buy pesos to spend in Cuba, they would want to be able to convert any unspent pesos back into foreign currency at the end of their stay in Cuba. But if the Cuban government allowed foreign tourists to do this, individual Cubans would use foreign tourists to convert their own pesos into dollars, just as they used to use foreign tourists to buy them goods in the dollar stores in the days when Cubans were excluded. And if the Cuban government did not allow tourists to reconvert pesos, the resulting inconvenience would make Cuba a less attractive destination.

Also, the tourism industry in Cuba relies heavily on imported inputs. If tourists exchange their foreign currency for pesos, which they spend in the hotel, which in turn has to convert those pesos back into foreign currency to buy imports, the transactions costs are much higher than if the tourists simply spend foreign currency in the hotels, which the hotel spends on imports.

Cuba's Monetary Future

Cuba's near-term monetary future will probably be much the same as Cuba's recent monetary past. The Cuban government will not deliberately abandon the peso. Quite apart from symbolic reasons, it simply cannot afford the loss of seigniorage. But neither will the Cuban government eliminate the use of the U.S. dollar. Quite apart from the failure of its past attempts to do this, forcing foreign tourists to use the inconvertible peso would seriously damage Cuba's tourist revenues. And introducing the euro will only further complicate an already complicated monetary system; the euro would not drive out the dollar.

But in the longer term some radical changes are possible to Cuba's monetary system. If Cuba became a market economy, which responded to price incentives, there would be a definite advantage to Cuba in having an independent national currency, freely convertible under flexible exchange rates. An independent central bank could then use monetary policy to pursue macroeconomic stabilization. But this is only feasible if budgetary discipline is accepted and a market in government bonds reestablished so that the central bank is not simply forced to monetize government budget deficits.

Alternatively, Cuba could forgo the advantages of an independent monetary policy in favor of the advantages of joining a common currency area. If there were a political rapprochement between the Cuban and U.S. governments, so that trade and investment were again permitted, Cuba's history, geography, and the existence of a large, wealthy, and entrepreneurial Cuban émigré population in the United States would make it natural for Cuba to join the dollar zone. And, very optimistically, the U.S. government may even make a free gift of the dollars needed to withdraw the pesos from circulation. Such a gift would cost the U.S. government nothing (except for paper and ink). A more pessimistic scenario is also possible, of course, in which a governmental, budgetary, and economic crisis causes the collapse of the peso and dollarization by default.

Notes

1. It established also a fixed exchange rate between the U.S. dollar and the gold Spanish and French coins. At that time, the silver Spanish coins were the most used in transactions. Note the coincidence between government (in this case the U.S. government) and individual (Cuban) decisions about currency. The silver Spanish coins were unstable so there was a risk and a cost associated with holding them.

2. The Cuban currency, although strong and stable, was not used and it was costly for the government. All the Cuban coins had the same value in terms of gold, silver, nickel, and copper as their equivalents in the U.S. monetary system. Both the Cuban gold peso and the U.S. dollar were legal tender. Furthermore, some of the U.S. certificates that had limited circulation in the U.S. were legal tender in Cuba. For two decades this was the monetary system in use.

3. The new Cuban certificates provoked an initial credit contraction as individuals were afraid of lending U.S. dollars and getting repaid in pesos that might depreciate. Also there were not enough Cuban certificates to cover big transactions.

4. This was especially true during the war and early postwar years when imports were hard to get. Estimates show that there were two hundred million pesos in "excess" in the hands of individuals and firms, and when dollar holdings are added it goes up to four hundred million. These holdings were a precautionary reserve in case of a recession due to the almost absolute dependence on the sugar crop. The other reason for holding dollars was the 2 percent tax on the export of money, so people would hold dollars in order to finance their tourist expenditures in the U.S. The dollar holdings of the public did not result in a reduction of the international reserves of the Central Bank. They came from withdrawals from the dollar deposits with the commercial banks and the transformation from dollar into peso deposits that freed dollar reserves in the commercial banks to sale to the public.

5. In the 1940s, when it became clear that the final switch to a full peso standard was only a question of time, a reduction in the dollar assets and liabilities in the banks had taken place. In 1951, after the creation of the Cuban Central Bank, the Cuban peso was going to be the sole legal tender for most transactions in Cuba.

6. The black market exchange rate has fluctuated widely, reaching a high of about 120 pesos per dollar during the crisis in 1995. Thereafter it stabilized for several years at around 20 pesos but jumped to 28 pesos in October 2001.

7. But in 2002 convertible pesos have been rationed or sometimes unavailable.

8. This passage was written before the collapse of Argentina's currency board. If Argentina cannot stick to a currency board, it is even more unlikely that Cuba can.

9. Again, this passage was written before the banking crisis in Argentina. The fears seem even more real now.

10. Gross foreign exchange earnings are probably larger for tourism, but given the high imports needed to sustain the tourist sector, net foreign exchange earnings may be higher from remittances.

11. It is interesting to note that the introduction of the euro in the tourist sector in 2002 coincided with a major price increase in the dollar stores.

12. Though we must allow the possibility that increased Cuban emigration to Europe, along with increased European tourism, may increase the use of euros in Cuba with or without encouragement from the Cuban government.

References

Carranza Valdes, Julio, Luis Gutierrez Urdaneta, and Pedro Monreal Gonzalez. 1995. *Cuba: La restrucuracion de la economía, una propuesta para debate.* Havana, Cuba: Editoriàl de Aéncias Sociales.

Edwards, Sebastian. 1993. "Dollarization in Latin America" *World Bank Discussion Papers* no. 207. Washington, D.C.: World Bank.

Fernandez Tabio, Luis Rene. 1997. "El problema de la dolarizacion en la economía Cubana." Unpublished paper. Havana, Cuba.

Foreign Policy Association. 1935. "Problemas de la Nueva Cuba." In *Informe de la comisión de asuntos Cubanos.* New York: Foreign Policy Association.

International Bank of Reconstruction and Development. 1951. *Report on Cuba: Findings and Recommendations of an Economic and Technical Mission.* Washington, D.C.

Sandoval, Raul. 1995. "Cuba: Dolarizacion, endeudamiento, proceso de ajuste y otras reflexiones." *Economía y Desarrallo,* no. 2:49–63.

CHAPTER 4

Export Processing Zones in Cuba

Larry Willmore

In a bid to attract foreign investment and increase exports, the government of Cuba inaugurated two export processing zones (EPZs) in the Havana area in May 1997, a third at the nearby port of Mariel in November 1997, and a fourth in the southern port of Cienfuegos. Although this represents a radical shift in post-1959 Cuban policy, it is a movement toward incentives long offered in the region by other governments, including that of prerevolutionary Cuba.[1] In some respects Cuba is a less than ideal location for export-oriented manufacturing, for the country is currently cut off from the U.S. market and lacks preferential access to markets outside of Latin America and the Caribbean. On the other hand, exporters are free to ship goods to any country other than the United States, and Cuba offers them an educated labor force, low wages, and the absence of independent trade unions, so development of export processing is by no means a far-fetched idea.

Cuba's EPZ Incentives

In June 1996, President Fidel Castro enacted Decree Law 165, which allows EPZs to operate in Cuba. In October of that same year the government set up a National Office of Free Zones to administer the law. The proposed Cienfuegos Free Zone and two of the free zones in the Havana area (Wajay and Mariel) are administered by Almacenes Universales S.A., a commercial venture of the Revolutionary Armed Forces that has concentrated on leasing space of in-bond warehouses to foreign producers and promoting sales of their goods. The fourth EPZ (City of Havana Free Zone, in Berroa, on the eastern outskirts of Havana) is administered by CIMEX, a large public enterprise responsible for the wholesale and retail distribution of a wide variety of local and imported goods. CIMEX, like Almacenes Universales, leases space for storage of imports in its in-bond warehouses. Both companies immediately began to convert existing warehouses for factory use and announced plans to make additional EPZ factory space available with an ambitious program of urbanization and construction of

Table 4.1 Export Processing Zones, 1997

	Land Area (hs)	Construction (m2)		Planned Construction (m2)
		Office	*Warehouse*	
Wajay free zone	21	1,100	13,000	5,000
Havana free zone	244	4,200	41,616	233,829
Mariel free zone	553	540	7,000	12,500
Cienfuegos free zone	432	9,800	11,800	13,000
TOTAL	1,250	15,640	73,416	264,329

Source: Business Tips on Cuba (July 1997), published by the National Office of Technological Information Promotion System in Cuba, available at that time on the Internet at http://www.tips.cu.

Note: Land area is in hectares (one hectare equals 2.47 acres) and construction is in square meters (one square meter equals 10.76 square feet). Planned construction is for 1997–2001.

new buildings. The Cuban authorities have set aside a total of 1,250 hectares for the four free zones. (See table 4.1.) To place this statistic in perspective, it should be noted that Panama's bustling Colon Free Zone occupies less than 400 hectares of land. Prior to the inauguration of Cuba's free zones, the Colon Free Zone was the largest in the Western Hemisphere both in size and in volume of shipments; it is now largest only in shipments, as both Mariel and Cienfuegos surpass it in land area.

In many respects, Cuba's EPZ legislation resembles that of other countries in the Caribbean Basin. Free zones are deemed to lie outside the customs territory, so the government does not in any way tax or restrict the exports or imports of firms operating in the zones. Similarly, with respect to capital flows, article 38.1 of Decree Law 165 provides for the unrestricted transfer abroad of profits. Investors are allowed as a matter of course to retain full ownership of EPZ plants; this is an important concession in Cuba, where all foreign investors so far have had to form joint ventures with public enterprises and are limited to a maximum participation of 49 percent.[2] Investors with plants in EPZs are also entitled to total exemption from Cuban income tax and taxes on labor utilization for twelve years, to be followed by a 50 percent exemption for another five years.

In one important way, Cuba's concessions to investors in EPZs exceed those of any other country in the region. Export processing zones are designed to promote exports. In this spirit, Caribbean countries invariably prohibit EPZ sales to the domestic market. In other words, they require producers to export all their output (Willmore 1996). Central American governments allow limited sales to the local market, but never in competition with domestic industry, never without payment of full import duties, and never without specific permission for each sale (Willmore 1992). In contrast, Cuba *automatically* allows EPZ plants, subject only to payment of duties, to sell up to 25 percent of their output in the national market. Moreover, Cuba exempts from payment of duty that portion of a product that is national value-added, and EPZ companies can sell an unlimited amount of their output in the domestic market with approval. Products that incorporate at least 50 percent Cuban value-added are totally exempt from payment of duty. No other country in the Caribbean basin offers these incentives for EPZ sales to the domestic market.

Wage Costs

Export processing plants are generally low-skilled, labor-intensive operations, so potential investors look carefully at minimum wages. The government of Cuba set the EPZ minimum wage at 163 pesos a month. This is more than 50 percent higher than the minimum wage in the rest of the economy, but it is still very low. Converted at the rate used by government exchange houses *(casas de cambio)* in October of 1997 for the purchase of foreign currency, it is equivalent to little more than U.S.$7.00 dollars a month. Assuming a forty-hour workweek and an average of 4.2 weeks in a month, this amounts to approximately U.S.$0.04 an hour. Average wages are somewhat higher, about 200 pesos a month, which is equivalent to U.S.$8.70 a month or somewhat more than U.S.$0.05 an hour. Cuban professionals, including medical doctors and university professors, seldom earn more than 400 pesos a month, so EPZ wages are high by Cuban standards. Nonetheless, they are far lower than take-home pay of workers in EPZs of other countries in the region (see table 4.2) and lower even than wages in export processing plants located in the People's Republic of China.

Table 4.2 Minimum and Average Wages for Sewing Machine Operators in Caribbean and Central American Countries *(in U.S. Dollars per Hour, 1990s)*

	Employee Take-Home Pay		Employer Cost	
	Minimum	Average	Minimum	Average
Caribbean				
Cuba*	0.04	0.05	1.50	1.75
Dominican Republic	0.42	0.71	0.55	0.94
Jamaica	0.32	1.08	0.40	1.34
Saint Lucia	0.75	1.20	0.87	1.41
Trinidad	0.38	1.00	0.38	1.00
Central America				
Costa Rica	0.65	1.02		
El Salvador	0.41	0.56		
Guatemala	0.33	0.46		
Honduras	0.41	0.57		
Nicaragua	0.21	0.60		

Source: Author's field research in Cuba in October 1997; Willmore (1996) for other Caribbean countries; Willmore (1992) for Central America.

*1997 wage data for Euro Latina, a plant that mixes and packages beverage powders, since no garment factory operates in any of Cuba's export processing zones.

Calculation of the foreign exchange equivalent of local wages is complicated by the fact that three currencies circulate side by side in Cuba: ordinary pesos (which fluctuate in value), convertible pesos (pegged to the U.S. dollar), and U.S. dollars. All three currencies are legal means of payment at least for some transactions, but wages are paid in ordinary pesos while many goods and services can be purchased only with convertible pesos or dollars.

Residents and tourists alike can buy and sell currency at commercial banks or at any of the many small exchange houses operated by the Cuban government in Havana and throughout the island. In October 1997 these houses purchased convertible pesos and U.S. dollars at the rate of twenty-three pesos and sold convertible pesos at the rate of twenty-five pesos. Customers could purchase ordinary pesos without limit. The exchange houses did not sell U.S. dollars, but many did sell convertible pesos, subject to a limit of four hundred convertible pesos per purchaser per day. Convertible pesos are accepted in Cuban shops and restaurants on par with the U.S. dollar, but they have no value abroad. The illegal black market price of U.S. dollars in October 1997 was close to the government's buying rate of twenty-three pesos, which indicates there was little or no excess demand for dollars.

Cuban workers are able to survive despite their low wages because they receive free health care and education from the government, and they pay no more than 10 percent of their income for housing. In addition, all Cubans are entitled to a subsidized monthly food ration. The rationed goods are limited, however, and do not cover all basic needs. Workers are free to shop at farmers' markets and in dollar stores where goods are not rationed, but prices in the open market are high for anyone who depends on a Cuban salary. Each adult is allowed, for example, to purchase each month, at very low prices, 6 pounds (2.7 kilograms) of rice and 20 ounces (570 grams) of beans. Rice and beans are basic to the Cuban diet; rice sold in October 1997 on the open market for about U.S.$0.20 a pound (U.S.$0.44 per kilogram) and beans sold for U.S.$0.39 a pound (U.S.$0.86 per kilogram). These are the prices Cubans must pay to supplement their monthly allotment of subsidized food.

Luxuries excluded from the ration card are also available on the open market, at a price. Fresh pork, for example, in October 1997 sold for the equivalent of U.S.$1.09 a pound (U.S.$2.39 a kilo), local ham for twice that price, and beer for U.S.$0.75 per twelve-ounce can or bottle. Large avocados could be purchased for the equivalent of U.S.$0.34 each, and oranges and limes for U.S.$0.02 each. Wages and prices did not change much in subsequent years. For the average worker, a single avocado represents nearly a day's wages, and a pound of fresh pork, almost all of three days' wages.

Nonwage Costs and Investor Response

Despite the availability of a large supply of educated workers at low wages, investors did not rush to Cuba's new EPZs. In May 1997, the first EPZ plant began operations: Euro Latina in the Wajay Free Zone near Havana International Airport. At the beginning of 1998 no other EPZ plant was even in the planning stage of operation, although dozens of foreign companies were alleged to have made inquiries. Euro Latina is a Jamaican-owned company that employs a Chilean manager and about forty Cuban nationals (all high school or university graduates) to mix and package powders that are dissolved in water in the home to make beverages. Euro Latina uses Argentine equipment and imports all packaging material, chemicals, and flavors from Argentina, but there is considerable backward linkage with the Cuban economy because sugar is a major ingredient in their soluble beverage powders. The government granted Euro Latina permission to sell all its output in the national market for an initial period of two years, after which it was supposed to begin to export to foreign markets, but this never happened.

EPZ plants are notoriously footloose and move in and out of countries in a matter of weeks. Such investments thrive in uncertain political environments that are too hostile for less reversible ventures. Haiti, for example, by 1990 was host to 145 export processing plants that employed approximately 140,000 workers. The owners of these plants quickly relocated production to the Dominican Republic and other countries following the 1991 military coup d'état. Haiti's civilian president was restored to power in October 1994; by the end of 1995, forty of the EPZ plants had returned to the country, despite the continued existence of political unrest and uncertainty. These forty plants generated about 12,000 jobs in Haiti, attracted by an abundant supply of labor and a minimum wage that was equivalent to only U.S.$0.30 an hour (United Nations 1996, 205). It was not unreasonable to expect EPZ producers similarly to move at least some of their operations quickly to Cuba's new export processing zones, yet Cuban authorities were disappointed. Publicly, promoters speak of hundreds of investors attracted to the EPZs, but they fail to mention that these investments are invariably commercial rather than industrial. A lengthy article in the magazine *Bohemia* (Alfonso 2002), for example, describes the exports of rum, fruit juice, coffee, and marmalade from the Wajay Free Zone, but these goods are not manufactured in the free zone; they are purchased from state-owned plants elsewhere on the island, stored in Wajay warehouses, then shipped without transformation to customers in Spain, Brazil, and other countries. Comercio Exterior Velenciano (CEXVAL S.A.), the free zone firm responsible for the exports, is a trading company and does not own or operate any manufacturing plants. This is the case for nearly all firms in Cuba's free zones.

One might argue that Cuba's failure to attract manufacturing investment to its EPZs is a consequence of the Cuban Liberty and Democratic Solidarity (Helms-Burton) Act signed into law by U.S. President Clinton in March 1996. But this is not plausible. The Helms-Burton Act targets only firms that traffic in properties confiscated from U.S. companies or from anyone currently a U.S. citizen. EPZ investors do not make use of any confiscated property, so they are not affected by provisions of the Helms-Burton Act.

Cuba's EPZ strategy has failed and will continue to fail, not because of the external embargo, but because of Cuba's own internal policies, which (1) do not allow foreign companies to hire workers directly and, most important, (2) impose a high implicit tax on wages. Regarding the first point, foreign firms operating in Cuba are required to hire all labor through an employing entity designated by the government. In practice, for plants located in an EPZ, this entity is the administrator of the free zone (Almacenes Universales, or CIMEX), which, technically, employs all workers in the zone. Both the 1996 Free Zone Law and the 1995 Foreign Investment Law (section 5) specifically forbid foreign companies to hire workers directly. This preserves the role of the Cuban state as sole employer and facilitates control of political dissidents, but it limits the freedom of firms to choose their own workers.

Even though the minimum wage in Cuban EPZs is only about $7.00 a month (U.S.$0.04 per hour), the cost to employers is U.S.$250.00 a month (U.S.$1.50 per hour). Nonwage labor costs amount to more than 97 percent of total labor costs, which means that labor in Cuba is quite dear compared to nearby countries. Most of the nonwage costs result from exchange rate losses: owners of EPZ plants are forced to purchase pesos at the official exchange rate, so it costs U.S.$163.00 to pay a worker 163 pesos that are worth only $7.00 at the market rate of exchange.[3] The worker gains nothing from this implicit payroll tax and would prefer to receive the U.S.$163.00 rather than 163 pesos. In addition, there are a number of legally mandated fringe benefits that add to labor costs. These employee benefits include a 14 percent contribution to social security, two weeks' paid vacation, six paid holidays, and a U.S.$2.60 daily lunch supplied by the administrator of the EPZ to each worker but paid for by his or her employer in U.S. dollars. Take-home pay is low that, to motivate workers, foreign-owned companies operating in Cuba find they must provide bonuses, such as monthly bags of toiletries or hard currency under the table, increasing labor costs even more.

The Future of EPZs in Cuba

What is the future for export processing in Cuba? With labor costs in excess of U.S.$1.50 an hour, Cuba is not likely to attract export-oriented investment. Import substitution is a different story, for the free zones are an attractive option for companies that want to enter the domestic market. Advantages of locating inside rather than outside an EPZ include the possibility of retaining full ownership of a firm and exemption from numerous duties and taxes, including an 11 percent labor utilization tax that joint ventures pay in U.S. dollars on top of the hard-currency payments they make to the Cuban state employing entity.

EPZ firms may well be willing to export some of their output at a loss in order to obtain preferential access to the domestic market. But, unless there is a drastic change in policy, it is access to the domestic market, not the possibility of exporting, that might attract some manufacturing activity to Cuba's free zones. Most likely, the free zones will continue to function almost exclusively as bonded warehouses for goods in transit to the domestic economy and, to a lesser extent, for goods in transit to foreign markets. In sum, the free zones will continue to be zones for transshipment, not export processing.

Notes

The opinions expressed are personal and do not necessarily reflect the views of the United Nations Secretariat. I conducted field research in October 1997 while employed as a lecturer in microeconomic theory for Carleton University's M.A. program in economics at the University of Havana. I am grateful to Prof. Elena Hernandez of the University of Havana for help and logistical support and to Ing. Pablo Torres, general manager of the Wajay Free Zone, for providing information; however, neither person has seen this paper nor, most emphatically, do they necessarily agree with the opinions expressed. On a subsequent visit to Cuba in November 1998, it was not possible to visit any of the free zones, but no developments appear to have taken place since the 1997 visit.

1. For an analysis of EPZs in other countries of the Caribbean basin, see Kaplinsky (1993, 1995) and Willmore (1992, 1995, 1996). For a brief description of EPZs in prerevolutionary Cuba, see Rodríguez (1997).

2. The 1995 Foreign Investment Law does contemplate wholly foreign-owned companies, but only one has been approved to date outside the EPZs, and the foreign ownership is specifically limited to a period of four and a half years. The investment consists of a $15 million electrical plant built on the Isla de la Juventud in late 1999 by a Panamanian-owned firm, Genpower Cuba S.A. Full ownership of the plant will transfer to Unión Eléctrica, a government-owned utility, in 2004 (see Rodríguez Molina 1999).

3. The Dominican Republic prior to 1985 used this same mechanism of a dual exchange rate to tax EPZ labor, but the implicit tax at its height was only 38.4 percent [100*(125–77)/125) in the Dominican Republic compared to 95.6 percent [100*(163–7)/163] in Cuba. See Willmore (1995, 529).

References

Alonso, Marcos. 2002. "Exportaciones: Inaplazable realidad." *Revista Bohemia* 1, no. 20 (11 September), at www.bohemia.cubaweb.cu.

Kaplinsky, Raphael. 1993. "Export Processing Zones in the Dominican Republic: Transforming Manufactures into Commodities." *World Development* 21, no. 11 (November): 1851–65.

______. 1995. "A Reply to Willmore." *World Development* 23, no. 3 (March): 537–40.

Rodríguez, Herminia. 1997. "Zonas francas: Hablemos con franquicia." *Bohemia* 89, no. 15 (18 July): 32–35.

Rodríguez Molina, Diego. 1999. "Avanza construcción de moderna central eléctrica," *Granma,* 5 November.

United Nations. 1996. "Investment in Post-Conflict Situations." Chapter 8, *World Economic and Social Survey 1996,* 189–213. New York: United Nations.

Willmore, Larry. 1992. "Industrial Policy in Central America." *Cepal Review* 48 (December): 95–106.

______. 1995. "Export Processing Zones in the Dominican Republic: A Comment on Kaplinsky." *World Development* 23, no. 3 (March): 529–35.

______. 1996. "Export Processing in the Caribbean: Lessons from Four Case Studies." *ECLAC Working Paper,* no. 42.

PART III

The Agricultural Sector

CHAPTER 5

Crisis and Reform in Cuba's Sugar Economy

Brian H. Pollitt

Between 1991 and 1994, Cuba's GDP fell by more than one-third. Such a collapse has been matched for Cuba only by the Great Depression of the 1930s. From the mid-1990s, however, economic recovery has been both significant and more or less sustained, although figures reporting very high recent growth rates are flattered by their depressed starting bases. The recovery process, moreover, has been structurally uneven. For example, from 1995 to 2002, while there was substantial absolute growth in the tourist sector, average annual sugar production remained only half that of the 1980s. Moreover, the persistently weak performance of the sugar economy up to 2002 coexisted with official statements that annual output was to be restored to some seven million tonnes—that is, to volumes close to those achieved in the heyday of Cuba's pre-1992 trading relations with the Council for Mutual Economic Assistance (COMECON). While lack of reliable data makes the appraisal of recent performance tentative, this essay considers some of the factors shaping output, organization, and policy in the growing and processing of Cuba's sugarcane from 1989 to 2002.

Background

From 1985 to 1989, Cuban sugar production averaged 7.6 million tonnes per annum.[1] Exports averaged 6.9 million tonnes. Of total exports, more than two-thirds were sold at premium prices on Soviet and other COMECON markets. In 1989 such premiums lifted the average value of Cuban sugar exports to all socialist countries to 642 pesos a tonne, or three times the 214 pesos a tonne received on 1.5 million tonnes shipped to market economies. Favorable terms of trade such as these encouraged a 20 percent growth of Cuban sugar production between the mid-1970s and the 1980s. This was attributable primarily to increased productivity in the cane-supply system made possible by large increases in imported inputs. Between 1980 and 1989, for example, field yields increased from 46 tonnes to 60 tonnes per hectare harvested due

Table 5.1 Cuban Sugar Industry Performance Indicators, 1950–59 and 1980–89

Crop Year	Sugar Produced (10^3t, 96° Basis)[a]	Harvest Days[b]	Milling Days[c]	Agricultural Yield[d]	Industrial Yield[e]
1950	5,621	100	87	35.9	13.06
1951	5,821	105	93	35.5	12.89
1952	7,298	130	115	41.8	12.19
1953	5,224	94	83	40.4	12.75
1954	4,959	90	80	41.0	12.62
1955	4,598	76	68	41.7	13.21
1956	4,807	87	72	37.2	12.91
1957	5,742	93	82	36.1	12.78
1958	5,863	109	86	43.6	12.62
1959	6,037	103	87	45.0	12.47
1980	6,665	149	109	46.0	10.82
1981	7,359	136	114	55.1	11.08
1982	8,210	152	124	55.1	11.17
1983	7,109	160	113	58.0	10.35
1984	8,207	166	126	57.4	10.47
1985	8,004	135	103	50.0	11.99
1986	7,255	137	104	51.6	10.62
1987	7,117	141	99	52.1	10.64
1988	7,415	128	100	56.8	10.85
1989	8,121	145	109	60.0	10.83

Sources: 1950–59, *Anuario Azucarero de Cuba;* 1980–89, *Anuario Estadístico de Cuba.*

Notes: a. Sugar statistics should not be interpreted too closely. The method used in Cuba to convert physical raw sugars into the 96° standard results, at the average polarization of Cuban raws reported in recent years, in values about 2.5 percent lower than the formula of the International Sugar Organization. Discrepancies between different Cuban publications can be found in other series but do not alter the trends discussed here. b. Total length of the harvest from beginning to end. c. Length of time in days in which mills are actually grinding. d. Tonnes of cane per hectare harvested. e. Sugar, basis 96°, percent cane.

mainly to the increased use of imported fertilizers and to more irrigation using both imported fuel and equipment.

Over the same period, there was increased mechanization in cane cultivation, harvesting, hauling, cleaning, and transshipment. By 1991, cane farms counted on 4,450 chopper harvesters to cut and load some 70 percent of the crop and all hand-cut cane was mechanically loaded. A park of more than fifty thousand tractors was reported for the same year, and over 85 percent of harvested cane was cleaned and/or transshipped by more than eight hundred dry cleaning stations (MINAZ 1990, 156). Cuban industry added value to a range of farm and factory machines, implements, and parts, but all depended to some degree on imported capital goods, fuels, and raw materials, mostly supplied by the USSR and other COMECON countries. The disintegration of these in 1991 brought both the loss of important East European markets and a deterioration in the terms of trade between Cuba and the new members of the Commonwealth of Independent States.

Table 5.2 Cane Yields Reported by Selected Cane Farms, 1989/90–1992/93
(Metric Tonnes per Hectare)

Sugar Mill	1989–90 tonnes/ha	1990–91 tonnes/ha	1991–92 tonnes/ha	1992–93 tonnes/ha	% Change 1989–90/ 1992–93
UBPC Fajardo, Habana	62	63	61	40	–35.5
CPA 17 de Mayo, Habana	86	90	79	54	-37.2
CPA Antonino Rojas, Habana	100	75	54	44	–56.0
CPA Revolución de Octubre, Matanzas	84	65	56	48	–42.9
CPA Manuel Ascunce, Matanzas	90	88	60	45	-50.0
CPA 17 de Mayo, Matanzas	99	96	69	59	–40.4
CPA Hermanos Almeida, Matanzas	89	87	75	39	–56.2
CPA Heroes de Moncada, Matanzas	82	67	64	40	–51.2
UBPCs Pedroso and Socorro, Matanzas	64	62	59	53	-17.2
UBPC Arratia, Matanzas	—	79	64	51	—
UBPC Ciege, Matanzas	47	40	37	36	–23.4
Average	80	74	62	46	42.5

Source: Author's fieldwork (1994).
Note: — = not known.

As Cuba's capacity to import needed inputs collapsed, so did productivity in both field and factory: production and exports were both held at over seven million tonnes in 1992 but then slumped to less than four million tonnes in 1993. Falling cane yields were the prime cause. According to official figures, these fell by over 30 percent between 1990 and 1993, from 52.5 tonnes to 35.6 tonnes per hectare harvested, primarily due to shortages of fertilizers and of fuel. Inadequate supplies of poor-quality cane in turn contributed to the disruption of factory operations. In 1990 the share of loss in potential milling time was 26.9 percent. By 1993 it had risen to 49 percent.

At the end of the 1980s, sugar generated three-quarters of Cuba's total foreign exchange earnings from merchandise exports. These were hit first by sharp falls in sugar prices from 1989 and then by the post-1992 slump in production and exports. The combination threatened the prospects for securing even a modest revival in the island's import capacity. Moreover, while constraints on the rapid development of nonsugar export earnings made some restoration of sugar production vital, the less favorable market conditions of the post-Soviet world inhibited any lavish deployment of costly imported inputs to achieve it. In Cuba's newly adverse circumstances, the island's planners had to address two key questions. The first was how to check a further decline in sugar production. The second was how to promote a recovery at a unit cost—and notably at an import cost—significantly below that of the 1980s.

The 1993 Reforms

Cuba sought the answers to these questions in its own history rather than in the experiences of the wider world. Up to the 1980s, field and factory operations had been separately managed by the ministries of agriculture and sugar. In the early 1980s, however, the state-owned lands producing the bulk of national cane supplies were integrated into large-scale mill-plantation complexes—CAIs—administered solely by the sugar ministry. This was justified at the time by a perceived need to improve and expand the organization of mechanized field operations and to ensure that agricultural practices were subordinated to the requirements of industrial processing (del Monte 1980). By 1993, however, acute shortages of imported inputs and a steady deterioration of existing machinery and equipment forced the adoption of different priorities. It was now hoped that smaller, more autonomous enterprises would achieve a more efficient use of scarce resources and foster labor-intensive practices, import substitution, and, where possible, increased labor productivity through better work organization and incentives. From the autumn of 1993, in the most radical structural change in Cuban agriculture since the agrarian reform laws of 1959 and 1963, the large-scale farm enterprises owned and operated by the state in both cane and non-cane agriculture began to be dismantled.

The alternative organizational form selected was the basic unit of cooperative production *(unidad básica de producción cooperativa)*, or UBPC. Its development was swiftest in the sugar sector and the 1993/94 harvest began with some 90 percent of CAI-administered land, embracing almost four-fifths of the country's total area under cane, transformed into UBPCs. UBPCs were part worker cooperatives, part collective farms, composed mostly of former state farm or CAI employees working for wages and distributed profits on lands leased in perpetuity from the state. In size, management structure, and organization these were largely modeled on the agricultural production cooperatives *(cooperativas de producción agropecuaria)*, or CPAs, that had been fostered among private farms since 1977.

The CPAs had been developed by pooling the holdings of individual farmers to achieve economies of scale through a more rational, specialized use of land and labor, combined with modern means and methods of production. By concentrating dispersed peasant households, they also simplified the provision of electricity, sanitation and better housing, schools, and medical care. By 1985 cane CPAs had become quite large, averaging 953 hectares and seventy-three members, and by 1989/90, some 63 percent of CPA canes were cut by machine, against 26 percent of private, non-CPA canes. Moreover, while private growers hired mechanized harvesting services from the state, the CPAs generally organized such operations on their own account, and by 1990 they owned 560 chopper harvesters together with all ancillary equipment (Pollitt 1994, 557; 1997a, 189–90). Most CPAs thus confronted the post-1989 import crisis not as simple peasant collectives employing predominantly traditional farming methods on lands now held in common, but as quite large agricultural enterprises, using machines, fertilizers, herbicides, and other imports on a scale approaching state farms and CAI lands.

But average CPA performance in terms of yields and unit costs was clearly better, and despite their adoption over the 1980s of more import-intensive farming techniques, they still combined new and traditional cultivation practices, notably in producing food crops for on-farm consumption. Here, they commonly used oxen to plough and cultivate, and the roots of CPAs in peasant farming were palpable. Compared with their larger counterparts in the state sector, CPAs in general got more work out of their labor and machines, and their equipment lasted longer to boot. To Cuba's political leaders, now forced to promote far less import-intensive farming methods, their example was compelling.

As Cuba's sugar marketing conditions deteriorated in the 1990s, the island's planners evidently reckoned that UBPCs should be able to assimilate poorer cash returns on cane production in much the same way as the *colonos* had done in prerevolutionary times. The *colono* system had also shown that appropriate availability of good-quality millable cane did not require agricultural operations to be directly owned or administered by the sugar factories. The prerevolutionary sugar economy had been characterized by low field yields, primarily because of scant use of fertilizers and irrigation. But cane supplies had been reliable, clean, fresh, and mature, and industrial yields in the 1950s averaged 12.75 percent of sugar, basis 96°, per tonne of cane ground, per annum. Largely as a result of longer, mechanized postrevolutionary harvests, this fell to an annual average of 10.88 percent over the 1980s and fell still further in the 1990s as field yields collapsed, cane quality deteriorated, and cane supplies became increasingly erratic.

Changed Circumstances

Whatever the past advantages of smaller-scale, less centralized field operations, it became swiftly apparent that they would be difficult to duplicate in the 1990s. The CPAs, for example, had been progressively developed from the late 1970s in a national context of profitable sugar prices and increasing availability of productive inputs. Cane UBPCs, by contrast, were formed abruptly and en masse for the 1993/94 harvest and inherited deteriorating plantations, falling cane incomes, and acute scarcities of key inputs. Moreover, the formation of CPAs had generally been accompanied by the construction of appropriate infrastructure such as workshops, offices, storage facilities, and the like. They were also supplied with materials for the improvement of social facilities—above all, of housing—to improve living conditions and to facilitate the recruitment and organization of cooperative labor. By contrast, most UBPCs were subdivisions of larger tracts of CAI cane lands, and many lacked the most basic facilities for the administration and maintenance of production, machinery, and equipment. Moreover, UBPC members were meant to acquire a peasantlike intimacy with the lands on which they worked. This required the construction of appropriately sited nuclei of housing, but a dearth of building materials meant that many if not most UBPC members continued to live far from the fields where they labored. And all UBPCs were required to establish or to expand areas dedicated to food production for on-farm consumption, sale, or exchange. On-farm consumption itself was to take place in worker canteens and via household distribution systems that in many cases needed to be built or established. The need for substantial resources for all productive and social investments of this kind peaked, of course, with the mass formation of UBPCs, in both cane and noncane agriculture, in the autumn of 1993 and throughout 1994. The prospects were remote for satisfying them adequately because the nadir of Cuba's national economic performance and import possibilities coincided precisely with this period.

The unfavorable material circumstances in which the UBPCs were founded meant they were unlikely, in the short term, to approach the performance of longer-established, better-endowed CPAs. But other disparities worked against them as well, especially in cane agriculture. If cane growing was their primary economic activity, both UBPCs and CPAs were defined as cane farms. The resources allocated within them for other purposes, however, could vary significantly. For example, a sample of five UBPCs studied in May 1994 reported an average of over 85 percent of their total area to be planted to cane. An average of less than 65 percent was reported for a sample of seven CPAs studied at the same time. In November 1996, a review of activities in the same CPAs and in a larger number of UBPCs confirmed that the share of cane in total farm income on cane UBPCs was substantially greater than that on cane CPAs. In many of the latter, while cane growing was the principal economic activity, it commonly generated only from 40 to 50 percent of total income, the remainder corresponding to livestock, cereals, and foodstuffs. In UBPCs, by contrast, where comparatively little land was available for pasture and food crops, cane income could account for 80 percent or more of total income. This meant, firstly, that UBPCs tended to be more exposed than CPAs to vicissitudes in the supply and price of inputs allocated to cane production, and their overall profitability depended far more on the ruling cane price. Secondly, the greater weight of meat, dairy produce, and other foodstuffs in total CPA production both diversified their commerce and gave better on-farm household food consumption. Thirdly, shortage of pasture land did not just restrict meat and dairy production in UBPCs but braked their participation in the government's well-publicized policy to substitute, where possible, animal traction—notably ox teams—for tractors and their imported fuels, parts, and equipment.

The UBPCs inherited the high percentage of cane in their total area from the CAIs from which they were formed at the end of 1993, and it proved difficult for them to reduce it thereafter. When the state leased its land to UBPCs, it ceded broad autonomy in the ways in which particular productive tasks could be performed and rewarded. But it did not cede the power to determine the UBPCs' primary economic activity and the strategic importance that higher-level planners might assign to a particular crop—to tobacco or cane, for example, as opposed to corn or plantains—tended in the last resort to be indicated not by relative prices and profitability but by administrative fiat. It was inevitable that this would create tensions both within UBPCs and between UBPCs and higher bodies authorizing their production plans.

Part of the problem was inequality in productivity and income between different UBPCs and between UBPCs and CPAs. These could reflect differences in natural conditions or infrastructure but might be exacerbated by the nature and degree of their productive specialization. For members of cooperatives of all kinds, a primordial measure of comparative living standards was the level and quality of household food consumption. On-farm food production assumed crucial importance in this as national food imports shrank from 1991 and possibilities to acquire foodstuffs locally by ordinary commercial means deteriorated. Where average household food consumption within given UBPCs was comparatively low but the area devoted to cane comparatively high, there was pressure from below to divert land from cane to food crops or pasture. This was resisted from above by the planners who wanted to maintain or increase cane and sugar production to meet obligations in international trade and finance. Inevitably this led to complaints that the autonomy of UBPCs was a myth.

State Interventions

Discontent was also caused by a different kind of intervention. In the early 1990s, cane yields fell not only through lack of inputs such as fertilizers and irrigation but through a decline in the proportion of total cane held over from one harvest to another. This was because the state, in the face of repeated foreign exchange crises, instructed farms to harvest almost all available cane. Since this reduced the average maturity of harvested cane, notably over 1992–94, yields were further lowered and unit costs increased in both field and factory. Less replanting led to yet more deterioration in the plantations over the same period (Pollitt 1997a, 185–87).

Ambitious sowing plans were announced for 1994 and 1995 to offset the damage, and UBPCs and CPAs were assigned additional resources—notably fuel—to demolish and replant the older, sparsely populated plantations on which yields had plummeted. But sowing targets were far too high to be met with the resources available, especially within a farming structure that had so recently been transformed. Furthermore, efforts within UBPCs and CPAs to lower costs by increasing the maturity of harvested cane continued to be frustrated, most painfully by injunctions to cut costly new spring sowings that managers had initially planned to hold over. Managers in all the UBPCs and CPAs visited by the author in Havana and Matanzas provinces in 1996 held the view that, in combination with a progressive resowing program, no less than 25 percent of the total area under cane should be held over for three consecutive harvests if the age structure of the plantations prior to 1992 was to be restored. But they did not think it likely in practice that they would be permitted to hold over more than 15 percent. Thus, while government spokesmen tended to blame setbacks in the recovery of cane yields and sugar production on input shortages, bad weather and poor field and factory organization, farm managers stressed the added aggravation of state-imposed harvesting policies. They well understood that these originated in a national economic crisis—but it was nonetheless demoralizing for good cane-growers to implement, time and again, what they knew to be poor technical harvesting practices that, moreover, discouraged rather than stimulated the necessary rejuvenation of aging plantations.

Some successful CPAs and small growers outside the co-operative sector evaded pressures to cut less mature plant cane by redistributing their sowings from the first to the second half of the calendar year. Autumn sowings were too immature to be cut in harvests taken in the months of December to May and, while commenting on the performance of growers who had maintained high yields in the face of severe input shortages, the president of the National Small Farmers Association pointed out that "with 11 and 12 month ratoons, one does not achieve high yields . . . (and) the most outstanding growers . . . skilfully shifted their sowings from spring to autumn so that they would not be cut before their optimum maturity. With (ratoons of) 14 and 15 months, the age-composition of plantations is maintained" (Lugo 1995, 8).

In fact, autumn sowings had traditionally been favored by many small growers because drier planting and growing conditions meant lower weeding costs than for cane sown in, say, May or June—a factor that could assume greater importance if labor or herbicides were dear or in short supply. But these very circumstances meant that if growers lacked irrigation, they needed considerable agility in the deployment of labor to sow successfully in less predictable, often short-lived, periods of soil humidity—and small-scale growers seemed generally better at this than large. It was in any event clear—but never explicitly acknowledged—that, in the 1990s, a shift from spring to autumn sowings was not a simple agronomic improvement. It was, rather, a tactical maneuver to frustrate higher-level harvesting plans that maximized short-run cane supplies only at damaging longer-run cost.

Loss-Making Farms

State worries about the newly formed UBPCs focused primarily upon their costs of production. After all, the new farming system had been created primarily to cut costs and use fewer imported resources so that Cuba could better confront less favorable international sugar markets. According to sugar ministry data, in 1988/89, with an average national cane yield of sixty tonnes per hectare harvested, costs of production were 17.53 pesos per 100 arrobas of cane (1 arroba = 11.5 kg; at the nominal exchange rate, one peso equals one U.S. dollar [MINAZ 1995]). By 1992/93, however, with yields having fallen to 35.6 tonnes per hectare harvested, the production cost of 100 arrobas of cane was reckoned to have risen to 29.30 pesos. The UBPCs were formed at the end of 1993 and their data are not strictly comparable with earlier figures either for national or state cane agriculture. However, costs for their first crop in 1993/94 were put at 26.45 pesos and for that of 1994/95 at 21.86 pesos. But of a total of 1,411 cane UBPCs enumerated for the financial year ending 30 June 1995, 1,087 (77 percent) were nonetheless reported to be unprofitable and their losses totaled 170 million pesos as compared with the 23 million pesos then reported as profits for 324 UBPCs (23 percent). The net losses of cane UBPCs as a whole hence amounted to some 147 million pesos, or more than 100,000 pesos per enterprise. Since the average price paid for UBPC cane in 1994/95 was 16.55 pesos per 100 arrobas and its cost of production 21.86 pesos, costs exceeded revenue by almost one-third (MINAZ 1995).

Moreover, fieldwork in the autumn of 1996 did not suggest any subsequent improvement. At first sight this was surprising since cane yields and production increased between 1994/95 and 1995/96. But for the most part, this reflected a greater use of inputs such as fuel, fertilizer, and herbicides in the 1995/96 crop. While the prices of all of these more than doubled between 1994 and 1996—prices of machine parts rose yet more steeply—cane prices over the same period remained constant. Thus many farms—CPAs as well as UBPCs—reported revived cane production to be accompanied by rising total losses (or falling total profits) in 1995/96 as compared with 1994/95. The official press reported on the progress and problems of cane UBPCs as these were discussed nationally or locally by party, administrative, or producer organizations. But one conspicuous grassroots complaint that went unreported was the difficulty faced by unprofitable farms in reducing their losses if the price of state-supplied inputs increased but cane prices did not.

A more complicated matter was an alleged lack of stability of the UBPC labor force. In December 1993, a total of 153,000 eligible and actual members were enrolled in cane UBPCs. According to (rounded) MINAZ data, membership fell by some 14 percent, to 132,000, by December 1994 before recovering slightly to 137,000 by October 1995. Adding 21,000 contract workers—a category that could not previously be separately identified—swelled the October 1995 total to 158,000, or slightly more than the workforce reported two years before (MINAZ 1995). These data understate the real volatility of UBPC membership since they do not report inflows and outflows occurring within a given year. Fieldwork in 1996 suggested that these could be substantial. Unequal income prospects between UBPCs—whether in money or real terms—encouraged both members and contract workers to move from less to more remunerative enterprises, commonly exacerbating labor shortages that already braked productive potential. Likewise, better-endowed CPAs were likely to recruit UBPC workers if they were both needed and tied by kinship to existing peasant members. And independent farmers were also reported to poach UBPC labor by offering shorter working hours and better wages in cash and kind. All this could exacerbate UBPC labor shortages made more acute by the pressure to adopt more labor-intensive techniques of cultivation. Most, but not all, UBPCs might succeed in replacing lost members or contract workers with new ones—but a high turnover of workers did not encourage the peasantlike familiarity with, and proprietary interest in, the land that was a major official motive in creating UBPCs in the first place.

Labor Problems

The ways in which UBPCs utilized their labor were obviously at least as important as instability in its supply in explaining why their wage costs might be relatively high or low. A key case in point was their success or failure in harvesting the cane with their own resources, as opposed to hiring in labor and/or equipment mobilized for the purpose by the state. In the 1960s, with the growth of alternative year-round employment opportunities in both town and countryside, there was a massive exodus from manual cane cutting, and by the end of that decade the number of professional cutters had fallen by two-thirds or more. Little progress had then been made in mechanized cutting, and the state had plugged the gap between the need for and supply of manual cutters by mobilizing tens, and sometimes hundreds, of thousands of workers from outside agriculture. By the end of the 1980s, however, some 70 percent of the cane was mechanically cut, loaded, cleaned, and transshipped, and virtually all hand-cut cane was mechanically loaded. Despite this, a sustained antipathy to manual cutting continued to erode the ordinary cane-cutting labor force, and the state continued to be obliged to mobilize significant numbers of nonfarm workers to bring in much of the hand-cut crop. In the harvest of 1989/90, for example, a total of fifty-nine thousand cutters brought in 27 percent of a crop that produced just over eight million tonnes of sugar. Of these, thirty-eight thousand—over 60 percent—were mobilized by the state. For the harvest of 1992/93, the total number of manual cutters deployed rose to sixty-five thousand to bring in 32 percent of a crop producing some 4.3 million tonnes of sugar. Of these, forty-seven thousand were mobilized workers, or over 70 percent of the total. The number of cutters ordinarily working in state and private farms was reported to have fallen by more than 15 percent over the period, from twenty-one thousand in 1989/90 to eighteen thousand in 1992/93 (Pollitt 1997b, 478).

For some observers, in Cuba and elsewhere, the island's shrunken capacity to import machinery and fuels meant that the scale of mechanized cane harvesting should be reduced and that of manual cutting increased. But this ignored the evidence that agricultural workers seemed unwilling voluntarily to increase their activities in manual cutting and continued to abandon that particular occupation whenever the opportunity presented itself. For all CPA and UBPC managers interviewed in 1996, a large-scale reversion to manual cane cutting by their members was simply out of the question. They did recognize, however, that the use of mobilized cutters jeopardized efforts to lower labor costs. The pay of mobilized nonagricultural workers was relatively high, and those who contracted them also had to meet the costs of their food and lodging and make a contribution to their central trades union organization or other mobilizing agency. From 1996 the state contributed toward the midday meal costs of mobilized workers, but even when they cut no more cane per day than ordinary UBPC members, their cost was still at least half as much again.

There were substantial variations in the man-land ratio and in the incidence of mechanized harvesting of different UBPCs. Fieldwork in 1996 included UBPCs and CPAs where all the cane was cut by machine. On others, 30 percent or more was cut by hand. In other parts of the country, UBPCs might hand-cut over half their crop. Such differences made it impossible to generalize as to how much UBPCs as a whole could reduce their use of mobilized labor and thereby their costs. But there was clear—sometimes spectacular—evidence to show that labor costs in some UBPCs were excessively swollen because their managers simply failed to mobilize the harvesting potential of existing members, opting instead to contract the expensive services of brigades of mobilized workers. This was simple capitulation to popular antipathy toward manual cutting and was made easier, of course, when UBPC members could obtain relatively high advance payments for less essential and less arduous tasks and where the losses resulting from such lazy management were written off by the state. A clear example from the province of Guantánamo was publicized in the newspaper *Granma* on 30 October 1996. It reported that of twenty-eight cane UBPCs in the province, twenty-seven were unprofitable. Data on the incidence of mechanized harvesting were not given, although the province's unfavorable terrain made it lower than the national average. It was noted, however, that the only profitable UBPC, with 250 members, brought in its entire crop without using any mobilized labor. This was contrasted with a UBPC making substantial losses that managed to deploy only 50 of its 300 members in the harvest while soliciting the additional assistance of three brigades of mobilized workers. Such practices were encouraged of course if an indulgent state simply wrote off UBPC losses. At the same time, however, official resistance in 1995 and 1996 to raising cane prices, despite steep increases in the costs of state-supplied inputs, was obviously reinforced by concerns that higher cane prices would simply conceal inefficiency or extravagance in the use or remuneration of labor.

As a general rule, whatever kind of labor was employed, the higher the share of machine-cut cane, the lower the harvesting costs of UBPCs. This was despite the more frequent breakdown rates, and deteriorating efficiency, of an aging stock of chopper harvesters. Many of these had been reconditioned over the years, and recent supplies of new engines included some made by Mercedes-Benz. But for the most part, the national park of cane harvesters was much the same in 1996 as in 1992 and 1993 and even by 2002 changes to the harvester stock consisted primarily of the reconditioning of existing machines rather than the production or import of new ones. In fieldwork in April and May 1994, the average age of the harvesters of a dozen CPAs and UBPCs visited worked out at eleven years. When the same farms were visited in October and November 1996, the same stock of machines was encountered and now averaged thirteen years of age. And even in April 2002, almost all the same harvesters—now eighteen years old or more—were still in operation, albeit commonly now hybrids, with new or reconditioned engines and a miscellany of new parts of both national and foreign origin. That such harvesters could still be kept at work—although with increasingly frequent and protracted breakdowns—reflected considerable ingenuity in repair and maintenance, facilitated by simple machine design. Particularly where hauling was done by tractor-drawn trailers as opposed to trucks, unit harvesting costs were far lower than for hand-cut cane, whether undertaken by cooperative members, contract workers, or mobilized brigades. This was well illustrated by the CPAs and UBPCs supplying cane to the Cuba Libre sugar factory in Matanzas province, studied in 1996. An average of more than 97 percent of their cane was machine cut from 1993/94 to 1995/96, and the percentage of profitable UBPCs was far higher than the national average. In fact, in 1993/94 and 1994/95 all six UBPCs studied were profitable, as compared with the national figure of only 23 percent in the latter year. The impact of higher prices for greater availability of inputs such as fertilizer, herbicides, and fuel was apparent in 1995/96 when three of these six UBPCs became loss-makers despite an average 25 percent improvement in their cane yields.

But the long-term success or failure of UBPCs did not lie solely, or even primarily, in the efficiency with which they managed to harvest crops. More decisive was how well they managed to sow and grow them. The UBPCs had been formed out of large state enterprises in which the use of imported inputs had been profligate and the labor force often work-shy. This situation had been tolerable only because of the premium Soviet and other COMECON prices paid for Cuban sugar. Stripped of such support, and of the abundance of imported inputs that went with it, the UBPCs had to acquire a new productive culture in which far more effort was squeezed out of labor and much better returns secured from newly scarce farm inputs. Some improvement was reported in the intensity and duration of the working day in UBPCs, notably in the afternoons, when absenteeism had been common in the old state cane farms. And while a dearth of essential consumer goods after 1991 had robbed money-wage systems of much of their incentive value, from August 1995 various schemes sought to link a fraction of the wages paid for the performance of particular tasks to the purchase of basic household goods. Such schemes weakened but by no means broke the vicious circle in which scarce consumer goods and low investment combined to depress labor productivity and, hence, prospects for more consumer and investment goods in the future.

Shoddy Farm Practice

It was evident both that there was still great room for productive improvement and that most of it lay not in adopting novel or sophisticated techniques of cultivation but in generalizing the mundane good tillage practice that could be observed on many small cane farms and CPAs throughout Cuba. First, for its long-run importance, was the achievement of a higher population density in younger plantations. This required UBPCs to display the same care in sowing and resowing as small farmers. Overambitious national replanting campaigns had encouraged shoddy sowings that left newly sown fields potentially underpopulated for five years or more. They also exhausted the nation's seed banks and thus stimulated the diffusion only of cane varieties already to hand in the fields. A low population density, whether attributable to poor-quality planting or simple aging of the plantations, lowered the yield of all inputs: land, labor, fertilizer, water, and all machinery and equipment engaged in cultivation and harvesting. It also increased the need for weeding, whether manual or chemical, since weeds ordinarily suppressed by the cover of growing cane in densely planted fields flourished in those where—as was not uncommon—the gaps within rows of plant or ratoon canes could amount to one-fifth or one-quarter of the whole. For the 1995/96 crop, Cuba had secured costly external finance that permitted substantially increased applications of balanced fertilizer to fields that had lacked them for up to three consecutive years. Predictably, yields improved. But the impact on the yields of deteriorated, poorly populated plantations fell well short of expectations, demonstrating that the productive potential of greater availability of costly inputs such as fertilizers would be realized only with prior improvements in tillage practices. The latter generally depended on the careful application of more and better-managed labor rather than on the lavish deployment of costly imported resources, and this focused attention once more upon factors affecting the incentives of workers to work and of managers to manage. Many of these factors had material origins, being conditioned by scarcities of both consumer and producer goods; but others originated in disruptive interventions from above that sacrificed the morale and long-term productive potential of the sugar sector to extricate the national economy from successive, and apparently unending, crises of foreign exchange.

The New Sugar Sector Regime

In October 1997 perceived inadequacies in crisis management prompted the replacement of both the Ministers of Agriculture (MINAG) and the Sugar Industry (MINAZ). The new head of MINAZ, Gen. Ulises Rosales del Toro, had previously been a prominent, and apparently well regarded, figure in the Cuban military. His primary objectives were soon apparent. The first was to reestablish basic, and mostly traditional, good practice in the sowing, growing, harvesting, and processing of the sugarcane. The second was to cut production costs to reduce, if not eliminate, massive state subsidies to the sugar sector while improving its competitiveness in increasingly difficult international market conditions. Success in the pursuit of these interrelated goals depended partly on the new minister's ability to resist the kind of outside interventions, previously discussed, that were inimical to technically sound agro-industrial practice. That he possessed the necessary political weight to achieve this seemed signaled by an early ministerial edict forbidding the harvesting of immature cane. While ostensibly addressed to the direct producers, the prohibition evidently reflected a growing recognition at far higher levels that a measure of protection of the sugar sector from the more damaging effects of macroeconomic emergencies was a precondition for its long-term recovery.

He grasped a second nettle in June 1998 by increasing, by 52.8 percent, and for a three-year period, the basic price to be paid to cane growers. The increase, from 16.30 pesos to 24.90 pesos per 100 arrobas, was backdated to cover the crop of 1997/98 (see Licht 1998). In the short term this decision seemed to conflict with the priority of cutting production costs, but in fact it recognized that this itself depended first and foremost on improving factory cane supplies. Better profitability prospects for cane producers, whether organized in UBPCs, CPAs, or less collective forms, played an obvious role in this and, unsurprisingly, 546 cane UBPCs were reported to be in profit by September 1999 as compared with 262 a year earlier (*Trabajadores,* 19 September 1999). But an improved cane supply did not mean just increased volumes of harvested cane. It also meant more stable deliveries of mature, clean, and freshly cut cane. This was essential for better performance and lower costs in industrial operations, as most notably expressed by a greater utilization of milling capacity and by higher sugar extraction rates per tonne of cane ground.

The routes by which improved cane supplies could be sought were varied and generally obvious. Basic per hectare yield increases were evidently crucial since they facilitated the increased productivity of all factors of production from field to mill. But it seemed out of the question that cane tonnages per hectare harvested could be restored to the levels of the 1980s. The latter had reflected a relatively lavish use of imported agro-chemicals in the now-vanished era of premium sugar-export prices and easy Soviet credits. But in current conditions, steady, year-on-year sowing programs, well-executed and with appropriate follow-up weeding, could improve plantation yields significantly—and relatively labor-intensive, not import-intensive, techniques could be chosen to achieve this. Crops of greater average weight and maturity could also be achieved by improving the relative balance within the plantations of plant cane and of ratoons of varying ages. The latter could be sought via new sowings to replenish plantations occupied by low-yield, older (or poorly sown) ratoons, supplemented by increases in the share of less mature cane held over from one harvest to the next. These measures were complementary, since holding over more cane on some plantations could release labor to renovate others.

Larger and more stable deliveries of better-quality cane permitted major gains in industrial efficiency, but these could be substantially augmented with two elemental changes in harvest organization. Firstly, the milling capacity that had produced the volumes of raw sugar of the 1980s was obviously greater than was needed to process cane yielding half those volumes since the early 1990s. During the years required for a substantial recovery of cane supplies, the least efficient sugar factories could be mothballed. When necessary, others could be demobilized for particular harvests in order to extend their repair and maintenance periods. The redirection of cane ordinarily delivered to these factories should enable a smaller number of others to grind at levels much closer to their full capacity. Secondly, improved sugar-extraction rates should, ceteris paribus, accompany a reduction in the duration of harvests. Given sufficient harvesting and processing capacity, a shorter grinding period would facilitate the milling of cane of higher average sucrose content. This did not imply a return to the ninety- to one-hundred-day harvests that were typical of the 1950s, but it did mean ensuring that almost all the cane it was planned to harvest was ground from December to April. Heavy rainfall during harvests—more probable in the months of May and June and a feature of the emergency extensions of harvests over 1993 and 1994—reduces the sucrose content of standing cane and can dislocate factory cane supplies by disrupting mechanized harvesting operations. Shorter harvests tend to reduce costly operational interruptions by cutting the wear and tear of all equipment used in cane harvesting, haulage, transshipment, and processing, and they extend the period available for essential out-of-season repairs and maintenance.

Recent Progress

The patchy availability and uncertain scope and methodology of official data dictate that any analysis of the recent performance of Cuba's sugar economy be both par-

Table 5.3 Selected Cuban Sugar Industry Performance Indicators, 1991–2000

Crop Year	Sugar Produced (10^3t, 96^0 basis)	Exports (10^3t, 96^0 basis)	Agricultural Yield	Industrial Yield
1990/91	7,729	6,596	49.1	10.59
1991/92	7,104	6,439	44.7	10.57
1992/93	4,365	3,968	35.3	9.85
1993/94	4,024	3,264	33.5	9.26
1994/95	3,419	2,778	28.2	9.92
1995/96	4,504	3,798	32.5	10.73
1996/97	4,316	3,622	32.0*	10.0*
1997/98	3,285	2,569	30.0*	9.9*
1998/99	3,851	3,121	35.0*	11.13
1999/00	4,134	3,431	37.7	11.1+

Note: For definitions of production, industrial, and agricultural yields, see table 5.1.
* = Data rounded from MINAZ estimates.
+ = Author's estimate.

tial and cautious. That said, the available, if fragmentary, statistical evidence suggests that since 1997 some progress has been made in the pursuit of the salient objectives reviewed above.

In the first place, while increases in annual raw sugar production from 1997/98 to 2001/2 have been extremely modest, the most recent harvests appear to have been carried out within a technically more rational recovery program, with correspondingly lower unit output costs. Cane yields per hectare harvested were reported to be around 35 and 37.7 tonnes for the crops of 1998/99 and 1999/2000, respectively. Though low by the standards of the 1980s, these yields were the highest since, respectively, 1992/93 and 1991/92. Industrial yields—that is, percent sugar extracted, basis 96°, per tonne cane ground—oscillated between about 9.3 percent and 10.7 percent between 1992/93 and 1997/98 but averaged less than 10 percent overall. Both of the harvests of 1998/99 and 1999/2000, however, apparently exceeded 11 percent, and while favorable harvesting weather conditions made their future extrapolation risky, this upward trajectory seemed based on improved harvest organization. There has certainly been a more rational use of industrial capacity. Cuba's sugar industry nominally comprises 156 sugar factories. By the harvest of 1999/2000, however, their active number was reduced to 110—but these then produced more than four million tonnes of sugar. An increased total output from fewer active mills, with higher field yields and better sugar extraction rates in the factories, clearly pointed to improved efficiency and lower unit costs of production.

Lower production costs are indeed affirmed in diverse official statements. For example, on 24 August 1999, MINAZ reported in *Granma* that the cost of producing a tonne of raw sugar in the harvest of 1998/99 was more than one hundred pesos below that of 1997/98. It claimed the corollary of a major cut in the state subsidy to the sugar industry. The following year, on 4 April, *Trabajadores* reported raw sugar production costs for the 1999/2000 crop to be fourteen pesos less than those of 1998/99. Progress in cutting cane production costs was less clear, however, and, on the basis of all the cost data so far made public, the inferences that can be drawn for the industry's future are demonstrably very limited.

Costs and Revenues and Levels of Production

The contemporary discussions of Cuba's production costs should, a priori, be assisted by the enormous, almost fetishistic, official public importance now ascribed to them. This is a new phenomenon in Cuban history and is obviously explained by the adverse conditions affecting both the production and marketing of sugar in the 1990s. According to the UN's Economic Commission for Latin America and the

Caribbean (UNECLAC), between the calendar years 1990 and 1995, Cuba's sugar exports fell 63 percent by volume (from 7.2 million tonnes to 2.6 million tonnes) and by no less than 84 percent by value (from $4.3 billion to $0.7 billion). With the value of merchandise exports of all kinds falling by 73 percent over the same period (from $5.4 billion to $1.5 billion), sugar's share in these fell from 80 percent in 1990 to 48 percent in 1995 (UNECLAC 1997, tables A.16–18). In subsequent years, from 1996 to 2000, world market (nonpremium) sugar prices have fluctuated between some $0.06 and $0.12 per pound, but within this range Cuba's raw sugar exports are unlikely to have bettered an average of some $0.07–0.09 cents per pound. By any standard, prices such as these were very low. By comparison with prices enjoyed by Cuba in the era of COMECON trade, however, they were catastrophic. It was evidently this acute and protracted depression in both production and prices that explained the terms in which the future of the sugar industry was discussed in the Economic Resolution of the Fifth Congress of the Cuban Communist Party of February 1998. As reported by *Granma International* on 15 February 1998, the resolution stated that the "sugar agroindustry must recover its strategic role in the economy by becoming a source of increased net resources from abroad and by reanimating the development of other branches and spheres of the economy." However, "production must be increased while appreciably lowering its costs with the aim of obtaining greater profits in relation to international prices. It should attain a minimum of seven million tonnes, with net earnings very much greater than current earnings, and it should boost the production of derivatives." But this seven-million-tonne target was evidently a long-term objective since "a medium-term strategy should be drawn up in the shortest possible time regarding the downsizing, development and upkeep of the sugar agro-industry, taking into account that its production is destined for a market with limited demand." Since he took office in October 1997, Minister Rosales del Toro's primary concern has been with the elaboration and implementation of this "medium-term strategy" and such successes as are so far to his credit relate to the "downsizing, development and upkeep" of the sugar economy rather than to any ambitious long-term reexpansion program envisaged for it. It is in this context that one must consider Cuba's present and prospective costs of production, for while the level and structure of costs during a period of productive retrenchment are one thing, those associated with an ambitious reexpansion program are quite another. This is most apparent when discussing the crucial question of net export earnings.

A major problem in appraising Cuba's official reports on levels and changes in year-on-year costs is that they give no hint of the mounting levels of new, predominantly hard-currency, investment needed to revitalize the productive potential of the sugar industry and its highly mechanized system of cane supply.[2] As one observer has aptly remarked, despite the fact that prices for Cuban sugar in early 1999 fell to their lowest level in twelve years, "when you separate the dollar and peso income and expenditure streams and set off dollar surplus against peso deficit, General Rosales del Toro is still delivering dollars for pesos at better than the 20:1 market rate. However, unless he can refurbish his equipment, he will have won a battle, but he will surely lose the war" (*Cuba Business* 1999).

In 1996, a one-time minister of Cuban foreign trade reported that specialists within the Sugar Division of the Ministry of the Economy and Planning put the import cost of a seven million tonne sugar harvest at US$500 million. This embraced everything from spare parts and replacement equipment for agriculture and industry, to fuels, fertilizers, and herbicides and the work clothes and footwear of cane cutters (see Fernández Font 1996, 88–95). But this estimate, though of impressive magnitude, refers to conditions in the mid-1990s and, since that time, the remorseless deterioration of plant, machinery, and equipment deployed in cultivating, harvesting, cleaning, transshipping, and processing Cuba's cane crops has pushed the import cost of renovation far higher. In addition, an increase in future production to the levels officially mooted would require substantial and costly increases in both the yield and sown area of cane. All this would have a formidable inflationary impact on both short- and medium-term unit costs, and, even less welcome, the escalating weight of dollars versus pesos in total costs would, ceteris paribus, sharply depress prospective net export returns. During the more acute years of economic crisis in the 1990s, the failing national economy swallowed up so much of the foreign exchange earnings generated by the sugar sector that it became quite impossible for the latter to reproduce itself. Any ambitious current expansion program for the sugar economy, however, would need an infusion of investment capital that would not only consume its own net foreign exchange earnings but also encroach upon those of rival, arguably more promising, sectors such as tobacco, minerals, or tourism. This might change were there to be a durable period of substantially improved sugar prices—but there is no sufficiently solid prospect of this at present to justify committing dramatic increases of scarce resources to the sugar economy to the detriment of its principal export-earning competitors.

Sugar, Land, and Labor

A preoccupation with sugar's hard currency costs and earnings naturally focuses attention on the domestic resources that might be used more effectively to cut one and thereby increase the other. In prerevolutionary times, it was commonly stressed that whatever natural resources Cuba might lack, it possessed both land and labor in relative abundance. In the case of land, although per hectare yields would also rise and fall, pre- and postrevolutionary periods of expansion and contraction of sugar production were generally associated with increases or decreases in the physical area under cane. Between 1950 and 1952, for example, sugar production rose by 30 percent (from 5.6 million tonnes to 7.3 million tonnes), linked partly to an increase in cane yields of a little over 15 percent, but more to an expansion of over 30 percent in the cane area (see table 5.1 and *Anuario Azucarero de Cuba* 1955, 101.) Between 1992 and 1995, on the other hand, while the fall of 63 percent in production was related to one of over 35 percent in per hectare yields (see table 5.3), the harvested area was also reported to have fallen by more than one-third (CEPAL 1997, table iv). There were obvious hard-currency limits to increasing cane yields by using more fertilizers, irrigation, and herbicides; but there seemed to be no comparably severe constraints regarding the availability of land.

Current labor supply data also suggest that increased sugar production based on traditional land-extensive techniques could be augmented by labor-intensive techniques that increased cane yields but used relatively few scarce imports. Conspicuous among these was the substantial but careful expansion of cane sowings already discussed and a more diligent manual weeding of both plant cane and ratoons. Most of the labor needs of these activities fell outside peak harvest periods, and reports of the size of the labor force currently associated with the sugar economy suggest that, in theory at least, there should be an abundant supply of workers to meet them. A recent census of the sector's peak labor force enumerated a total of 499,000 workers for 1998. Half of these were attached to the various types of cane cooperatives; 110,000 were in industrial production; and another 140,000 were state employees in unspecified activities that presumably included those working in cleaning and transshipment stations, railroads, storage, and other infrastructural facilities.

There was strong a priori evidence to indicate that a workforce of this large size must include substantial reserves of underutilized labor. To make a historical comparison, the sugar sector's peak labor force in the 1950s was generally reckoned to have totaled no more than 400,000–500,000. But the annual average of five million tonnes of sugar produced at that time came from cane crops that were all cut, cleaned, and loaded by hand, most being then carted by oxen to factories or railroads. In addition, of the total labor force then referred to, only 25–30 percent was employed year round. This minority of so-called permanent workers was joined, for harvests of no more than three or four months' duration, by an army of seasonal labor. These workers migrated both from town to countryside and from one province to another to work in the newly activated sugar mills and their ancillary transportation systems or to bring in the cane crop using labor-intensive methods little changed since the times of slavery. By 1990, in stark contrast, 70 percent of the crop was cut and loaded by machine; all of it was mechanically loaded; some 85 percent was then further processed in cleaning and/or transshipment stations; and animal traction for cane haulage had effectively disappeared. Moreover, with the exception of a few tens of thousands of harvest workers, mobilized mainly by trade unions and the military, the labor force of the 1990s was nominally employed year round, ordinarily residing in the environs of the sugar factories or of the cane areas that supplied them. And it was this permanent labor force—almost half a million strong—that ostensibly showed no reduction in size throughout the 1990s, despite the fact that sugar production was halved, with the same system and level of mechanized harvesting delivering far less cane to progressively fewer active factories. Viewed from any angle, this could not but suggest high levels of industrial and infrastructural overmanning accompanied by low and falling levels of agricultural productivity—a combination that made increasing the productivity of Cuba's cane lands by using more labor-intensive techniques such a plausible option. However, familiar problems swiftly showed that matters were not that simple. In July 2000 serious shortfalls were reported in the manual weeding program for the cane. These promised to be doubly damaging since their threat to cane yields, and therefore sugar production, for the ensuing harvest would also jeopardize prospects of then taking full advantage of a significant, and possibly short-lived, improvement in world market sugar prices (Licht 2000). This was the kind of problem that forcefully posed the question "So where does all the labor go?"

The Labor Force

The answer to this question lies in myriad factors that transformed the conditions of labor supply and demand for the sugar economy after 1959. There are two interrelated issues. One concerns the spatial distribution and mobility of labor of Cuba's sugar economy since the revolution. The other is the nature and process of mechanizing the island's cane harvest. As has been stressed, the bulk of the labor force active in both sugar agriculture and industry in the 1950s was seasonal in character. With the end of the harvest, in the dead season, many workers returned to occasional work in the ubiquitous urban service sector or to open urban unemployment. More eked out a living in low-productivity agricultural work on land plots or small-scale family farms. This labor supply situation was transformed with the revolution of 1959. Rural labor was drawn to urban areas by the growing opportunities for work or education that also checked the seasonal outflow of urban dwellers into agriculture. At the same time, the agrarian reforms of 1959 and 1963 provided stable year-round employment in an expanding state farm sector while improving the conditions of living and production of the landholding peasantry. In consequence, the army of workers and peasants that had previously migrated each year to cut cane in historically underpopulated regions such as Camagüey and Oriente was literally demobilized. An acute consequential shortage of harvest labor was felt as early as 1963 and was progressively exacerbated thereafter by a remorseless exodus of agricultural workers from manual cane cutting that has endured to this day. The costly, complex, and ultimately successful program of mechanizing the cane harvest had its origin in these years, as did the prodigious annual mobilizations of nonagricultural labor to cut cane by hand during the ill-fated campaign to produce ten million tonnes of sugar in 1970 (Pollitt 1973).

By the 1970s and 1980s, rising levels of mechanization meant that tens and not hundreds of thousands of mobilized nonagricultural workers were sufficient to bring in progressively larger cane crops, which, moreover, were now taken in harvests of substantially greater average duration. These longer harvests reduced sugar extraction rates in the factories, but they also permitted a greater, more extended use of industrial capacity and machinery, equipment, and labor employed in cane supply. It was clear from all this that much of the labor saved by harvest mechanization was not ordinary agricultural labor at all, but was of seasonal urban origin, mobilized prior to 1959 by force of economic circumstances and by state-organized mobilizations thereafter.

Moreover, little if any labor was saved by the mechanization of cane loading since it did not increase the productivity of those continuing to cut cane so much as it eased their task by shortening the workday. While it was claimed in the 1970s and after that one chopper-harvester did the work of twenty-five, thirty, or even forty *macheteros,* the complex logistics of deploying mechanized harvesters, with their supporting labor and transport, meant that the number of harvest workers of all kinds actually saved per machine was nearer to four (Pollitt 1994, 562–63). In addition, a major reconfiguration of the cane fields accompanied the growing use of chopper-harvesters in the 1970s and 1980s. At the same time, a rising number of skilled workers was required for the repair and maintenance of the expanding machine park. The mechanization of Cuba's cane harvests was not thus a simple substitution of capital for labor but wrought profound changes in the sources, distribution, and skills of labor, both in and out of harvest. Its primary objective was greatly to reduce the number of nonagricultural workers annually mobilized for manual cane cutting. It achieved this. But it also created a large on-farm cohort of skilled workers to operate or maintain the machinery, equipment, and installations associated with this complex process of technical transformation, as well as employing much unskilled labor in related tasks of pre- and post-harvest field preparation.

At the same time, while the longer harvests of the 1970s and 1980s extended the employment of workers in harvest-related activities, they shortened the period in which out-of-harvest tasks could be performed. The latter could be important in the sparsely populated areas that had depended heavily on substantial seasonal imports of harvest labor both before and after 1959. Here, harvest mechanization cut the number of cane cutters mobilized outside the region but did not substantially enlarge the permanent resident workforce. Where this was small, it was difficult to increase labor-intensive cultivation practices such as manual weeding to save scarce imported inputs such as herbicides.

We have seen that a simple comparison of the size of the sugar sector's peak labor force before and after 1959 suggests that labor supplies should have been abundant by the late 1980s. This becomes less clear-cut, however, with the introduction of some of the complexities of the mechanization process, together with changes in the postrevolutionary mobility and spatial distribution of labor. But even so, any reasonable appraisal of the sugar workforce in 1989 would conclude that it was at the least large enough to carry out its productive tasks without excessive strain. How, then, could one account for the fact that, over the next decade, such a workforce remained constant or even increased in size despite the fact that annual sugar production was halved? Since the rate of harvest mechanization was maintained over the period, the obvious conclusion was that the sugar economy must now incorporate an extravagantly large, and barely disguised, reserve army of labor. But, as the impact of collapsing cane yields on the employment of labor and other means of production between 1992 and 1995 illustrate, even this was not as clear as it appeared at first sight. Cane yields are obviously influenced by both the quantity and quality of labor invested in sowing, weeding, and harvesting the crop. However, there may be no great change in the number of workers needed—whether for manual or mechanized tasks—if yield variations are determined primarily by weather conditions or by the availability of imported fuels, fertilizers, and other agrochemicals. For example, other things being equal, the performance of a chopper-harvester may differ little whether it operates in fields yielding fifty or eighty tonnes of cane per hectare. Similarly, there is little difference in the effort required of manual cane cutters whether harvesting individual canes weighing two or three kilograms apiece. In industrial processing, for its part, collapsing cane yields mean inadequate, oft-disrupted supplies of poor-quality raw material, with consequentially frequent operative interruptions and lower sugar-extraction rates. Hence the plummeting cane yields of 1992–95 cut the average productivity of the workers needed in field and factory rather than their absolute number.

In addition, the establishment en masse of cane UBPCs in 1993 diverted substantial numbers of workers into new infrastructural projects and into programs to increase on-farm food production. The latter were both labor intensive and import substituting in nature and were crucial in reducing the impact on cane workers and their families of precipitous falls in national food-imports. They enabled more ox-drawn and fewer tractor-drawn implements of cultivation to be used and consumed only meager allocations of fertilizer and other imported inputs. At the same time, they cut the costly transportation within Cuba of root crops and vegetables from surplus to deficit food-producing regions.

With falling levels of investment from 1991 onward, the condition of the capital stock in cane agriculture, transport, and the sugar industry became more and more precarious. In conjunction with increasingly unstable cane supplies, this brought more frequent breakdowns in the process of production. The breakdowns did not just immobilize the operatives of the machinery and equipment directly affected but also made idle whole chains of workers in mutually dependent field and factory operations. As with falling cane yields, up to the mid-1990s rising breakdown rates did not create a growing pool of permanently unemployed labor but instead depressed the productivity of a constant number of workers. And, of course, the progressively aging capital stock now required a still larger skilled workforce for its increasingly laborious and often improvised repair and maintenance.

Up to the mid-1990s, one could add to factors such as these the lack of any official interest in seeking out and shedding potentially redundant labor in the sugar economy. With the rupture of Cuba's privileged structure of international trade in the early 1990s came nationwide scarcity, disorganization, and demoralization, and shortages of imported fuels, raw materials, and other intermediate goods brought widespread infrastructural paralysis and the mass closure of factories. Outside the sugar sector, hundreds of thousands of urban workers became effectively redundant, subsisting on what were, in monetary terms at least, generous state benefits. In such a context, identifying and shedding surplus labor in the sugar sector seemed likely to achieve little more than the transfer of beneficiaries from one state payroll to another.

By 1995 state policy on this began to change. The worst effects of the national economic crisis had by then been assimilated and a more or less coherent process of economic restructuring and recovery began. To sustain it, it was necessary to curb a rampant inflation to which the swelling wage bills of underproductive workers had given significant impetus. Moreover, it was recognized that worker discipline—already weakened by deteriorating real wages—could be further corroded by the mass featherbedding of labor. For example, within a given enterprise, it was hard to keep up the morale of the labor force when vital tasks demanded the intensive efforts of some workers while unnecessary activities were created to give a semblance of productive employment to others. Management morale was undermined as well, for if wage bills were uncontrollably high, enterprise losses were inevitable, and this did not encourage managers to improve other standards of technical and economic efficiency. Taken as a whole, such a climate did not favor the radical reorganization and cost-cutting rationalization of the sugar economy made imperative by Cuba's persistently unfavorable international sugar markets.

It has been shown that the most diverse factors—some structural and some more ephemeral—could explain why, from 1959 onward, there was never quite so much labor available for additional employment in the sugar economy as workforce censuses might suggest. Between 1992 and 1995, however, it was reported that in addition to falling per hectare yields, the total area planted to cane fell by about one-third (See UNECLAC 1997, table IV.15). Such a reduction must have lowered labor requirements in both the cultivation and harvesting of the crop. Complementing this, a growing number of sugar factories—peaking at forty-six in 1999/2000—were withdrawn from harvest activity where inadequate cane supplies or the precarious condition of industrial equipment made tolerably efficient factory operations impossible. Such mill closures were not reported as permanent, nor their labor force declared redundant, but the process must have freed tens of thousands of workers for alternative employment. Even so, as the reports of weed-infested cane fields in the summer of 2000 exemplified, the theoretical availability of growing numbers of field and factory workers was one thing; their effective deployment in labor-intensive agricultural activities such as manual weeding, however, was evidently quite another.

Labor Organization, Discipline, Adaptability, and Incentives

How to extract substantially greater productive effort from a manifestly underutilized labor force is one of the thorniest questions in Cuban political economy. Its treatment here is necessarily perfunctory, touching on interrelated problems of the organization, discipline, adaptability, and incentives of labor.

From 1997, as discussed, the Sugar Ministry, headed by Gen. Rosales del Toro, sought to retrench the sugar economy via the restoration of good technical practice in agricultural operations and a more efficient use of industrial capacity. Such policies improved both the organization and discipline of labor not least by cutting the morale-sapping wastage of effort associated with earlier stratagems that maximized output in one harvest only by increasing costs and lowering productivity in others.

What it did not and could not do, however, was restore the draconian disciplinary mechanisms that, prior to 1959, had ensured that labor worked intensively at the right time and in the right place and at a wage rate permitting profits to be earned in both field and factory. In agriculture, for example, workers put in a full day of hard labor supervised by *mayorales.* These were exacting taskmasters, able to fire workers for diverse disciplinary infractions and to replace them by tapping a resident pool of unemployed labor. The disciplinary function of mass unemployment in the post-harvest dead season was at least as potent, for it compelled seasonal workers to maximize effort and income in the few months when wage work was available in order to subsidize their consumption during the months when it was not. But all this vanished with the agrarian reforms of the early 1960s. The intensity of the working day on the new state farms slackened and its effective duration came to last no more than an average of six hours or so year round. As in socialist agricultural systems elsewhere, an elite of publicly lauded vanguard workers emerged, but the productivity of the mass of workers it headed lagged far behind. One attraction of agricultural mechanization in this context was that the boost it gave to overall productivity tended to mask the pervasively inadequate performance of labor in ancillary operations and in widespread administrative overmanning. Finally, Cuba's insertion into the so-called socialist international division of labor underpinned the whole system with generous net material and financial transfers, most notably from the USSR, that wrested urgency from efforts to increase labor efficiency and cut wage costs.

Of course, the members or workers of UBPCs, CPAs, and CAIs in the 1990s could all be sanctioned by their respective administrations. But offenses of some gravity or persistence needed to be committed if workers were to be fired or membership rights were to be lost, and, in these cases, if administrative decisions were required to be ratified by enterprise assemblies. Working at only moderate intensity for a relatively short workday was clearly not an offense of this kind. Indeed, in many enterprises it was normal conduct. A somewhat different problem was the reluctance of workers to do jobs considered inferior to those they had performed hitherto. This was exacerbated in the 1990s by what has elsewhere been described as the technical regression of Cuban agriculture (Pollitt 1997, 197–99). For example, while numerous tractors, cane loaders, and chopper-harvesters were decommissioned by shortages of fuel or parts, their erstwhile operators were generally unenthusiastic about taking up a hoe or machete or driving a team of oxen instead. And, unsurprisingly, many industrial workers from the newly mothballed sugar factories were disinclined to become unskilled agricultural laborers.

Labor problems such as these can be treated partly as matters of organization or discipline, but underlying them all, of course, is the crucial question of incentives. During the worst of the crisis years of the 1990s, the primary material objectives of most urban and rural workers were to secure the food supplies necessary for personal and family subsistence together with the pharmaceutical and hygiene products considered essential for family health. Other priorities varied with the material conditions and family circumstances of workers at the onset of the crisis and ranged from the provision or maintenance of adequate lighting, shelter, clothing, and footwear to the functioning of domestic electrical appliances. In the most difficult years, workers pursued these objectives in a context of acute shortages of basic household consumption goods and a precipitate decline in the real purchasing power of money. Such shortages were felt with unequal severity by different sections of the population. Those who directly produced basic wage goods—that is, essential items of household consumption—could put up some resistance to the onslaught of material scarcities and monetary depreciation. Farmers able to produce or exchange staple foodstuffs were notable examples. But the majority of workers lacked such defenses, and the comparative deterioration in their basic living standards was more acute. These workers initially included most of those engaged in cane cultivation and sugar production. Both the volume and variety of consumption goods supplied through the state rationing system became desperately limited, and deliveries of even basic items became increasingly erratic. The prices of scarce goods on private markets escalated beyond the reach of ordinary workers no matter how hard or long they might work in cane fields or sugar factories. For a system of material incentives to be effective in such conditions, it was obvious that individual or collective work performance had to be linked to real wages, not money ones.

This was hardly a novel problem: national policy makers had grappled with it (albeit in less acute form) on and off since the early 1960s. In 1993 they foresaw that the labor force in specialized cane farming might disintegrate if subsistence food supplies could not be guaranteed. The promotion of greater self-sufficiency in staple food production within the new UBPCs was important in averting this. But it was an essentially defensive policy for while it kept the plantation labor force in existence, it did not of itself radically improve the quantity or quality of its work in the cane fields. Indeed, it had at least one major unwanted side effect: the performance of a cane UBPC in its peripheral activities of rearing livestock and growing food crops could matter more to its members than its commercial success in the production and sale of sugarcane. The same was true for many cane CPAs and for farmers and workers engaged in more individual forms of cane farming.

The most important material needs of field and factory workers, for both work and personal consumption, were recorded for a number of the crisis years of the 1990s in surveys carried out by MINAZ (see, for example, MINAZ 1995), and this data can be complemented by material gathered by independent researchers (see, for example, Deere et al. 1998). Such inquiries show that the provision of adequate on-farm housing—or of the materials for house construction, improvement, or maintenance—ranked high among the felt needs of both UBPC members and administrations. Indeed, such provision was clearly a strategically important complement to on-farm food production in recruiting and retaining essential UBPC workers. These and other findings suggested that persistent shortages of all or any items that workers or management considered essential for consumption or production engendered poor worker morale and productive inefficiency. An obvious corollary was that the latter would improve if such shortages were eased. Experience showed, however, that when some priority needs were satisfied, others were promoted to take their place and—a large problem—the point at which this process might be checked remained quite obscure.

As the national economy emerged from the trough of the depression in the mid-1990s, the availability of many consumer goods increased. Their import content tended to be high, however, and diverse methods were used to link their distribution to greater productivity, most notably in export production. For example, fractions of wages or salaries might be paid in forms of currency that conferred access to restricted retail outlets. Or, reminiscent of a successful scheme to bring back high-productivity cane cutters into the sugar harvest of 1965, competitions might be organized to offer prizes to outstanding workers in the form of scarce consumer durable goods. The legalization and diffusion of U.S. dollar transactions at increasingly stable exchange rates were less discriminating in their effects but increased both the volume and variety of consumer goods sold on a growing number of state and informal markets.

However, the large size, low average productivity, and poor post-1991 international trading conditions of the sugar economy severely constrained the scope and efficacy of the material incentives that could be offered its workers in comparison with those in other foreign exchange earning sectors. This reflected the same harsh facts. Firstly, the labor force in tobacco growing, tourism, or mining and extraction was to be counted in scores of thousands, while that of the sugar economy was formally put at half a million. Secondly, in any competition for resources, whether for production or consumption, the sugar sector was much less attractive than some of its rivals, whether this was viewed from the standpoint of its interest to foreign investors, its net export earnings potential, or its general outlook for growth and development. Such a context made unlikely any substantial short- or medium-term increase in the average real wages of sugar workers and restricted the possibilities of enhancing and extending material incentives schemes to embrace more than a small minority of its higher-productivity representatives.

The most obvious route out of the various difficulties associated with overmanning in the sugar economy appeared to be the large-scale shedding of surplus labor—one that pared perhaps 20 percent (or some 100,000 workers) from the peak workforce, as reported by the most recent censuses. This route would cut agricultural and industrial wage costs; lower or eliminate state subsidies (which remained high for cane cultivation); free up resources to improve the incentives and efficiency of a trimmer, more productive workforce; and generally erode the disincentives associated with the large-scale featherbedding of both managers and workers. But while obvious enough, such a route was also full of pitfalls. In UBPCs and CPAs, for example, the identification and discharge of members whose services were deemed to be dispensable would have to be implemented and approved by the administrations and memberships of the self-same cooperatives. The closure of factories—which had obvious knock-on effects for the cane farms supplying them—was a simpler and more spectacular way of making workers redundant, but the problem of creating alternative employment for them could be acute. The typical agro-industrial complex of the sugar economy was located in a semirural setting where it generated overwhelmingly the greatest share of total local employment. The permanent closure of a sugar factory—like closing mining or extractive enterprises elsewhere—could hence destroy the economic raison d'être of entire local communities. This is why mass mill closures in Cuba in the 1930s were accompanied by widespread social violence and by a political opposition that extended well beyond the sugar interests directly affected. Large political and social issues such as these made the whole business of identifying and shedding surplus labor in postrevolutionary Cuba a far broader and more complex issue than that encompassed within the narrow criteria of economic profit and loss.

From Retrenchment to Retreat

Nonetheless, by the harvest of 2001/2, it was clear that progress in improving agricultural and industrial performance in the sugar economy had stalled and that a major restructuring of the sector was imperative. This was primarily because of a failure to secure the substantial and sustained increases in cane yields necessary for any notable future improvement in the efficiency of field and factory operations. The harvests of 1998/99 and 1999/2000 had seen encouraging increases in yields from the 30 tonnes per hectare harvested estimated for 1997/98 to some 35 tonnes and 37.7 tonnes, respectively. But such increases proved to be ephemeral: both cane yields and industrial recovery rates fell back in the harvests that followed, the crop of 2000/2001 producing only an estimated 3.6 million tonnes of sugar and that of 2001/2 some 3.7 million tonnes.[3] A review of harvest performance over the decade 1992/93 to 2001/2 showed that in only one season yields exceeded 35 tonnes per hectare harvested.

The main causes of persistently low cane yields were well known. The supply of imported agrochemicals was inadequate for land often exhausted by unbroken year-on-year cultivation. Active irrigation capability was insufficient. And there were obvious shortcomings in the planting and weeding of what was recognized to be an inferior mix of cane varieties.[4] If such problems were evident enough, their short-run solutions were not. Dramatic increases in the availability of agrochemicals and of fuels and equipment for irrigation, cultivation, and harvesting were ruled out by their prohibitive import cost, and neither the chronic underperformance of agricultural labor and machinery nor the shortcomings in the development and diffusion of better cane varieties could be resolved overnight.

It was notable, however, that the unacceptably low average cane yields reported, whether at national, regional, or local level, concealed substantial deviations from the mean. For example, the author's fieldwork in April 2002 gathered data from sixteen CPAs and UBPCs in Matanzas and Havana provinces and their average yield for the 2000/2001 crop was shown to be thirty-five tonnes per hectare harvested. At the individual farm level, however, yields among suppliers of the CAI Cuba Libre varied from forty-seven tonnes (for both the CPA Revolución de Octubre and the UBPC Las Mercedes to nineteen tonnes (for the UBPC Flora). Yet greater variations could be reported for farms supplying other factories. During the harvests of 2000/2001 and 2001/2, moreover, there were growing complaints of disrupted factory cane supplies attributable to a rising incidence of breakdowns in the aging and increasingly hybridized park of chopper-harvesters.

It was, in fact, the coexistence, past as well as present, of comparatively high and low cane yields within national and regional averages that seemed to offer a way out of this apparently intractable productive impasse. It could be shown that plantations currently producing, say, forty or forty-five tonnes per hectare harvested had achieved yields well in excess of sixty or seventy tonnes in precrisis years. The sixteen CPAs and UBPCs surveyed in April 2002, for example, reported average yields of thirty-five tonnes per hectare harvested in 2000/2001 but were comprised of cane areas averaging seventy-three tonnes in 1989/90. If, as was inevitable, fertilizers, fuels, parts, and other key inputs were to remain in short supply, would it not make better sense to restrict their allocation to cane farms with the best levels of current and/or precrisis performance? Plantations with poor prospects for improvement could be demolished, and the scarce resources hitherto assigned to their cultivation could then be redeployed to much better productive effect. The obvious corollary to this was that there should be a substantial further cut in the national area devoted to cane cultivation accompanied by additional mill closures. As discussed, such closures carried with them profound social and political implications. In the event, however, the cogency of the economic argument proved decisive and was reflected in the drastic restructuring plan for the sugar economy announced by Minister Rosales del Toro at the conclusion of the harvest of 2001/2.

Firstly, the official objective of restoring sugar production to annual levels of six or seven million tonnes was formally abandoned. A new target pitched production at the far more modest figure of four million tonnes per annum. Scarce resources would be switched from enterprises with substandard performance to farms and factories where actual or potential cane yields and sugar recovery rates were demonstrably and substantially superior. This would enable cane of higher yields and better quality to be grown on a smaller physical area that would in turn permit the more efficient, full-capacity operation of a smaller number of mills. This would cut unit costs drastically even though output would remain at a level comparable with the average annual production of previous postcrisis years.

The Sugar Ministry affirmed that with cane yields of fifty-four tonnes per hectare harvested and industrial recovery rates of 12 percent, four million tonnes of sugar could be produced on "38 percent of the land now dedicated to cane"—an area put by several sources at some two million hectares. The latter figure reflected a confusing use of language (whether in original or translated versions), for it implied that the reduction in the area actually planted to cane would be far greater than was envisaged in reality. The figure of two million hectares almost certainly referred to the cultivable area for cane on land overseen by MINAZ rather than the area actually planted with the crop. But this writer would estimate the area harvested in 2000/2001 to have been no more than one million hectares—perhaps a little less—with the area actually planted to cane at the end of that year being of the order of 1.2 million hectares. The restructuring plan seemed to contemplate a reduction in the latter figure to some 750,000–800,000 hectares planted to cane with a harvested area of 600,000 hectares or so. This would be a reduction in the area actually planted to cane of roughly one-third.[5] The alternative uses to which the diverted area were to be put ranged from forestry and pasture to the growing of diverse food crops. Of these, it seemed likely that pasture for the extensive grazing of cattle would be the most prominent in terms of physical area since it would permit a reversion to traditional—and much needed—

practices in the rotation of cane land as well as expansion of the national cattle herd.

Along with the proposed reduction in the cane area, it was announced that 71 sugar mills would also be closed. This greatly magnified the real extent of mill closures over the proposed restructuring period. Cuba's nominal total of mills was officially put at 156. The closure of 71 would thus leave 85 in continued operation—a truly dramatic reduction. But, as previously noted, in the course of the 1990s, a growing number of the nominal total of factories had already been taken out of service. Some had been temporarily inactive in a particular harvest for the completion of vital repairs and maintenance—the CAI Cuba Libre was a case in point during the crop of 1993/94—but an increasing number had been closed for more protracted periods. By 2000/2001, the crop was reportedly processed by only 110 factories and that of 2001/2 by only 104. Since the formal restructuring program began with a total of 104 active sugar factories and was to end with 85, the de facto closure program thus amounted some 19 mills. It was further proposed to divert 14 of the 85 surviving factories from manufacturing raw sugar to producing only cane by-products and derivatives—a proposal reflecting the perceived implausibility of any substantial improvement in long-term world sugar prices.

Some Costs and Complications of Restructuring

It was formally estimated that the restructuring program would make redundant some one hundred thousand workers and farmers currently gaining their livelihood from the sugar economy. Of these, fifty thousand were reported to be factory workers, although a significant, if unspecified, number of them were evidently on the payrolls of factories that had already been taken out of service but not yet definitively shut down. The acute economic and social costs of the unemployment of so many mill workers was explicitly recognized with the award of continued full pay while they were retrained and placed in other occupations.[6] It was suggested, further, that some factories scheduled for closure might be reactivated in the event of unexpected boosts to world sugar prices. This was a somewhat tenuous proposition, but it hinted at the concern felt at the highest official levels about the angst palpable in the mill communities now threatened with disintegration. More tangible was a MINAZ guarantee that community services and amenities, up to and including the local baseball league, would be maintained.

The farmers and agricultural workers of the sugar economy were obviously better positioned than their industrial counterparts to be absorbed into alternative agricultural activities. Cane CPAs, credit cooperatives, and UBPCs already devoted a variable but significant part of their members' land and labor to the cultivation of food crops and the rearing of livestock. But how easily and on what scale their land or labor could be so absorbed could not be assessed without far more explicit information than was currently publicly available or, indeed, officially known. It was not yet clear, for example, just what plantations were to be demolished and when, and the composition of the alternative activities proposed for affected areas remained obscure. It was factors such as these, of course, that would shape employment prospects. Land devoted to forestry, for instance, or to pasture for the extensive grazing of cattle, used relatively little labor. By contrast, food crop production could be far more labor intensive than cane farming.[7] Great variations in the techniques of production of the same food crops were also to be expected. Crops grown for on-farm consumption or local rural or urban markets might be produced—as was currently widespread—with animal traction and with very limited agrochemical resources.

By contrast, the burgeoning growth and increasingly widespread geographical dispersion of centers of foreign tourism might permit the adoption of far more import-intensive techniques to enable more of their year-round food needs to be met by local suppliers. The costs in foreign exchange of using more irrigation, fertilizers, herbicides, and fungicides for this purpose could be more than offset by cutting the hard currency component in the total earnings from foreign tourism.[8] The alternative uses to which cane areas might be put, together with the varied techniques of production that these might employ, would shape (and be shaped by) the number and skills of the workforce they would need. But, like much else in the restructuring program, just what relative balance of options would actually be adopted (or prove practicable) remained obscure.

It was clear, however, that the speed, scale, and skill with which restructuring was carried out would determine how large a short-run fall in cane supplies and raw sugar output could be expected and how quickly rising yields on a substantially smaller but more productive physical area might restore them. As to speed, a period of no more than two or three years appeared to be envisaged for the entire reconstruction program, stated in one report to have begun in March 2002 and to be finished at the end of 2004.[9] Given the scale of demolition envisaged for low-yield plantations, this meant substantial cane losses that could not immediately be offset by supplies from higher-yield producers. Moreover, not all cane plantations with above-average yields could be kept in production or all those with poorer ones demolished. The complex of plantations that supplied cane to a given mill had to make logistical sense and could not be comprised of a patchwork of fields with acceptable yields but anarchic field-to-factory transport routes. Moreover, past mill closures had shown that processing their cane in other factories—even from plantations with acceptable yields—

tended to increase transport costs and, since the quality of the cane deteriorated when delivered via routes that were excessively long or convoluted, sugar recovery rates could also suffer.

Whether or not the reconstruction program was carried out skillfully depended on myriad factors, some specific and others amorphous. A crucial one was the quality of the research carried out to determine which factories possessed the best conditions for greater efficiency—the sine qua non being a sufficient and stable supply of fresh, clean, and mature cane. Such research would show that high-capacity mills were not necessarily more efficient than smaller ones. The oft-cited CAI Cuba Libre of Matanzas Province, for example, had a daily grinding capacity of six thousand tonnes of cane. This was twice that of the CAI Cmdte. Manuel Fajardo in the province of Havana. Nonetheless, key performance indicators—most notably sugar recovery rates—showed the smaller factory to be the more efficient, reflecting not the higher caliber of its industrial installations but its better conditions of cane supply. Moreover, comparatively small factories with few cane suppliers were obviously less taxing to manage than larger ones where greater potential efficiency might fail to be realized because of deficiencies in the organization of more complex field and factory operations.

An accurate appraisal of cane supply conditions to determine which factories should remain operational and which not was formidably difficult to achieve. It encompassed an amalgam of technical, economic, and social factors, some with important political or ideological ramifications. For example, should not the UBPCs be made to bear a disproportionate share of the cuts to be made in the area under cane? After all, despite a number of privileges they enjoyed in the provision of material inputs and finance, their average yields were significantly lower than those of cane growers in CPAs and credit cooperatives. This was because the memberships of cane CPAs and other cooperatives tended to be more adept, versatile, and resilient as cultivators. But of course it was these very qualities that made the latter better placed to divert plantations to their most productive alternative uses. The case exemplified one of the many apparently simple questions to which the answer could only be "It all depends."

The empirical research underpinning the reconstruction program will almost certainly turn out to be highly uneven in scope and quality. The numerous mill closures that preceded the formal announcement of the reconstruction program in 2002 contributed valuable experience on which to base a more far-reaching reorganization of the industry. But up to 2000/2001, such closures were effected in a context in which the oft-stated official objective was the recovery and subsequent further expansion of production. As somewhat abruptly announced in 2002, therefore, the new reconstruction program appeared to be a strategic volte-face that in both scale and tempo took many by surprise. Long experience, moreover, had taught most managers, workers, and farmers to be skeptical of great leaps—whether backward or forward—as the best means to achieve advances in productivity. Overly ambitious cane yield targets were a case in point. At the risk of seeming to make a virtue of necessity, this skepticism—if not antipathy—toward policies perceived to seek too much too fast, and/or to lack a sound empirical base, could prove beneficial. When acting as a check—however limited—on the momentum of change at a local level, it could give pause for thought and enable many small but important blunders to be avoided. This was not likely to be unwelcome at higher levels of political and economic management, even where military tradition influenced the manner in which instructions were transmitted. This was because at the level of the localities where the cane was actually grown and processed, the practical implementation of the reconstruction program manifestly involved transactions that were far too intricate to be known, let alone directed, by loftier levels of administration. For example, complex local negotiations were needed to decide which specialized machinery and equipment should be transferred from one farm—whether private or collective—to another, and tracts of land, often with resident labor, would be transferred or bartered as well.

The precise number of factories to be closed or kept active (albeit for modified ends) could and had been predetermined in a national plan. But the reconstruction and diversification of the sugar economy viewed more broadly could not be so planned. It would instead be a process consisting of many both more and less devolved provincial, regional, and municipal exercises. And those exercises that most skillfully assimilated very disparate material, social, and institutional circumstances were the ones most likely to minimize their inevitable social and economic costs.

Conclusion

The focus of this discussion has been restricted to the sugar economy as a producer of raw sugar. Its direct productive role in the national economy is, of course, far more extensive, and the greater prominence recently assigned to the production of cane by-products and derivatives is likely to emphasize this. In the first place, the cane crushed in industrial processing—the bagasse—is also the industry's basic fuel, as well as an alternative to wood pulp in paper and furniture production. Cane-tops, leaves, and molasses, in crude or processed form, are important sources of animal feedstuff. Raw sugar, alcohol, and molasses are not only exported but underpin important national industries in brewing, distilling, canning, and confectionery. And the more specialized use and potential of cane by-products in biotechnology has attracted the interest of foreign investors. To this selection of the better-known by-products of cane production must be added the sugar economy's role as a major market for the output of the country's engineering and chemical industries. The ability of these industries to supply this market has been constrained by their dependence on key imports of capital and intermediate goods, but they remain major sources of domestic employment and value added. Whether they grow or decline depends in no small measure on the expansion or contraction of the sugar sector.

Since 1991, both at home and abroad, Cuba's sugar economy has often been viewed as an unwelcome historical relic. Its growth and sustained dominance was explained up to 1959 by the colonial or neocolonial forces to which Cuba was subservient. After 1959 it was given a potent but artificial breath of life by the geopolitical eccentricities of Soviet-Cuban ties in a Cold War world. Nonetheless, two factors ensure its continued importance for Cuba's national economic well-being. The first is that, despite unpropitious sugar marketing conditions, it continues to generate scarce hard-currency earnings in an international trading environment warped by U.S. hostility. The second is that, in an economy with limited alternative resources, it generates a crucial volume of employment and income both in the sugar sector and in the multiplicity of ancillary activities to which it is structurally linked. There is no doubt that its influence over time will progressively wane—but the transition period in which it continues to play a prominent, if no longer a leading, role is likely to be prolonged.

Notes

1. Unless otherwise noted, all data cited are from tables 5.1, 5.2, and 5.3.

2. L. Peña Castellanos reports that a working figure of US$200 per tonne is used to represent production costs in agreements securing foreign finance for territorial sugar production in Cuba from 1995. It is suggested that this same figure is used in analyses of Cuba's sugar recovery programs (Peña Castellanos 2001). To complement this, it could be noted that in 1996 Carlos Lage reported the import component of Cuba's raw sugar production to cost "between US$120–160 per tonne" (Lage 1998).

3. Data for 2000/2001 and 2001/2 are taken from estimates of Licht (2002).

4. The statistics and quotations cited to portray the reconstruction program are extracted from diverse reports published in the Cuban press from June to September of 2002. The most informative is an interview with Manuel Cordero, general secretary of the Sugar Workers Trade Union, published in *Trabajadores*, 8 July 2002. These reports are discussed by G. B. Hagelberg in Licht (2002, 493–99).

5. These estimates would be consistent with the MINAZ projections of cane yields, industrial recovery rates, and total sugar production cited above. They do not, however, explicitly include cane to be grown and processed exclusively for by-products.

6. President Castro announced in a speech on 21 October 2002 that almost eighty-five thousand sugar workers were already enlisted in formal study programs (*Granma*, 22 October 2002).

7. In the CPA Antonino Rojas of Havana Province, for example, some four hundred hectares were under cane in 1991. Between 1991 and 1994, however, the food needs of the capital city forced one-third of this area to be diverted to the production of food crops. Together with a more labor-intensive cultivation

of the reduced cane area, the change in land use required the membership of the cooperative to be increased over the same period from 70 to 120 (author's fieldwork, cited in Pollitt 1997a, 195 n. 57).

8. Cuba's most popular and extensive tourist complexes were located on the peninsula of Varadero in the north of Matanzas Province. Together with a historical legacy of numerous small sugar mills, the size and propinquity of this foreign tourist market may explain why Matanzas had the highest number of mill closures planned for any province. Only eight out of a nominal provincial total of twenty-one factories were to remain operational. Six of these were to continue to produce raw sugar and two were to produce only molasses and derivatives.

9. Manuel Cordero, *Trabajadores,* 8 July 2002.

References

Álvarez, J., and L. Peña Castellanos. 2001. *Cuba's Sugar Industry.* Gainesville: University of Florida Press.

Anuario Azucarero de Cuba. 1955.

Cañaveral. 1995. Vol. 1, no. 4, (October–December).

Cuba Business. 1999. Vol. 13, no. 3 (April).

Carmen, Diana, Niurka Pérez Rojas, Ernel González, and Miriam Garcia. 1998. *Güines, Santo Domingo y Majibacao—Sobre sus historias agrarias.* Havana, Cuba: University of Havana.

Comisión Económica de America Latina (CEPAL). 1997. *Reformas estructurales y desempeño en los noventa.* Mexico D.F.: CEPAL.

Fernández Font, M. 1996. "Perspectivas del mercado mundial azucarero hasta el ano 2000: Participacion de Cuba." Pt. 2. *Cuba Foreign Trade* 2: 88–95.

Lage, C. 1998. "Intervention in the Asamblea Nacional del Poder Popular of 21 December 1998." *Granma,* 23 December.

Licht, F. O. 1998. *International Sugar and Sweetener Report* 130, no. 22.

_______. 2000. *International Sugar and Sweetener Report* 132, no. 24.

_______. 2002. *International Sugar and Sweetener Report* 134, no. 31.

Lugo, Orlando. 1995. *Cañaveral* 1, no. 4. (October–December): 8.

Ministerio de Azúcar. 1990. *Anuario Estadístico.* Havana, Cuba: Ministerio de Azúcar.

_______. 1995. *Balance del Trabajo y la Situación de las UBPC.* Havana, Cuba: Ministerio de Azúcar.

del Monte, A. 1980. "La integración agro-industrial azucarera." *ATAC,* no. 2 (March–April).

Peña Castellanos, L. 2001. "La agro-industria acucarera Cubana y su competitividad." Paper presented at Development Prospects in Cuba workshop, London University, 25 January 2001.

Pollitt, B. H. 1973. "Employment Plans, Performance, and Future Prospects in Cuba." In *Third World Employment,* edited by Richard Jolly, Emanuel de Kadt, Hans Senger, and Fiona Wilson. London: Penguin.

_______. 1997a. "The Cuban Sugar Economy: Collapse, Reform, and Prospects for Recovery." *Journal of Latin American Studies* 29, pt. 1 (February): 171–210.

_______. 1997b. "Cuba's Cane Cooperatives: Background, Trials, and Tribulations." *International Sugar and Sweetener Report* 129, no. 24 (August): 473–79.

Pollitt, B. H., and G. B. Hagelberg. 1994. "The Cuban Sugar Economy in the Soviet Era and After." *Cambridge Journal of Economics* 18:547–69.

Sulroca, F. 1990. "La agricultura canera y su papel en la eficiencia agro-industrial azucarera en Cuba." Paper presented at Asociación de Técnicos Azucareros de Cuba, Havana, Cuba, November 1990.

UN Economic Commission for Latin America and the Caribbean (UNECLAC). 1997. *La economía Cubana—Reformas estructurales y desempeño en los noventa*. Mexico, D.F.

CHAPTER 6

Cuban Agriculture in Transition

The Impacts of Policy Changes on Agricultural Production, Food Markets, and Trade

William A. Messina Jr.

The creation of basic units of cooperative production (*unidades básicas de producción cooperativa,* or UBPCs) from the former state farms in 1993 and the opening of agricultural markets (*mercados agropecuarios,* or MAs) in 1994 were significant steps in a process of reform and transformation for the agricultural sector in Cuba. Some analysts argue that, as a result of the Cuban government's failure to continue its process of economic liberalization beyond these two important policy changes, the transition for the Cuban economy in general and for Cuban agriculture in particular can be characterized as a dismal failure. This chapter reviews the most current available data to characterize the present situation in the agricultural sector in Cuba and to assess the impacts these policy changes have had on Cuba's agricultural production, consumption, and import patterns.

The Changing Structure of Production

Following the loss of Soviet economic support and subsidization in 1990, Cuba faced a severe economic crisis. Recognizing the extent of the economic pressures to come, Fidel Castro warned the Cuban people that they were facing a time of austerity, which he labeled as the Special Period in Time of Peace. Cuba's agricultural sector was a pivotal element of the economy at this point, with more than 6.8 million hectares of land dedicated to agricultural production. Over 5 million hectares of this land (about 75 percent) was held in large, highly mechanized, and input-intensive state farms. With only limited access to fertilizers, pesticides, fuel for tractors, and spare parts for agricultural equipment after 1989, agricultural production in Cuba plummeted.

Facing ever increasing food shortages in the early 1990s, the Cuban government recognized that the less input-intensive agricultural cooperatives had not experienced production decreases as dramatic as those of the state farms. In response, the Cuban government passed legislation in September 1993 authorizing the breakup of large state farms into a new form of cooperative known as the basic units of cooperative production. Nova Gonzalez wrote, "The positive experience over more than 20 years with smaller Agricultural Production Cooperatives (Cooperativas de Producción Agropecuarias or CPAs) provided the foundation for the planning and creation of the UBPCs. Even during the early years of the *Special Period*, the CPAs had demonstrated their ability to better adapt to difficult economic conditions" (1998, 1). This policy change marked the beginning of a significant process of transformation in the structure of agricultural production in Cuba.

The transition from state farms to UBPCs occurred rapidly following the passage of legislation authorizing their creation in the fall of 1993. By the end of 1995, more than 2,800 UBPCs had been created, encompassing about 42 percent of total agricultural land in Cuba. State farms, which held nearly three-quarters of total agricultural land area in Cuba in 1989, represented less than one-third of the land area by 1995 (ONE 1996).

While this extraordinary transition from state farms to UBPCs was taking place in Cuba during the mid-1990s, land area in other forms of tenancy for agricultural production remained fairly stable overall.[1] Land area in dispersed private farms increased somewhat over the period, although their share of total agricultural land area was largely offset by decreases in acreage held in CPAs. Even after the increases, the dispersed private farm share of agricultural land area remained at less than 5 percent of total agricultural land area.

In their 1993 work Puerta and Alvarez documented how, in the late 1980s, CPAs, CCSs, and dispersed private farms utilized their land more intensively (that is, cultivated higher proportions of their agricultural land areas) than the state farms. This pattern continued into the late 1990s, and UBPCs demonstrated a similar pattern, showing notable increases over state farms in the proportion of their agricultural land under cultivation. In 1997, on average, state farms had 18.7 percent of their available agricultural land idle, compared to 8.9 percent for UBPCs, 7.5 percent for CPAs, 4.6 percent for CCSs, and 5.9 percent for dispersed private farms.[2] Viewed another way, state farms had more than twice as large a percentage of their agricultural land area left idle as UBPCs and CPAs, more than three times as large a percentage as dispersed private farms, and more than four times as large a percentage as the CCSs.

The breakup of the state farms for the creation of UBPCs also brought about an important shift in average farm size in Cuba. In 1997 the average size of UBPCs for producing sugarcane, livestock, and tobacco was less than 10 percent of the average size of state farms producing the same crops. The average size for UBPCs for production of vegetables, roots, and tubers was only slightly more than 10 percent of the average size of state farms producing those crops, and rice UBPCs were less than 20 percent of the size of state rice farms (ONE 1994; Nova Gonzalez 1996; and "Las soluciones" 1997). As UBPC farm sizes more closely approximated those of the CPAs, the view in Cuba was that the decrease in scale of agricultural production on the UBPCs would provide the basis for more efficient and sustainable production systems under conditions of limited availability of agricultural inputs. In examining shifts in the patterns of agricultural production, the following section will attempt to assess the degree to which this is the case.

Shifting Production Patterns

As discussed previously, the loss of economic support from the Soviet Union brought about a crisis in the Cuban economy that was characterized by, among other things, abrupt and significant declines in Cuba's agricultural production. Table 6.1 provides a summary of the declines in the production of some of Cuba's most important staple crops for feeding its population.[3] The second column of this table shows 1994 domestic production of each of Cuba's basic agricultural crops as a percentage of domestic production volumes in 1988. In 1994, production of such important crops as rice and beans was only 46 and 73 percent, respectively, of 1988 production volumes. Over the period, root and tuber production had fallen to less than three-quarters of its 1988 level, and vegetable production was less than half of the volume produced in 1988. Conversely, Cuba's corn production more than doubled between 1988 and 1994, although this increase occurred from a relatively low base level. The only other crop to show a production increase over the period was plantain, with an increase of slightly over 50 percent.

Table 6.1 also documents the recovery in Cuba's agricultural production that took place in 1994 as the Cuban economy began a slow recovery from its economic freefall. Not coincidentally, these increases in agricultural production began the year following the formation of UBPCs and the year when the farmers markets (*mercados agropecuarios,* or MAs) were opened. The third column in the table shows production volumes achieved in 2000 as a percentage of the production levels from 1988. For all commodities, Cuba's production volumes were higher in 2000 than in 1994. In fact, in 2000 only peppers, rice, bananas, mangoes, and guavas failed to exceed production volumes from 1988. Of particular note is the nearly sixfold increase in corn production, a fourfold increase in bean production, almost a tripling of plantain production, and a doubling of vegetable production.[4] Corn and bean production improved as initiatives to expand production offset Cuba's loss of food import capabilities after 1990 due to critical foreign exchange shortages. However, the fact that rice production in 2000 was still less than two-thirds of its 1988 level was particularly disappointing given that rice is such an important part of the Cuban diet and that Cuba is a net rice importer.

Table 6.1 Cuban Agricultural Production Decline and Recovery, Selected Commodities, 1994 and 2000

	1994 Production Volume as % of 1988 Production	2000 Production Volume as % of 1988 Production
Roots and tubers	74.2	152.0
Potatoes	68.0	132.9
Boniatos	81.6	134.3
Malangas	17.3	171.7
Vegetables	47.7	216.2
Tomatoes	28.6	101.0
Onions	10.8	164.7
Peppers	13.7	55.7
Cereals	57.1	97.1
Rice	46.2	62.6
Corn	207.3	574.1
Beans	73.0	402.7
Bananas and Plantains	104.5	170.1
Bananas	70.6	91.4
Plantains	152.8	282.3
Other Fruits	33.1	103.1
Mangoes	36.7	82.9
Guavas	16.4	30.1
Papayas	23.8	121.3
TOTAL	62.8	156.5

Source: Anuario Estadístico de Cuba (1989, 1996, 2000).

One way of providing a broad assessment of overall fluctuations in production of these basic staple crops is to compare the percentage changes in the production volumes for these crops in total between years. In 1994 total production of Cuba's staple crops fell to 63 percent of the 1988 production level. By 1996 total production volume recovered to about 95 percent of the 1988 level, suggesting that, while the composition may have changed somewhat, food volumes from domestic sources moving through Acopio (the state agency in charge of food collection and distribution) in that year should have approached those in 1988. While production volumes of staple crops in 1997 fell below those of 1996,[5] they recovered in 1998 and increased significantly from 1998 through 2000 to the point where domestic production of these crops in total was over one and a half times as large in 2000 as the production volumes achieved in 1988.

Unfortunately, data is not available to disaggregate production areas, production volumes, or yields among the state farms, UBPCs, CPAs, CCSs, and dispersed private farms. The data does, however, show that for all of the staple crops examined, there has been a steady transfer of acreage and thus production from the state to the nonstate sector, the nonstate sector being made up of the UBPCs, CPAs, and CCSs ("Anuario Estadístico de Cuba" 2002). Lacking more specific data on acreage transfers to the UBPCs, given that from 1994 through 1997 all of the agricultural land transfers from the state farms went to create new UBPCs, the vast majority of this transfer of agricultural land area from the state sector to the nonstate sector between 1997 and 2000 likely continued to take place with the UBPCs. Thus, the increasingly important role of the nonstate sector generally and the UBPCs in particular in Cuba's agricultural sector is apparent.

In reality, though, it is unlikely that this change in the structure of production alone could drive the increases in production that Cuba has experienced without the influence of some other factor(s). Enter the role of the agricultural markets.

The Role and Function of Agricultural Markets

In the early years of the Special Period prior to the opening of the MAs, food availability was an increasing problem in Cuba.[6] As the food shortages became more prevalent, black market sales of food and agricultural products expanded rapidly. These transactions were conducted almost exclusively in dollars and, as a result, individuals and families without access to hard currency (either through tips in the tourist sector or remittances from overseas) were not able to obtain food products through the black market. When the food shortages approached crisis proportions in the summer of 1994, the opening of the MAs enabled purchases of "surplus" food supplies (agricultural production in excess of quota obligations for sale to Acopio) in pesos, which was a particularly important development, as it broadened the availability of food outside of the ration system within Cuba.

In 1995 the author heard a Cuban scholar refer to the opening of the MAs as an attempt by the Cuban government to, among other things, "bleach" the black market. Empirical evidence suggests that the MAs have been somewhat successful in this regard.[7] Armando Nova Gonzalez (1998) refers to the way in which the reopening of the free market for agricultural products (October 1994) deflated prices of products that had previously been sold in the underground economy or black market by reducing the *risk premium* for such sales.[8]

The importance of the MAs in Cuba is perhaps most clearly demonstrated by the fact that in the city of Havana in the late 1990s, ration markets only were able to supply about 60 percent of daily caloric consumption for the population. Social meals provided another approximately 8 percent of caloric consumption.[9] This means that Havana's population was relying on the MAs and other sources for about one-third of their caloric requirements (Nova Gonzalez 1998). However, because the prices in the MAs were high relative to average salaries in Cuba, these food purchases consumed a significant proportion of the total monthly income of the average Cuban household.

MAs exist throughout Cuba. There are about fifty MAs in Havana. Sales in the Havana markets represent roughly two-thirds of the value of sales of all MAs of the country. For this reason, the agricultural markets in Havana often are considered to be the most representative. They are attractive for the producers and sellers because of their relatively large sizes, the higher income levels in the city; and the lower sales taxes (5 percent compared to 15 percent in townships and 10 percent in provinces).

During the first three years following the establishment of the MAs, the sale of agricultural products and meats steadily increased. Between 1995 and 1996 there was an increase of 19 and 5 percent respectively in sales of agricultural and meat products in the MAs (ONE 1998a). A slight decrease in the sales of agricultural and meat products moving through the MAs was experienced in 1997, which was attributed to the effects of hurricane Lili.

Nova Gonzalez provides some especially interesting statistics regarding the main suppliers to the MAs. The CCSs, and dispersed private farms were especially active and important in the MAs following their reopening in October 1994, holding between 40 and 62 percent market share for agricultural products and between 60 and 79 percent market share for meat products. Interestingly, the state has been another important participant in the markets through Acopio, with its market share steadily increasing between 1995 and 1997 to approximately 40 percent for both agricultural and meat products. This was presumably part of an effort by the government to keep prices in the MAs low so that food supplies outside of the ration stores would be more accessible to the populace since the ration stores were not able to supply all of the food needs.

Nova Gonzalez notes that, over time, there was a steady reduction in the presence of UBPCs, CPAs, and the EJT (Ejército Juvenil del Trabajo, or Working Youth Army) as participants in the MAs. These trends may be a bit misleading, however, as he reported that it is likely that some of the increase in the activity of the state (Acopio) in the MAs represented purchases from UBPCs, CPAs, and/or the EJT that had decreased their direct participation in the MAs.

Prices of staple food products sold in the MAs declined consistently between 1994 and 2000 to the point where prices of many products in 2000 were between one-half and one-third of their level in 1994. Prices in the MAs in Havana are consistently higher than the prices in the MAs throughout the rest of the country, and they tend to fluctuate more than the prices of markets outside the city (Nova Gonzalez 1995, 2002).

In the final analysis, it is the very real and significant incentives provided by the MAs that have been a primary stimulus for the recovery in Cuba's agricultural production, even with the severely constrained input availabilities that agricultural producers face. The breakup of the state farms into UBPCs facilitated this process in the sense that small cooperatives with about sixty to eighty members were much more capable of responding to and empowered to take advantage of the opportunities offered in the MAs than were the large state farm.

The transfer of over 2.5 million of agricultural land to the UBPCs in the short span of two years, coupled with the same dynamic influencing the CPAs, CCSs, and dispersed private farms, which held another 1.6 million hectares of agricultural land, translates into a very significant amount of productive capacity. The gains in agricultural production that Cuba has experienced are a clear demonstration of the power of markets and incentives, even in the presence of the constraints and rigidities facing producers as discussed previously.

In another development affecting food distribution within Cuba, in 1999 the Cuban government introduced a new form of government-sponsored market (under the Ministry of Agriculture) for sales of food products outside of the ration system. As of 2002 there are 2,380 of these markets operating throughout the country at locations other than those where the MAs operate. As distinct from the MAs, the majority of which are in Havana, the majority of these markets are located outside of the city. These markets operate in parallel with the MAs as another source of food outside of the ration system. Data is not available regarding the volumes moving through these markets, though their prices are generally lower than the MAs. These markets also are reported to have problems with product quality and the assortment of products offered (Nova Gonzalez 2002).

This discussion of Cuba's dynamic agricultural markets also serves to highlight what may be the quintessential enigma of Cuba's agricultural and food system: how is it that food supplies in the MAs, which are supposed to be surplus production (that is, production in excess of quota obligations for sale to Acopio), remain high while food supplies in the ration stores are not sufficient to meet the needs of the population? The Cuban government acknowledges this condition but offers no explanation. The full explanation for the situation is undoubtedly complex and may, in part, involve the supplying of products to the MAs by Acopio if those stocks were diverted from the ration stores. However, this likely only would provide a partial reason for the extensive supply of food and agricultural products in the MAs when ration requirements are not being met. The last section of this chapter will examine the role Cuba's agricultural and food import patterns may play in the shortages in the food ration system.

Agricultural and Food Imports

Shifting import patterns for agricultural and food products also must be examined to have a full perspective of the changes in Cuba's food situation. Table 6.2 contains

Table 6.2 Value of Cuban Agricultural and Food Product Imports and Total Imports, 1989–2000 *(in Thousands of Pesos)*

Year	Agricultural and Food Product Imports	Total Imports	Agricultural and Food Imports as % of Total Imports
1989	908,762	8,124,224	11.2
1990	827,341	7,416,525	11.2
1991	825,377	4,233,752	19.5
1992	498,569	2,314,916	21.5
1993	474,146	2,008,215	23.6
1994	467,331	2,016,821	23.2
1995	610,890	2,882,530	21.2
1996	718,212	3,568,997	20.1
1997	724,581	3,987,256	18.2
1998	704,200	4,181,192	16.8%
1999	722,396	4,349,090	16.6%
2000	671,801	4,829,050	13.9%

Source: Anuario Estadístico de Cuba (1991, 1998, 2002).

data on the value of Cuban agricultural and food imports and total Cuban imports from 1989 through 2000.

Between 1989 and 1994, the value of Cuba's total imports fell by more than 75 percent, reflecting the economic crisis that gripped the nation following the loss of its preferential trading relationships with the Soviet Union and Eastern European countries. Over the same period, Cuba's agricultural and food imports fell by only about 50 percent. As a result, agricultural and food imports doubled their representation as a proportion of the total value of Cuban imports, from 11 to 23 percent. This clearly demonstrates that the government of Cuba placed a priority on maintaining agricultural and food import volumes to the extent possible during the crisis of the Special Period in an effort to meet domestic food requirements.

In 1993/94, the Cuban economic collapse reached its low point and the economy began a slow recovery. At the same time, the value of Cuba's agricultural and food product imports began to increase. In fact, the value of agricultural and food imports jumped by over 30 percent between 1994 and 1995 and increased another 18 percent between 1995 and 1996. The fact that this growth in imports was occurring at the same time as Cuba's production volumes for staple crops was increasing is a reflection of the extent of the crisis in food supplies that had developed as well as, to a lesser extent, the increases in food imports required to supply Cuba's rapidly expanding tourist sector.

While Cuba's agricultural and food imports were experiencing this rapid growth, the total value of Cuba's imports grew even more rapidly so that the agricultural and food import share of total imports began to decline after 1994. Between 1996 and 1999 the value of Cuba's agricultural and food imports remained fairly constant; over the same period, continued increases in the total value of Cuba's imports resulted in a steady decline in the proportion of total imports represented by agricultural and food products. By 2000 the agricultural and food product share of the total value of Cuba's imports had declined to the point where it was approaching the levels of the late 1980s, although the nominal dollar value of these imports remained well below levels of a decade earlier.

These import patterns offer at least a partial explanation for the shortages in Cuba's food rationing system at a time when surplus food supplies in the MAs were plentiful. Shortages in the food ration system were, to some degree, the result of Cuba's diminished capability to import the necessary products. Even given the increased production levels Cuba's agricultural sector achieved between 1994 and 2000, with ration system food requirements increasing along with population, agricultural and food product import levels at only about three-quarters of their 1989 value, and an increasing proportion of these imports going to the tourist sector, the pressures on the ration system are not likely to diminish in the near term.

Conclusion

Following the establishment of UBPCs in 1993 and the opening of MAs in 1994, the Cuban government has done little to remove the obstacles that hinder the efficient functioning of the agricultural sector in Cuba. Nevertheless, these institutions both play important roles in Cuba's agricultural sector and the food system at the present time.

Increases in the production of staple food crops experienced in Cuba after 1994 are not entirely attributable to the formation of UBPCs. Even the Cuban government reports "unprofitability" of a large proportion of the UBPCs (Nova Gonzalez 1998). The fact remains that the large-scale, highly mechanized, input-intensive state farms were no longer viable following the loss of Soviet support. In light of that situation, the UBPCs appear to have achieved some level of success in terms of expanding agricultural and food production to feed the Cuban people, despite the fact that many structural rigidities remain in place in Cuba that have hindered further improvements and efficiencies in the functioning of the agricultural sector.

In a particularly noteworthy development, the Cuban National Assembly reportedly approved legislative revisions in November of 2002 to allow agricultural cooperatives and farmers expanded flexibility and incentives to increase food production for the government's food distribution system. Included among the initiatives included in this legislation is a provision to allow agricultural producers more autonomy in determining which crops they will produce on their land. Interestingly, long-standing restrictions on this sort of decision making at the producer level was identified by Cuban analysts as one of the important barriers constraining Cuba's agricultural sector from achieving increased productivity and efficiency (Nova Gonzalez 1998). While details on how these new policies will be implemented were unclear at the time of the preparation of this chapter, this legislation has the potential to stimulate important additional increases in agricultural production in Cuba, which would help improve food availabilities both inside and outside of the food ration system. As such, this legislation may well represent the most important policy development for Cuba's agricultural sector, and for the nation as a whole, since the opening of the MAs in 1994.

With the MAs providing about one-third of the caloric requirements of the Cuban people, these markets have played and are expected to continue to play an important role in feeding the population even though food costs in the MAs remain expensive relative to general income levels. Thus, opening of the MAs has been another successful, and perhaps even pivotally important, policy change implemented by the Cuban government.

An examination of Cuban food import patterns suggests that significantly lower food import volumes offer a partial explanation for the shortfalls being experienced in the food rationing system in Cuba at a time when surplus food supplies (supplies in excess of quota requirements for sale to Acopio) in the MAs appear relatively plentiful. With its chronic and ever increasing trade deficits and continuing economic difficulties, questions remain regarding Cuba's ability to continue its present level of agricultural and food imports. This is an especially important and pressing issue for the Cuban government with important implications for its food system.

In October 2000, President Bill Clinton signed historic legislation allowing U.S. firms to sell food and medicine to Cuba for the first time in forty years. Because of a number of provisions in the legislation, among them the requirement that all sales be on a cash basis and that Cuban exports to the United States would not be permitted, the Cuban government responded by refusing to purchase any products from U.S. companies under the legislation, thus this legislation had no influence on Cuba's trade patterns in 2000. However, the Cuban government's position changed in November 2001 after Hurricane Michelle struck Cuba with the most destructive winds and rains that the island nation had experienced in half a century. Damage from the storm to the agricultural sector was extensive, and while the Cuban government refused U.S. offers of emergency food aid, it did begin purchasing agricultural and food products from U.S. companies on a cash basis. These sales expanded in 2002 to the point where, as of the early fall of 2002, Cuba had purchased in excess of $170 million in agricultural and food products from U.S. companies on a cash basis. While the Cuban government and U.S. firms speak in optimistic terms about continued growth in these sales transactions, the aforementioned situation regarding the shortage of Cuba's hard-currency reserves to fund these cash purchases remains an issue.

The evidence presented in this chapter suggests that the establishment of UBPCs and the opening of MAs have had positive impacts on food production and availability in Cuba from the deficient levels experienced in 1993–94. However, their influence has not been sufficient to offset all of the problems experienced in the agricultural and food sector as a result of the loss of Soviet aid. While the agricultural and food situation in Cuba at the present time does not appear to be as difficult as it was in 1993 and 1994, the aforementioned factors suggest that the present equilibrium, such as it is, may indeed be fragile.[10]

Notes

1. Agricultural production cooperatives (*cooperativas de producción agrogecuarias,* or CPAs), credit and service cooperatives (*cooperativas de créditos y servicios,* or CCSs), and a category referred to in the Cuban statistics as dispersed private farms. For additional detail on the forms of tenancy for agricultural production in Cuba, see Alvarez and Messina (1996) and Puerta and Alvarez (1993).

2. Cuba has not published an update on this data series since 1997.

3. Cuba's sugar production recorded similar declines. For a detailed examination of Cuba's sugar industry, see Alvarez and Peña Castellanos (2002).

4. To levels more than twice as high as the highest production volumes over the previous twenty-five years.

5. Reports from Cuba indicate that this is, in part, the result of damage caused by Hurricane Lili in late 1996, which is not implausible.

6. This section draws heavily from Nova Gonzalez (1998).

7. While black market sales undoubtedly continue to take place in Cuba, it is likely that food volumes moving through the black market now are smaller than the volumes sold on the black market in 1993 and early 1994. However, there is no information or basis whatsoever upon which to base even the roughest of estimates of black market food sales.

8. An implicit reference to the previous experience with free agricultural markets in the early 1980s.

9. Meals provided for workers and students, or sales to workers.

10. With the possible exception of the sugar subsector, which is presently undergoing dramatic restructuring.

References

Alvarez, Jose, and Lazaro Peña Castellanos. 2001. *Cuba's Sugar Industry*. Gainesville: University Press of Florida.

Alvarez, Jose, and William A. Messina Jr. 1996. "Cuba's New Agricultural Cooperatives and Markets: Antecedents, Organization, Early Performance and Prospects." In *Cuba in Transition, Volume 6*. Washington, D.C.: Association for the Study of the Cuban Economy.

Alvarez, Jose, and Ricardo Puerta. 1994. "State Intervention in Cuban Agriculture: Impact on Organization and Performance." *World Development* 11:1663–75.

Anuario Estadístico de Cuba 1989. 1991. Havana, Cuba: Oficina Nacional de Estadísticas.

Anuario Estadístico de Cuba 1996. 1998. Havana, Cuba: Oficina Nacional de Estadísticas.

Anuario Estadístico de Cuba 2000. 2002. Havana, Cuba: Oficina Nacional de Estadísticas.

"Las soluciones están en cada colectivo laboral." 1997. *Trabajadores,* 22 September.

Nova Gonzalez, Armando. 1995. "Mercado agropecuario: Factores que limitan la oferta." *Cuba: Investigación Económica* 3.

______. 1996. "Cuba: Modificación o transformación agrícola?" Centro de superacion del MEP.

______. 1998. "Las Nuevas Relaciones de Producción en la Agricultura." Paper presented at the Twenty-first Congress of the Latin American Studies Association, October.

______. 2002. "El mercado interno de los alimentos." *Cuba: Reflexiones Sobre su Economía*. Havana, Cuba: University of Havana Press.

Oficina Nacional de Estadísticas (ONE). 1994. "Caracteristicas de las UBPC y algunos cambios producidos in el sector agropecuario con su introducción." Havana, Cuba.

______. 1998a. "Ventas en el mercado agropecuario." Havana, Cuba.

______. 1998b. "Estadísticas seleccionadas." Havana, Cuba.

Pampín Balado, Blanca Rosa, and Clara María Trujillo Rodríguez. 1998. "Los cambios estructurales in la agricultural Cubana." Asociacion Nacional de Economistas de Cuba (ANEC).

Puerta, Ricardo, and Jose Alvarez. 1993. "Organization and Performance of Cuban Agriculture at Different Levels of State Intervention." International Working Paper No. IW93-14. International Trade and Development Center, Department of Food and Resource Economics. Institute of Food and Agricultural Sciences, University of Florida, Gainesville.

PART IV

Entrepreneurship and Economic Reform

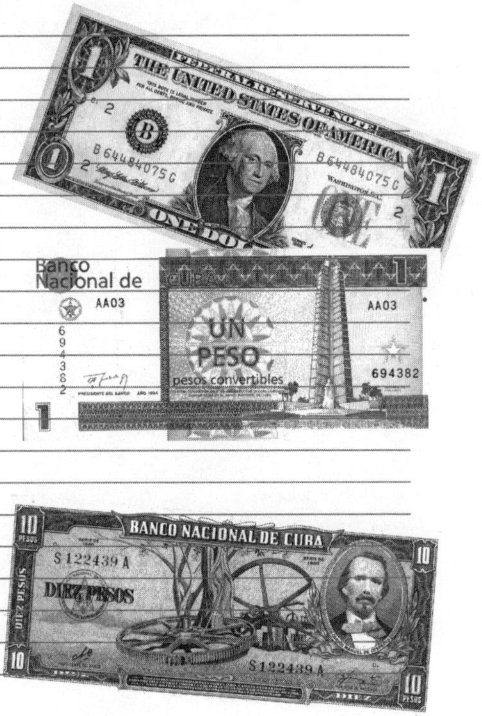

CHAPTER 7

The Taxation of Microenterprise

Archibald R. M. Ritter

In September 1993, in the depths of the economic crisis, Cuba liberalized self-employment—legalizing many of the economic activities Cubans were already practicing in clandestinity as part of their personal and family survival strategies. This permitted a surfacing of many activities previously conducted in the underground economy and an explosion of new entrepreneurial creativity. The need for a tax regime to tap the incomes generated in the self-employment sector was immediately obvious and a tax system was adopted in September 1993 and fully implemented in 1996.

The tax regime, as designed and implemented, indeed has extracted revenues from the sector. However, the design of the tax regime has a number of weaknesses that reduce its fairness, damage the efficiency of resource allocation, and limit its viability. The objective of this study is to analyze the impacts of the tax regime for the microenterprise sector in terms of the equity of income distribution; the efficiency of resource use; and the viability, effectiveness, and sustainability of the collection of revenues for the government. Following an analysis and evaluation of the microenterprise tax regime are a number of observations on how it could be modified in order to achieve more fully the objectives of fairness, efficiency, and viability.

The Microenterprise Sector

Despite the nationalizations of small- and medium-scale enterprise in the Revolutionary Offensive of March 1968, a small self-employment sector continued to exist mainly in areas of personal services, transport, artisan work, and various types of fabrication. The number of officially registered nonagricultural microenterprises was placed at 28,600 in 1988 with 12,800 employees, accounting for 1.1 percent of total employment (Comité Estatal de Estadisticas 1988). The underground economy also included many microenterprise activities, and it continued to operate on a large scale from 1968 to 1993. However, its size is virtually impossible to ascertain. From 1989 to

Table 7.1 Registered Microenterprise Self-Employment in Cuba

	December 1994	December 1995	March 1996	January 1998
Approved and registered	169,098	208,786	206,824	159,506
Total applications for registration	248,552	390,759	439,268	(268,295)
Applications rejected	10,675	11,519	12,665	(108,789)
Applications withdrawn	64,586	148,491	195,023	
Applications in process	4,193	21,963	8,789	

Source: Ministerio de Trabajo y Segundad Social and UNECLAC (1997).

1993, the volume of clandestine self-employment increased rapidly, as people's family survival strategies required that they earn real incomes beyond those provided by employment in the state sector. The latter were increasingly insufficient to acquire the daily necessities that were no longer available through the rationing system (Ritter 1998, 74–76).

The liberalization of self-employment on 8 September 1993 permitted many microenterprises to surface from the underground economy and permitted new ones to become legally established. Decree Law 141 and the accompanying resolution legalized 117 types of activities in six general areas, including transportation, house repair, agricultural related areas, family and personal services, housing services, and other activities. By early 1997, a total of 157 types of activities had been legalized, including "gastronomic services," which encompassed street vending and private restaurants, or *paladares.* The legislation of 1993 limited self-employment to retirees, housewives, and laid-off workers but excluded professionals and enterprise managers. In time, professionals who were declared redundant in their professional activities were permitted to enter one of the self-employment categories but not as self-employed professionals. In order to enter self-employment, regularly employed workers in the state sector also required the permission of their work centers. A variety of other restrictions on microenterprise activity were imposed as well, as discussed below.

The number of registered and legal microenterprises rose rapidly, reaching 169,098 by December 1994 and peaking at 208,786 in December 1995 (table 7.1.) The real level of employment was higher than the number of microenterprises, as family members were frequently employed and others often provided some of the inputs needed by registered microenterprises. One estimate by the United Nations Economic Commission for Latin America (UNECLAC 1997) placed the total volume of private sector employment at 400,000, or 9.4 percent, in 1996, but the number may have been higher.

Indeed, if one includes informal, nonregistered *part-time* self-employment, the number of self-employed could reach 30 percent or more of the labor force. This is because virtually all families in Cuba, except those receiving remittances from relatives or other access to dollars, such as foreign travel, must supplement their state sector wage incomes with additional incomes from a secondary activity. The state sector wage incomes are insufficient for necessary purchases from the higher-priced agricultural markets and dollar stores.

Registered self-employment and all the other unregistered self-employment activities have made a valuable contribution to the Cuban economy and people. They create employment. They have helped families earn the incomes necessary for their survival. Although some self-employment activities have generated higher incomes, the vast majority provide significant but modest income supplements. The self-employment activities constitute a massive school for entrepreneurship. They also provide basic services and goods for the satisfaction of essential needs of virtually all Cubans.

The sector also generates large volumes of revenues for the state through the taxation system and the imposition of fines, which are onerous and apparently frequent. The monthly tax payments of one dollar sector restaurant are U.S.$520. (This is calculated as $300 for the basic monthly payment, plus $100 for an alcohol license, plus $60 for each of the minimum required two family employees. This is almost fifty times the average monthly salary in the state sector (which was 214 pesos in 1997) at the exchange rate relevant for Cuban citizens, namely 1 U.S. dollar = 20 pesos (see table 7.2).

The Policy Environment

The tax regime for microenterprise is but one element of the general policy environment within which microenterprises operate. The first element in the policy framework is the broad range of detailed regulations that affect their size and operations. The regulatory environment includes the following general features as summarized in Decreto-Ley 174 (1997):

Table 7.2 Taxation Rates for Gastronomic Services
Monthly Lump-Sum *(Cuota Fija)* Payments

	National Economy (Pesos)	Tourist Sector (U.S.$)
Food and drink vendor *(al detalle)*	100	—
Food vender from home	200	100
Private restaurants *(paladares)*	400	300
Alcoholic beverage sales at private restaurants	100	100
Tax for required minimum two employees at private restaurants	120	120

Source: Ministerio de Trabajo y Seguridad Social y de Finanzas y Precios, Resoluciòn Conjunta No. 4/95, *Granma,* 14 June 1995.

• a prohibition of "intermediaries" of any sort: producers must sell their own output, sellers must produce what they sell with no specialized retailers, no wholesalers, and no producers selling their output to others for sale;

• a prohibition of self-employment in all professional areas;

• restrictions on access to markets, with prohibitions on sales to all state entities except where specifically permitted;

• a prohibition on public marketing;

• no access to credit, foreign exchange at the official parity rate, or directly imported inputs;

• prohibition on the hiring of labor outside of the family;

• prohibition of associations of own-account workers;

• additional specific limitations on private restaurants: a twelve-seat maximum;

• confinement of input purchases to the dollar stores and agricultural markets, where prices are large multiples of input prices in the state sector;

• limitations on products available;

• additional specific limitations on the vending of food products in the streets—for example, prohibition of the use of benches, seats, or tables;

• prohibition of using any location for a microenterprise activity aside from one's home or, in some cases, a rented market stall.

There are also a variety of regulations on health, sanitary, and safety conditions for gastronomic services and private transportation. Some regulations in these areas are of course necessary. However, the definition of the relevant standards appears to be open-ended so that whatever an inspector feels is appropriate could be the operational standard. The character of fines and punishments also appears to permit discretionary punishment for infractions with the intensity of the punishments being at the discretion of the relevant inspectors (Decreto-Ley 174, 1977). For the twenty-eight microenterprise infractions of an economic operational character, the fines can be significant—up to 1,500 pesos, or about seven times the national average monthly income, although perhaps not unduly onerous for the most lucrative types of self-employment. This compares with traffic offenses that are in the area of 2 pesos for an illegal left turn to 10 pesos for a dangerous offense such as running a red light. The suspension of an offending microenterprise's license for a minimum of two years in many cases is a heavy punishment, as it destroys the livelihood of the offending individual and the relevant family. Some private restaurant owners argue that the license suspension is in fact permanent. The possible seizure of equipment, instruments, machinery, or materials involves the confiscation of the accumulated capital of the microentrepreneur, modest though it might be. Multiple or repeat infractions receive harsher punishments. If the fine is not paid within thirty days, it is doubled. If it is not paid in sixty days, the relevant authorities are empowered to seize the wage, salary, pension, or any other income, then the bank account, and then any movable property.

The regulations are enforced by a corps of inspectors including those who enforce the economic regulations and others who enforce the health, safety, environmental, and labor regulations. The inspectors can levy fines, seize equipment, and cancel licenses immediately and put any microenterprise out of business at any time, apparently with minimal chances of successful appeal.

There are a variety of economic consequences of these regulations. First, they constrain the normal growth and expansion of individual microenterprises, condemning them to a small size. The results of this are that indeed the incomes of the entrepreneurs are limited considerably. The microenterprises are thus prevented from providing serious competition to the state sector enterprises in some areas such as food services, transport, and taxis. Second, the microenterprises operate inefficiently as a result of the economic regulations. The prohibition of intermediaries, for example, compels artisans or fabricators of various products not only to retail their products on a day-to-day basis but also to find time to produce the products they sell—and no other products. The prohibition of specialized retailers thus wastes the time of the artisans and reduces the quantity and quality of their production. Or, more likely, it encourages various infractions of the rules in daily operations, despite the activities of the inspectors to enforce the regulations. The overall result of the regulations is therefore to waste the energies of many of the entrepreneurs, to lower their productivity, and to reduce the quality and quantity of their production. The general impact for Cuba is thus to waste its human energies as well as its capital and material resources.

Another area where public policy appears to be aimed at the containment of parts of the microenterprise sector is the specifically targeted competition from state enterprises, which often face structures of input costs that are but a small fraction of those facing the microenterprises (Ritter 1998.)

The general political environment within which the microenterprise sector has operated has been uncertain since its legalization in 1993. The original legislation included a clause that could be used at any time to eliminate parts of the sector (Decreto-Ley 141, 1993). In a speech given in April 1997, Fidel Castro criticized the reforms of 1993–94 on the grounds that they generated incomes "ten times, twenty times, or thirty times those earned by a worker" and stated that they were implemented, "never imagining that we would have to learn to live with them for a period of time that is difficult to predict, and that depends on many factors" (1997). This statement was widely interpreted to mean that the continued existence of the microenterprise sector was in question.

The microenterprise sector is also criticized vigorously by the state-controlled press. Articles critical of the sector have appeared with regularity (for example, Lee, 1996; Del Barrio Menendez 1998; Mayoral 1995, 1997; Ricardo Luis 1998). Such press coverage usually emphasizes the illegalities perpetrated by the sector, the alleged high incomes in the sector, the evasion of taxes, and the ostensible need for stronger enforcement, greater vigilance, and tighter controls.

The Microenterprise Tax Regime

Structure of the Tax Regime

The microenterprise tax regime consists of compulsory lump-sum fees paid each month to the tax authority, the Oficina Nacional de Administracion Tributaria (ONAT) together with a self-administered correction for the annual tax payment carried out by each microenterprise. A key feature of the system is the 10 percent maximum allowable deduction from taxable income for purchased inputs.

The first element in the tax regime is the monthly *cuota fija mensual,* or monthly fixed lump-sum payment. This payment was imposed initially in 1993 when Cuba entered the first phase of microenterprise liberalization. The ministries of finance and prices and of labor and social security set the minimum rates, but the administrative councils of the municipal governments are empowered to establish rates above these minimum levels, with the approval of the relevant ministries. The rates can be changed every six months, in January and July. The legislation permits the councils to raise the rates if it considers that the incomes of the microenterprises are excessive, although this is not defined (Decreto-Ley 141, 1993). But, again, the ambiguous character of the law increases the uncertainty for the microenterprises. The law permits increases only and not decreases in the tax rates. This also adds to uncertainty and makes the system inflexible for the microentrepreneur who must pay the full fixed lump sum in both fat and lean months and years. However, the microentrepreneur may leave the activity at the beginning of any month and can cease the monthly payments immediately.

The rates were set at relatively low levels in September 1993 but have been increasing steadily since then. Especially noteworthy is the distinction between those microenterprises that operate in the dollar economy vis-à-vis those in the peso economy, the former being taxed at a rate which is twenty times that of the latter (at the exchange rate relevant for Cuban citizens).

At the end of each year, microenterprises must pay a tax on their revenues on the basis of an escalating tax schedule, the second feature of the tax regime. However, they can deduct the total of the monthly lump-sum *cuota fija* payments from the amount of tax owed according to the schedule. The procedure is as follows:

1. The microenterprises add up their gross revenues.
2. They subtract 10 percent of the gross revenues (20 percent in the case of private transport) as an allowable deduction for purchased inputs in order to arrive at net taxable income.
3. They calculate the tax owed according to the scale in table 7.3. The payments are cumulative, with each component of income falling within each bracket being taxed at the rate for that bracket.
4. They deduct the sum of the monthly lump-sum payments from the tax that is owed according to the tax scale or schedule.
5. If the amount owed according to the tax scale calculations exceeds the amount already paid through the monthly lump-sum payments, they must pay taxes equal to the difference.
6. If the amount owed is less than the amount already paid, they do not receive a rebate for the excess tax already paid.

The official tax scale is presented in table 7.3. One of the scales is for income and taxes in the national currency, while the other is for income and taxes in U.S. dollars or convertible pesos. The tax scale applies to income net of the 10 percent of gross revenues, which is the maximum allowable for purchased inputs. The progressivity of the tax scale for dollar incomes is not too far out of line in the context of an international comparative perspective. It also seems reasonable from a Cuban perspective.

Table 7.3 Tax Scales Applied to Personal Income

Peso Scale		U.S. Dollar Scale	
Tax Bracket	Tax Rate %	Tax Bracket	Tax Rate %
0–3,000	5	0–2,400	10
3,000–6,000	10	2,400–6,000	12
6,000–12,000	15	6,000–9,600	15
12,000–18,000	20	9,600–13,200	20
18,000–24,000	25	13,200–18,000	25
24,000–36,000	30	18,000–24,000	30
36,000–48,000	35	24,000–36,000	35
48,000–60,000	40	36,000–48,000	40
60,000 and over	50	48,000–60,000	45
		60,000 and over	50

Source: ONAT (1997, 1) and Ministerio de Finanzas y Precios (1996)

On the other hand, for peso incomes the scale increases from 5 percent for the first three thousand pesos and reaches 50 percent for the tax bracket for income exceeding sixty thousand pesos. The peso tax scale does appear to be steep, as the 50 percent marginal tax rate comes into effect at an annual income of sixty thousand pesos, which is about three thousand U.S. dollars.

A third feature of the tax system is that a maximum deduction of 10 percent from gross income is permitted for purchased inputs in the determination of taxable income. In other words, net income for tax purposes or taxable income is always considered to be 90 percent of gross income regardless of the real value of purchased inputs. The only exception is in transportation, where the maximum deduction for purchased inputs is 20 percent (ONAT 1997, 6). This is referred to here as the 10 Percent Maximum Cost Deductibility Rule. This feature of the tax system is problematic in that those microenterprises that face high costs for purchased inputs are in effect being taxed on these purchases. This means that the true tax rate on value added by the firm on its actual net revenues can be much higher than those illustrated in table 7.3, which show the true rates only for a microenterprise with actual costs of purchased inputs of 10 percent of gross revenues.

What proportion of microenterprises have net revenue equal to or more than 90 percent of gross revenue? Perhaps a significant proportion. Many microenterprises involve labor-intensive activities with minimal equipment or purchased material inputs. The following microenterprises may be of this type: messenger, bicycle guard, child care, building attendant, manicurist, masseuse, shoe repair, domestic service, sports or language instruction, and some repair services. On the other hand, other activities (such as food vending, shoemakers, artisans, flower cultivators and sellers, used book or record sellers) involve the purchase and processing of substantial amounts of material inputs. Some private restaurant operators estimated their input costs as being above 60 percent.

The Rationale for the Current Tax Regime

There are three factors that explain the adoption of this tax regime. First, when self-employment was legalized in September 1993, prices, revenues, and net profits were often exceedingly high. This was the result of (1) the excess purchasing power in the hands of citizens (because the government was financing a large deficit—about 28 percent of GDP in 1993—through the creation of money, while the prices in the state sector were fixed at low levels), and (2) the limited number of microenterprises initially. The imposition of the tax regime and the escalation of tax rates were therefore designed to remove a substantial proportion of this income for equity reasons. It may be noted again, however, that a majority of the microenterprises are involved in the provision of simple goods and services for low-income Cubans in the peso economy and generate only modest incomes, albeit probably higher than the average in the state sector.

Second, the microenterprise tax regime was established at a time when there was not yet a well-established administration for this type of taxation. Nor had there been an established and transparent tax system and popular habit of paying taxes, because the tax rates and payments had been hidden previously. Moreover, prior to the legalization of much microenterprise, many such firms had operated in clandestinity, avoiding tax payments and other types of regulations. The tax system that was implemented seems to have been designed to enforce a high level of compliance in a context in which noncompliance (in the underground economy) previously had been the norm and in which there had been no established practice of paying taxes openly.

Third, there was a significant amount of theft of products from the state sector of the economy, especially in the 1990s. A proportion of these found their way to the microenterprise sector as production inputs. One of the novel elements of the tax system—the 10 percent limit on the deduction from taxable income for purchased inputs—appears to be designed to handle this situation. If it were impossible to know for sure the true value of purchased inputs, it would be risky to permit microenterprises to calculate their own input costs for determining taxable income. It was administratively easier to simply declare a maximum of 10 percent of gross income for purchased inputs for all microenterprises regardless of their true level of purchased inputs.

A popular view among the *cuenta propistas* is that the tax system is designed to punish them for ideological reasons and ultimately to put them out of business. This is a possibility and there are statements of the leadership that seem to support this view. The heavy reliance on regulations and the severe punishment for "infractions" also suggests that this is the case. It is not likely that the current microenterprise tax regime was designed to kill the microenterprise sector. Instead, it was designed to actually collect taxes in a difficult environment in which open and transparent tax paying was not the established practice.

A Quantitative Analysis of the Microenterprise Tax Regime

There are two complications in analyzing the microenterprise tax regime: first, the up-front lump-sum tax, and second, the requirement in the income tax act that net income for tax purposes always must be fixed at 90 percent of gross income. To analyze the implications of these factors for the microenterprise tax regime, a step-by-step approach is used. First, a brief section is presented deriving mathematically the relationship between (1) the "true" tax rate and (2) the value added by the microenterprise (or conversely the value of purchased inputs as a percent of total revenue). The implications of the up-front tax payments combined with the tax scale are then analyzed using a graphical presentation.

The relationship between the true tax rate, which is imposed on the microenterprise and the value of purchased inputs by the microenterprise (or its net value added) is analyzed, beginning with a mathematical derivation of that relationship, as follows:

Definitions:

c:	Percent of gross income used for input purchase
GY:	Gross income
GYk(1–.1):	Officially determined tax brackets
GYk(1–c):	True value added or net income for tax bracket
NYk:	Taxable income for tax bracket
TNYk:	True net income for tax bracket
Tk:	Tax rate for specific tax bracket
Mk:	Amount of tax payment in tax bracket
NAYk:	Net after-tax income in tax bracket
Vk = Mk/TNYk:	Tax rate as percent of true net income in tax bracket

True net income is defined as gross income less the costs of purchased inputs—that is, net value added:

$$TNYk = GYk^{*}(1-c) \qquad [1]$$

Taxable income is defined by the tax legislation as gross income less 10 percent for purchased inputs (regardless of the true value of purchased inputs)—that is, net value added for tax purposes is always considered to be 90 percent of gross income:

$$NYk = GYk * (1-.1) = GYk^{*}.9 \qquad [2]$$

The amount of the tax payment is then the tax rate for the relevant tax bracket, times the taxable income for that bracket:

$$Mk = (Tk/100) * NYk \qquad [3]$$

From [2],

$$Gyk = NYk/0.9 \qquad [4]$$

and, substituting [4] in [1],

$$TNY = (NY/0.9) * (1-c) \qquad [5]$$

or,

$$TNYk = (NYk/0.9) * (1-c) \qquad [6]$$

Thus, given a value for "c" there is a corresponding value of TNYk for every value of NYk:

$$Vk = Mk/TNYk \qquad [7]$$

That is, the actual tax rate is the tax payment divided by the true net income for each tax bracket. Then, substituting [3] in [7]:

$$Vk = \{(Tk/100) * NYk\}/TNYk \qquad [8]$$

Again, substituting [6] in [8]:

$$Vk = \{(Tk/100) * NYk\}/\{(NYk/0.9) * (1-c)\}$$

or,

$$Vk = (Tk/100) * 0.9/(1-c) \qquad [9]$$

Using the relationship of equation 9, the official ONAT tax scale of table 7.3 is adjusted so as to represent the true tax rates on true net income. Section A of table 7.4 is then constructed, showing the revised tax brackets in terms of true net income and the tax rates as proportions of true net income. Then, when different values are assigned to *c* different tax rates and brackets are the result. In table 7.4, the revised scales and tax rates are presented for values of *c* of 10 percent, 40 percent, and 60 percent.

The rapid escalation of the true marginal tax rate is apparent in table 7.4. For the case of true net value added of 40 percent (that is, $c = 0.6$) the highest tax bracket reaches 112.5 percent. This occurs at tax bracket *h*, at a level of taxable income of 48,000 pesos or 21,333 pesos in terms of true net income.

If the 10 percent rule were abolished so that every microenterprise could deduct its real costs of purchased inputs from taxable income, then the official tax scale would represent the true burden of the tax system on the microentrepreneur. As it stands, however, the official scale understates the true tax burden for all those microenterprises with purchased inputs exceeding 10 percent of gross revenues.

The lump-sum cuota fija tax payments can be examined using the three cases presented in table 7.4, with purchased inputs accounting for 10 percent, 40 percent, and 60 percent respectively of gross income. These three cases are illustrated in figures 7.1, 7.2, and 7.3. The third case is explained in detail below, with only a quick reference to the other two.

In figure 7.3, with gross income on the horizontal axis and the percent of gross revenues on the vertical axis, the horizontal line at the 60 percent level indicates that 60

Table 7.4 Tax Rates for True Net Income for Various Levels of Purchased Inputs or Net Value Added

A. With *c* as Purchased Inputs as % of Gross Income

Tax Brackets in Terms of True Net Income (Pesos)		
From	To	Tax Rate for True Net Income
0	$3{,}000 \times (1-c)^{(-1)}\, 0.9$	$0.05 \times (1-c)^{(-1)}\, 0.9$
$3{,}000 \times (1-c)^{(-1)}\, 0.9$	$6{,}000 \times (1-c)^{(-1)}\, 0.9$	$0.10 \times (1-c)^{(-1)}\, 0.9$
$6{,}000 \times (1-c)^{(-1)}\, 0.9$	$12{,}000 \times (1-c)^{(-1)}\, 0.9$	$0.15 \times (1-c)^{(-1)}\, 0.9$
$12{,}000 \times (1-c)^{(-1)}\, 0.9$	$18{,}000 \times (1-c)^{(-1)}\, 0.9$	$0.20 \times (1-c)^{(-1)}\, 0.9$
$18{,}000 \times (1-c)^{(-1)}\, 0.9$	$24{,}000 \times (1-c)^{(-1)}\, 0.9$	$0.25 \times (1-c)^{(-1)}\, 0.9$
$24{,}000 \times (1-c)^{(-1)}\, 0.9$	$36{,}000 \times (1-c)^{(-1)}\, 0.9$	$0.30 \times (1-c)^{(-1)}\, 0.9$
$36{,}000 \times (1-c)^{(-1)}\, 0.9$	$48{,}000 \times (1-c)^{(-1)}\, 0.9$	$0.35 \times (1-c)^{(-1)}\, 0.9$
$48{,}000 \times (1-c)^{(-1)}\, 0.9$	$60{,}000 \times (1-c)^{(-1)}\, 0.9$	$0.40 \times (1-c)^{(-1)}\, 0.9$
$60{,}000 \times (1-c)^{(-1)}\, 0.9$		$0.50 \times (1-c)^{(-1)}\, 0.9$

Source: Calculated on the basis of equation 9 and table 7.3.

B. Where *c* = 10%

Tax Brackets in Terms of True Net Income (Pesos)		
From	To	Tax Rate %
0	3,000	5
3,000	6,000	10
6,000	12,000	15
12,000	18,000	20
18,000	24,000	25
24,000	36,000	30
36,000	48,000	35
48,000	60,000	40
60,000		50

C. Where *c* = 40%

Tax Brackets in Terms of True Net Income (Pesos)		
From	To	Tax Rate %
0	2,000	7.5
2,000	4,000	15.0
4,000	8,000	22.5
8,000	12,000	30.0
12,000	16,000	37.5
16,000	24,000	45.0
24,000	32,000	52.5
32,000	40,000	60.0
40,000		75.0

D. Where *c* = 60%

Tax Brackets in Terms of True Net Income (Pesos)		
From	To	Tax Rate %
0	1,333	11.3
1,333	2,667	22.5
2,667	5,333	33.8
5,333	8,000	45.0
8,000	10,667	56.3
10,667	16,000	67.5
16,000	21,333	78.8
21,333	26,667	90.0
26,667		112.5

Source: Calculations based on part A of this table.

percent of gross income is always expended on the purchased inputs. The true value added is then that 40 percent of gross revenues lying above the 60 percent line. The escalating marginal tax rates for the sequential tax brackets are represented by the steplike tax rate function. The area between this function and the 60 percent line represents the tax owed by the microenterprise, while the area above the tax rate function but below the 100 percent line represents the after-tax net revenues retained by the microenterprise. It can be seen that the tax rate function escalates rapidly and exceeds 100 percent at the last tax bracket (66,666.67 pesos per year and above). The tax rate function escalates quickly due to the fact that the tax is levied on 90 percent of the gross revenues, but the microenterprise only receives 40 percent of the gross revenues as net income.

Fig. 7.1 Effective Tax Rates with Lump-Sum Payment (of 620 Pesos per Month or 7,440 per Year) with True Net Value Added at 90% of Gross Revenues ***(c=0.1)***

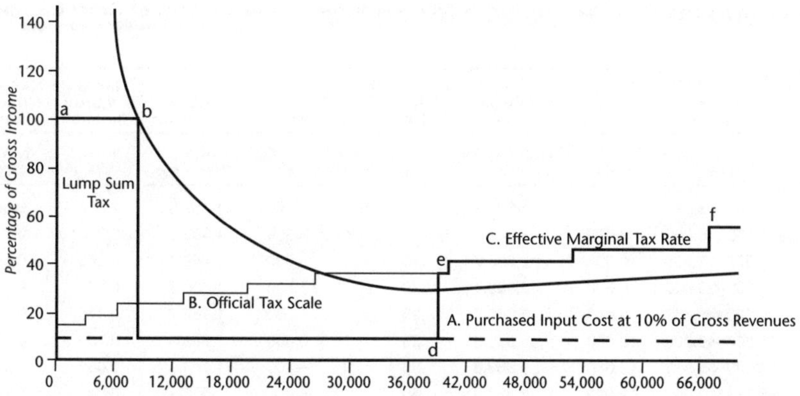

Fig. 7.2 Effective Tax Rates with Lump-Sum Payment (of 620 Pesos per Month or 7,440 per Year) with True Net Value Added at 60% of Gross Revenues ***(c=0.4)***

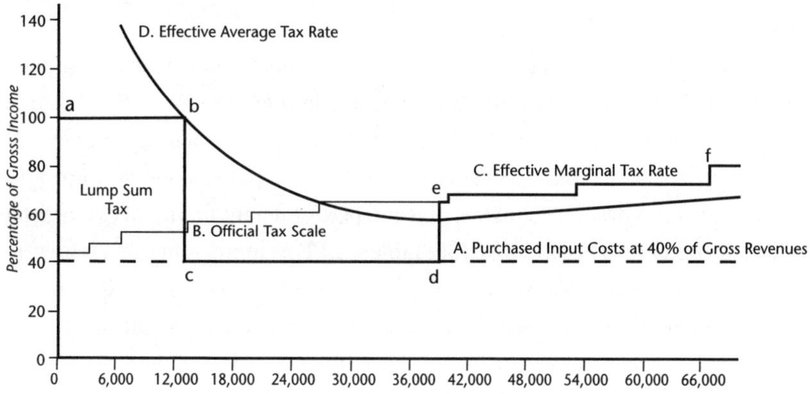

Fig. 7.3 Effective Tax Rates with Lump-Sum Payment (of 620 Pesos per Month or 7,440 per Year) with True Net Value Added at 40% of Gross Revenues ***(c=0.6)***

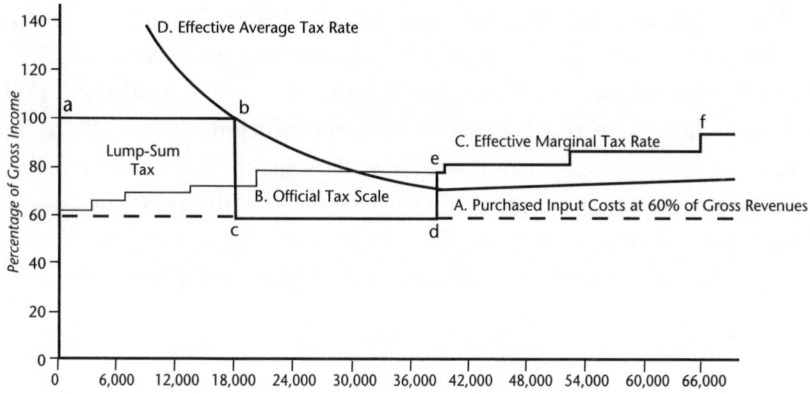

Table 7.5 Microenterprise True Tax Rates with True Net Income at 40 Percent of Gross Income *(or c = 0.6)*

Tax Bracket	Gross Income	Taxable Inccome	True Net Income	Tax Rate	Tax Payment	Net After-Tax Income	NAY as % of Gross Income	NAY as % of True Net Income	True Tax Rate
GYk (1–.1)	Gyk	Nyk	TNYk = GYk (1–c)	Tk	Mk = TkxNYk	NAYk = TNYk – Mk	NAYk/ GYk	NAYk/ TNYk	Mk/ TNYk
0–3,000	0–3,333	3,000	1,333.3	.05	.05x3,000=150	1,183.3	0.355	0.887	11.3
3,000–6,000	3,333–6,667	3,000	1,333.3	.10	.10x3,000=300	1,033.3	0.31	0.775	22.5
6,000–12,000	6,667–13,333	6,000	2,666.7	.15	900	1,766.7	0.265	0.663	33.7
12,000–18,000	13,333–20,000	6,000	2,666.7	.20	1,200	1,466.7	0.22	0.55	45.0
18,000–24,000	20,000–26,667	6,000	2,666.7	.25	1,500	1,166.7	0.175	0.44	56.0
24,000–36,000	26,667–40,000	12,000	5,333.3	.30	3,600	1,733.3	0.13	0.325	67.5
36,000–48,000	40,000–53,333	12,000	5,333.3	.35	4,200	1,133.3	0.085	0.21	79.0
48,000–60,000	53,333–66,667	12,000	5,333.3	.40	4,800	533.3	0.04	0.10	90.0
60,000– e.g. 100,000	66,667–111,111	40,000	17,777.8	.50	20,000	–2,222.3	–0.05	–0.125	110.5

Note: Key assumption: c = 0.6, or purchased inputs = 60% of gross income.

The additional complication arises because the microenterprises must pay the cuota fija or lump-sum taxes in advance. Consider here the example of a private restaurant in the peso economy. For this case, and on an annual basis, the amount of the lump sum tax could be 620 pesos per month, or 7,440 pesos per year (400 pesos cuota fija, plus 100 pesos alcohol tax, plus 120 pesos for a minimum of two registered workers, or 620 pesos per month). (See table 7.2.) This lump-sum tax is represented by the area "LST," which shows that a gross income of 18,600 pesos is required to generate enough net revenues (40 percent of the gross income) to pay the tax. However, the tax owed, as calculated by the tax scale, can be deducted from the lump-sum taxes already paid. This means that no additional taxes need to be paid until the total tax payable according to the scale reaches the lump-sum tax payment. In this case, the level of gross income at which the taxes owed equal the lump-sum payments is 39,743 pesos at point *e*.

The coexistence of the lump-sum tax that can be deducted from the tax owed according to the tax scale produces a curious pattern of marginal tax rates. Instead of the rates pictured by the steplike tax function, the effective marginal tax rate (MTR) function follows line *abcdef*. For the first 18,600 pesos of gross income, the MTR on net income is 100 percent. (This is an MTR in the sense that within this range of its gross income, the microenterprise must pay 100 percent of its net income as taxes on a month-by-month basis.) However, the MTR then falls to 0.0 percent from *c* to *d* for that gross income for which no additional tax needs to be paid because it has already been paid via the lump-sum tax. Only after an income level of 39,743 pesos is surpassed at point *e* does the tax scale again become effective.

This pattern of marginal tax rates cannot fail to have a variety of impacts on microenterprise behavior. When the lump-sum tax is included in the picture as in figure 7.3, it can be seen that the net after-tax revenues in this case could include only the area above line *bcdef* and below the 100 percent line. The possibilities for this microenterprise for earning sufficient net revenues to survive appear to be limited.

The calculations for the case illustrated in figure 7.3 are shown in table 7.5. In this table, column 1 shows the tax brackets defined as they are in terms of gross income less the allowable 10 percent deduction for purchased inputs. Column 2 then shows the true gross income relevant for the tax brackets. In column 4, the true net income for each tax bracket is presented, taking into consideration the assumed 60 percent cost on purchased inputs. With the tax rates of column 5, the tax payments are calculated in column 6, noting that the gross income (less 10 percent for purchased inputs) is what is actually taxed. The tax payments of column 6 are then presented as proportions on true net income (from column 4) to yield the actual or true tax rate, shown in column 10. In column 7, net after-tax income is calculated as true net income less the tax payment (column 6). Then the net after-tax income is calculated in column 8 as a percentage first of gross income (from column 2) and second in column 9 as a percentage of true net income. (The complications of the lump-sum payments are not included in the table.)

The escalation of the marginal tax rates as proportions of the true net income in this case are dramatic. With true net income equal to only 40 percent of gross income, the tax scale reaches high levels quickly. By the eighth tax bracket, 96 percent of every peso earned goes to input-suppliers and the tax authority. And in the last tax bracket, the tax payment reaches 112.5 percent on true net income, and net after-tax income is negative.

The case of actual input purchases of 10 percent is illustrated in figure 7.1. This case presents no complications, as the true net income is equal to the taxable income permitted by the official tax scale of the tax legislation—that is, allowing for a 10 percent reduction from gross income for purchased inputs. For this case, the tax rates applied by the tax scale are in fact the same as the tax rates for true net income. An intermediate case, in which input purchases constitute 40 percent of gross income, is presented in figure 7.2.

Without presenting other possible cases, it can be concluded that the higher is the level of purchased inputs by the microenterprise (or, in other words, the lower the true net value added by the firm, the more onerous is the true tax burden). The tax rates do not appear out of line for those enterprises with purchased inputs around 10 percent (true net income or value added as a proportion of gross income of 90 percent) and especially for those with even lower relative values of purchased inputs. However, as the level of value added or true net income as a proportion of gross income declines, the average tax rates begin to increase rapidly and ultimately become impossible.

When the lump-sum tax is included in the analysis, the average tax rate (ATR) is high at first, reflecting the up-front character of the payment. (The ATR function is measured from the cost line upward.) As can be seen in each of figures 7.1, 7.2, and 7.3, the average tax rate declines up to the point where the official tax rate becomes effective at point *e* in each of the charts. The ATR schedule is especially important as a measure of the burden of the tax as it expresses what percentage of gross income is paid as taxes (from the cost line upward). Thus the declining ATR and MTR indicate regressivity in the incidence of the tax system—that is, the tax is higher on low-income earners and declines as income rises up to point *e* in the charts.

A final feature of the lump-sum tax not illustrated in the charts is that as the up-front lump-sum tax payment increases in magnitude, the point at which the official tax scale becomes effective shifts toward the right in figures 7.2 and 7.3. This means that as the lump-sum payments increase, the tax system becomes more regressive.

Implications for Equity, Efficiency, and the Viability

The microenterprise tax regime has a variety of impacts in terms of fairness, the efficiency of the economic system, and the viability of the tax collection system itself. These impacts are explored here at the levels of the microenterprise, the microenterprise sector, and Cuba's society and economy more broadly.

The Microenterprise Level

First, the lump-sum payments involve a marginal tax rate of 100 percent of true net earnings until they are paid off, at which level of income the marginal tax rate falls to 0 percent (point *c* in figures 7.3, 7.4, and 7.5). This 0 percent rate prevails until gross income reaches the level at which the tax payments owed under the official tax scale—but deductible from the lump-sum payments—is just equal to the total lump-sum payments. At this point (*e* in the charts) the official tax scale becomes effective again.

When faced with this pattern of marginal tax rates, the microenterprise will likely try to avoid paying the higher tax rates. It will try to locate itself often at point *d* in figures 7.1, 7.2, and 7.3, the highest revenues with a marginal tax rate of 0 percent, and it will try to earn gross income just below *d*. This will be especially relevant for those microenterprises facing high levels of purchased inputs (see fig. 7.3), where the marginal tax rate jumps from 0 percent to 67.5 percent at point *e*. It can do this by restricting its output to this level and/or underdeclaring income. If the firm restricts its output, society loses the goods and services forgone, the microenterprise sector loses income, and the government loses tax revenues. On the other hand, the microenterprise can also try to underdeclare its income. In this case, the government loses tax revenues.

With the high barrier to entry created by the 100 percent initial marginal tax rate, some microenterprises may refrain from registering and may decide to operate in clandestinity. There can be no doubt that this has occurred in Cuba. Numerous tradesmen undertake house repairs; private car owners provide occasional taxi services, despite the risks involved; some households provide unofficial rental accommodation; and many people provide personal services unofficially. In this case, the government loses tax revenues. Indeed, it may lose its tax base if the numbers of microenterprises diminish.

The tax administration is not unaware of the lost revenues and uses inspectors and the *comités por la defensa de la revolución* (CDRs) to try to prevent enterprises from operating in the underground economy. However, clandestine microenterprise is widespread and the members of the CDRs (which include most people) are also involved in the underground economy, so that controlling it is difficult.

Despite the ostensible progressivity of the official tax scale or schedule, the tax structure is in fact regressive for the lower- and middle-income microenterprises. Because the lump-sum tax creates a 100 percent marginal tax rate for the first amount of income earned followed by a 0 percent marginal rate, relatively lower net incomes in this range are taxed more heavily than higher incomes. The average tax rate declines as income increases up to that level where the official tax scale becomes effective (point *e*). This result is inequitable in that lower incomes are taxed more heavily than higher incomes in this range.

The Microenterprise Sectoral Level

The tax regime is inequitable in terms of its impact *among* microenterprises. Because of the 10 Percent Maximum Cost Deductibility Rule, firms with higher levels of purchased inputs pay higher marginal and average tax rates in terms of their net income than other firms with the same net incomes but lower levels of purchased inputs. A second element of unfairness is that the tax structure discriminates against new entrants to any part of the sector, because the marginal tax rate is initially 100 percent due to the lump-sum monthly cuota fija. New entrants must earn revenues immediately that would permit them to pay these taxes. Established microenterprises are more likely to have reached income levels that permit them to experience the range of gross income where the marginal tax rate is 0 percent. Thus they have an advantage that shields them in part from new competition by helping to keep out the new firms.

From the standpoint of the microenterprise sector, the tax regime also results in a variety of inefficiencies. By creating a high barrier to entry because of the 100 percent marginal tax rate, the number of new firms entering the sector is reduced. High levels of uncertainty and risk for new entrants also serve as a barrier keeping out potential new participants. Therefore, there may be less legal competition, higher prices, and lower volumes of production than if these barriers to entry were lower. On the other hand, for some other types of microenterprise where entrance into the clandestine economy is easier, the result may be increased competition from tax-evading lower-cost suppliers of certain goods and services.

The 10 percent rule also has negative effects in terms of efficiency. Because of the high true taxation levels for those microenterprises that have higher levels of purchased inputs, the volume of production of goods and services from these firms is probably unduly low. The prices of their outputs also are probably unduly high, reflecting the high tax burden but not necessarily reflecting the real efficiency and true costs of production of such firms.

There is an additional negative effect of the 10 percent rule. As an economy evolves, there normally is an increasing articulation of production among enterprises as they become more specialized and as intra-enterprise trade expands. With the 10 percent rule, there is a disincentive for a microenterprise to make purchases from other enterprises, as the tax treatment of such purchases is so harsh. The result is that enterprises try to avoid purchases of inputs from other firms. On an economywide basis, this would be to block the evolution of specialization among firms and interenterprise exchange.

The Societal Perspective

Taxation of the microenterprise sector is necessary from the standpoint of equity. The sector, like all others, must pay its share of the costs for public goods and services. It is difficult to know what a fair level of taxation for the sector is in the period when it was getting established. This is because for at least a transitional period, the incomes earned in the sector were high for a number of reasons mentioned. The high taxation rates in real terms—in relation to true net incomes in the sector—reflected the desire to tap these high incomes for both revenue-raising and social justice reasons.

Table 7.6 Comparison of Tax Regimes for Cuban Microenterprise and Foreign Enterprise Operating in Joint Ventures

	Microenterprise Sector	Joint Ventures
Effective tax rates	May exceed 100% of net income	30% of net income (50% for mining and petroleum)
Effective tax base	90% of gross income	Net income after deduction of costs
Deductibility of investment	Not deductible from taxable income	Fully deductible from taxable income
Lump-sum taxation	Up-front *cuota fija* tax payments necessary	None
Rebates for tax overpayment	No rebates for overpayment	Not applicable
Tax holidays	No	Yes
Profit expatriation	No	Yes

However, from a social perspective, it is inequitable to tax those with lower incomes more heavily than those with higher incomes, but this is what the lump-sum cuota fija perpetrates in the lower ranges of microenterprise incomes—those ranges where perhaps a large proportion of the firms are operating. It is also inequitable to tax microentrepreneurs or anyone else with the same net incomes at different rates, but this is what the 10 percent rule achieves.

Perhaps one of the more disturbing inequities of the microenterprise tax regime is that it is more onerous than the tax regime facing foreign companies operating in joint venture arrangements with Cuban state firms. The contrasting tax regimes are summarized in table 7.6. It is clear from this table that while foreign enterprises in joint venture arrangements receive a fairly standard tax treatment from a comparative international perspective, their treatment is much more favorable than domestically owned and oriented microenterprise.

The tax regime for microenterprises damages the rationality of resource allocation and in consequence lowers living standards. First, the onerous levels of taxation inherent in the tax regime lead enterprises to go out of business or, in some cases, to restrict their own production in order to avoid higher tax brackets. Both of these results reduce the volume of goods and services produced in the sector and raise prices. Second, the microenterprise tax regime restricts entry into the sector, thereby restricting competition, reducing output, and raising prices. Third, the movement of microenterprises into clandestinity or the refusal for many self-employed to register and pay taxes also results in inefficiencies of resource use. Such enterprises must operate on a very small scale and continuously undercover. This probably lowers the quality of their products and increases their prices in comparison with those firms operating legally (and allowing for the impact of taxes on the prices of the legal microenterprises).

By blocking the entrance of new microenterprises and promoting their exit, the tax regime also reduces productive employment and the generation of incomes. (Open unemployment was stated to be 6.8 percent in 1996, while the open-unemployment equivalent of underemployment was estimated by the UNECLAC [1997, 378] at 27.3 percent in the same year. This latter figure emphasizes the loss to the nation arising from labor underutilization.)

One surprising result of the microenterprise tax regime is the discrimination inherent in it against domestically oriented economic activity or domestic value added. Microenterprises have little or no access to imported inputs except those acquired from recycled materials, or purchases from the dollar stores or special state sellers of inputs. The effective exchange rate for them in 1998 was approximately twenty pesos for one U.S. dollar's worth of imported inputs (plus taxes of 140 percent normally). For enterprises in the state sector, on the other hand, one U.S. dollar's worth of imported inputs cost only one peso when the importation was approved by the planning authorities. This means that state enterprises can obtain access to imports more cheaply than microenterprises. The result of this is that often the microenterprises use domestically available inputs to a higher degree than the state enterprises. An example of this occurs with the private restaurants where close to 100 percent of all of the inputs are of Cuban origin, in contrast to the state fast-food chains such as Burgui (a Burger King look-alike), which import almost everything: tables, potatoes, hamburger, chicken, trays, paper cups, and many of the specialized building materials. In discriminating against microenterprise, the current tax regime discriminates against domestic value added and in favor of the more import-intensive state firms.

Implications for Tax System Viability

There are some important implications of the microenterprise tax regime for the functioning and viability of the general tax system. The tax regime leads to reduced revenues in comparison with a standard type of tax regime. This is due to a number of factors:

1. Because the true tax rates are so high for those microenterprises with higher levels of purchased inputs, some firms are put out of business with a loss of revenues.
2. When faced with high real tax rates, some microenterprises cease legal operation and enter the underground economy.
3. The true level of the marginal tax rate is so high when it becomes effective for

those microenterprises with higher levels of purchased inputs that they have an incentive to underdeclare their gross incomes. This leads to revenue losses for the government.

4. When faced with high lump-sum taxes when contemplating the establishment of a new microenterprise, or reregistering an established one, some potential microentrepreneurs may enter the clandestine economy or refrain from starting or continuing their business.

The perceived unfairness of the microenterprise tax regime has resulted in high levels of noncompliance. Indeed, the survival of some microenterprises depends on noncompliance, especially if they are unable to retreat to the underground economy due to a location or profile incompatible with clandestine operations. Some microenterprises may underdeclare their incomes.

The result of the character of the tax system and the noncompliance it engenders is that the tax system lacks credibility and respect. Rather than leading to the gradual development of a tax culture in which people willingly and honestly pay their taxes, the system has provoked the habit of cheating. To some extent this is part of people's survival strategies in the difficult circumstances of the late 1990s. The nature of the tax regime leads some people to think that tax evasion is not unethical even if it is illegal.

In the long term, it may be difficult to change the current culture of tax evasion to one of compliance. This could continue to be a problem even after a reasonable microenterprise tax regime has been established.

Policy Recommendations

There are a number of changes in the tax regime that could reduce or eliminate some of more harmful effects of the microenterprise tax regime. A few of these are not complicated and could be implemented quickly. Others are more complicated and would take longer to generate positive results.

Recommendation 1: Establish a Normal Tax Base

The first change might be to establish net income rather than gross income as the tax base. This means abolishing the 10 percent rule, which limits the allowable deduction from taxable income to a maximum of 10 percent of gross income. This would improve the equity of the system and end the discrimination against those microenterprises with purchased inputs exceeding 10 percent of gross income. By making the tax regime fairer in this way, noncompliance would be reduced and tax collection facilitated. This change would permit an expansion of output of the microenterprises that were more dependent on larger proportions of purchased inputs.

Recommendation 2: Eliminate the Up-Front Lump-Sum Cuota Fija Payments

The elimination of the monthly cuota fija payments would have a variety of positive results. It would remove a barrier to the entry of new enterprises, thereby increasing numbers of firms, intensifying competition, increasing output, and reducing prices in the sector. This would also, in time, lead to an increase, not a decrease, in tax revenues. These would increase as more microenterprises entered the sector and as more microenterprises surfaced from the underground economy because the high cost, risk, and uncertainty created by the cuota fija would be eliminated. Moreover, elimination of the cuota fija would also eliminate some of the obvious unfairness of the tax regime. No longer would the incidence of the tax in the lower and middle income ranges be regressive. The nonrefundability of tax overpayments would no longer exist. The corrections of these two inequities would help to establish the credibility in the tax regime, facilitate tax compliance, and reduce tax evasion.

Recommendation 3: Build the Credibility of the Tax System

At present, the tax regime is perceived to be unfair and unreasonable, so that cheating and noncompliance seem to be morally acceptable as well as necessary for survival. Therefore, any other policies that would help to build the credibility of the tax system would be desirable. Some such changes could include reasonable financial penalties for noncompliance and the refunding of tax overpayments to the microentrepreneur. The surfacing of some of the economic activities that previously had gone or remained in clandestinity would also help make the system fairer by reducing the number of unregistered microenterprises that were able to evade taxes totally.

Recommendation 4: Lower Barriers to Entry into the Microenterprise Sector

A further set of changes concerns the large number of rules and regulation mentioned earlier. These are designed to contain the sector, to limit incomes in the sector, and perhaps to provide protection to some state sector enterprises. This policy environment provides an incentive for microenterprises to remain underground, with a variety of harmful consequences, as discussed earlier. The solution, however, is not to impose more regulations. Instead, it would probably be wiser to lower the barriers to entry into the legal microenterprise sector. This would involve dropping many of the restrictions on the microenterprises and permitting most applicants for entry to the sector to enter. It would involve changes in the structure of incentives, which at this time encourage microenterprises to remain in the underground economy or out of business.

By lowering the barriers to entry and changing the incentive structure so as not to penalize legality, the number of microenterprises will increase. With increased competition in the sector, production will increase and prices will decline. The average income level of the microentrepreneurs will approach the national average. Employment in the sector should increase but should decrease in the underground economy. Finally, the tax revenues actually collected by the tax system should increase.

Summary and Conclusion

Cuba's tax regime for microenterprise has a number of shortcomings that make it inequitable, which damages the efficiency of resource allocation in the economy and reduces its effectiveness in collecting revenues.

The problems with the tax regime stem mainly from the 10 percent rule and the character and size of the cuota fija or lump-sum tax payments that must be made each month regardless of revenues. The analysis of this essay has shown that the actual incidence of the tax is much higher than the official tax scale when actual production costs exceed the 10 percent maximum cost deductibility rule. Indeed, for microenterprises with costs of purchased inputs in the 60 percent range, the true marginal tax rate on true net income (rather than gross income less the maximum allowable 10 percent) can reach levels in excess of 100 percent. Moreover, the up-front lump-sum tax payments result in what are in effect marginal tax rates of 100 percent for initial levels of revenue. Then the marginal tax rate falls to 0 percent until that level of taxable income is reached where taxes payable with the tax scale are equal to the lump-sum payment. This creates a pattern of declining marginal and average tax rates in the lower and middle-income ranges—that is, the tax in this range is regressive. The tax rates in the official tax scale also turn out to be steep for the vast majority of the microenterprises that operate in the peso rather than the dollar economy.

From the standpoint of equity, the tax regime discriminates against those microenterprises that have costs of purchased inputs in excess of 10 percent of gross revenues. It is regressive in that the tax rates are higher for lower income microenterprises. It discriminates against potential new entrants vis-à-vis established firms because the former must pay the up-front lump-sum taxes even without earning revenues. Much of the microenterprise sector also faces a more onerous tax regime than foreign firms in joint venture arrangements.

From the standpoint of its impact on the efficiency of resource use in Cuban society, the tax regime has unfortunate results. It restricts the entry of new firms into the sector and puts some out of business, thereby reducing production, raising prices to Cuban citizens, reducing employment in the sector, and probably reducing the generation of incomes. It discriminates against domestic value-added in the microenterprise sector, which uses inputs almost entirely of domestic origin in contrast to the lower-taxed state sector, which is highly dependent on imported inputs and permits profit repatriation.

While the tax regime collects revenues from the microenterprises, there are a number of effects that actually reduce the volume of taxes collected. First, the lump-sum tax payment arrangement and the high tax rates for those with purchased inputs exceeding 10 percent of gross revenues encourage firms to go underground or to refrain from formally registering. The size of the clandestine economy is immense and the loss of revenues comparably large. The nature of the tax regime has bred a culture of tax evasion and not of compliance.

However, there are ways in which the microenterprise tax system could be improved. First, a normal tax base should be established—that is, the 10 percent rule should be dropped and taxable income should be gross revenues less actual costs of production. Second, the up-front lump-sum tax payment should be canceled. Third, compliance with the tax regime in the long term needs to be developed by making it as fair and reasonable as possible. And, fourth, artificial policy-generated barriers to entry to new microenterprises should be dropped. A more effective tax administration would also be necessary to prevent abuses of a "cost deductibility from taxable income" arrangement and in the absence of the up-front lump-sum tax payment.

Generally, while the microenterprise sector must pay its share of taxes, it should also have a tax regime that is not more onerous than that facing joint ventures and foreign firms and which is equitable among microenterprises. A well-designed microenterprise tax regime could help permit the sector to make a more valuable role in the Cuban economy in terms of employment and income generation and the production of needed goods and services at lower relative prices. It could also generate more revenues than the current system, which pushes microenterprises into clandestinity and into tax evasion.

Note

Shoemakers, artisan workers, taxi operators, carpenters, house repairmen, *tricycletistas*, restaurant operators, and other microentrepreneurs were interviewed by the author during the preparation of this chapter.

References

Castro, President Fidel. 1997. Speech of April 4. *Granma International*, 23 April.
Comité Estatal de Estadisticas. 1998. *Anuario Estadístico de Cuba*. Havana, Cuba.
Decreto 192 del comité ejecutivo del consejo de ministros. 1994. *Granma*, 26 October.

Decreto-Ley 141 del consejo de estado, gobierno de Cuba. 1993. *Acerca del ejercio del trabajo por cuenta propia,* 8 September.

Decreto-Ley 174. 1997. *De las contravenciones personales de las regulaciones del trabajo por cuenta propia. Gaceta Oficial,* 30 June.

Del Barrio Menendez, Emilio. 1998. "Sin extremismo, pero con toda firmeza." *Granma,* 12 November.

Lee, Susana. 1996. "Trabajo por cuenta propia: Una reflexion necesaria." *Granma,* 13 September.

Ley no. 77, Ley de inversion extranjera. 1995. *Gaceta Oficial,* 6 September.

Mayoral, María Julia. 1995. "La ilegalidad no tiene futuro." *Granma,* 14 February.

______. 1997. "Debaten sobre el trabajo por cuenta propia en la capital." *Granma,* 14 April.

Ministerio de Finanzas y Precios, Gobierno de Cuba. 1996. *Instruciòn No. 11/96, Declaracion Jurada, Divisas*. Havana, Cuba.

______. 1997. *Resolucion no. 20, establecen procedimiento para el pago del impuesto por el arrendamiento de viviendas, habitaciones o espacios.* Havana, Cuba.

______. 1998. *Presupuesto del estado, anteproyecto 1998 Informe.* Havana, Cuba.

Oficina Nacional de la Administracion Tributaria (ONAT). 1997. *Declaracion jurada, impuesto sobre ingresos personales moneda nacional.* Havana, Cuba.

Ricardo Luis, Roger. 1998. "Continúa enfrentamiento or ilegalidades en la vivienda." *Granma,* 14 February.

Ritter, Archibald R. M. 1998. "Entrepreneurship, Microenterprise, and Public Policy in Cuba: Promotion, Containment, or Asphyxiation." *Journal of Inter-American Studies and World Affairs* 40, no. 2:63–94.

United Nations Economic Commission for Latin America and the Caribbean (UNECLAC). 1997. *The Cuban Economy in the 1990s: Structural Reform and Economic Performance*. Santiago, Chile.

CHAPTER 8

Foreign Investment in Cuba

Jorge F. Pérez-López

In the second half of the 1990s Cuba intensified its campaign to attract foreign direct investment (FDI). In September 1995 the Cuban government adopted a long-awaited foreign investment law aimed at giving additional assurances to foreign investors that Cuba welcomed their participation in the economy and that their investments would be secure ("Ley No. 77" 1995; Ossman 1996; Burguet Rodríguez 1995; Vega Vega 1997; Fábregas i Guillén 1998). The economic resolution adopted by the Fifth Congress of the Cuban Communist Party in October 1997 called for greater promotion of foreign investment, particularly with regard to "projects that can make the greatest contribution to the achievement of national development plans" (*Resolución* 1997). Cuban officials have been very active in publicizing the advantages of investing in the island through visits to foreign countries, participation in international investment fora, and hosting of potential investors.

Socialist Cuba's record in attracting FDI is mixed. On the one hand, Cuba has been successful in attracting some FDI, particularly since the mid-1990s. These capital flows contributed to arresting the economy's free fall of the first half of the 1990s and to enabling the economic recovery that has occurred since 1995. FDI has also had other positive effects on the Cuban economy: promoting technology transfer, generating some productive employment, and opening up foreign markets to Cuban exports, particularly tourism services. On the other hand, FDI flows into the island have been very modest, both in comparison with Latin American and Caribbean countries and with the massive foreign financing needs of the country. FDI has shown that it can contribute to preventing further economic deterioration and to generating some positive economic growth, but it cannot pull the Cuban economy out of the current economic crisis absent meaningful systemic change.

Quantitative evaluations of the magnitude of FDI flows into Cuba and their contribution to Cuban economic performance are hindered by a lack of information. This chapter therefore takes a largely qualitative approach to analyzing FDI in Cuba. The first part uses the best available information to attempt to quantify FDI flows and stocks as well as their distribution by country of origin of the foreign investor and economic sector. To place Cuba's record in attracting FDI in context, information on FDI flows to Latin American countries is also considered. The second part of this chapter illustrates some issues that have affected Cuba's FDI performance in the second half of the 1990s and that will continue to pose challenges in the foreseeable future.

Cuban Foreign Investment Performance

Quantitative information on FDI flows and stocks in Cuba is scarce and inconsistent. The lack of transparency on the part of Cuban authorities regarding incoming FDI is officially attributed to concern that the U.S. government, as part of its policy of economic sanctions against Cuba, would use the information to punish foreign investors operating in the island or those considering doing so.[1] However, it may also reflect an interest on the part of these authorities to give the impression that FDI flows are more significant than they actually are, and many investors are eager to locate in Cuba, thereby improving the investment climate.

Cuba's jealousness in safeguarding information on foreign investment intensified with the enactment by the United States in 1996 of the Helms-Burton Act,[2] which, among other things, allows U.S. nationals to file suit in domestic courts against third parties trafficking in property confiscated by the Cuban government on or after 1 January 1959 and directs the U.S. secretary of state to deny visas to enter the United States to such traffickers and their families. Thus, Cuba's antidote to the Helms-Burton Act—Law No. 80, the Reaffirmation of Cuban Dignity and Sovereignty Act, enacted in December 1996—directs Cuban government agencies to take action to protect foreign investors in the island, including through the transfer of foreign investors' interests to fiduciary companies, financial entities, or investment funds to conceal their origin (Article 6), and proscribes Cuban citizens from collaborating in the implementation of sanctions against foreign investors in Cuba pursuant to the Helms-Burton Act—for example, by supplying information on foreign investments to U.S. authorities (Article 8). A complementary law, Law No. 88, the Law for the Protection of Cuba's National Independence and Economy, enacted in February 1999, proclaims punishment of up to twenty years' imprisonment for Cuban citizens who collaborate in the implementation of the Helms-Burton Act—for example, through leaking of confidential information that results in the imposition of sanctions against a foreign investor (Articles 4 and 5). As an adviser to Cuba's minister for foreign investment and economic cooperation has stated, "we follow a policy of discretion regarding the identity of investors in the island" in order to prevent their interests in the United States or in other countries from being adversely affected by the Helms-Burton Act ("Dan garantías a los inversionistas" 1999).

Latin America and Caribbean FDI Flows and Stocks

Annual inflows of FDI to Latin America and the Caribbean tripled between 1994 and 1999, reaching nearly $93.6 billion in the latter year. In 2000, FDI inflows into the region slowed down to $74.2 billion, nearly 20 percent lower than a year earlier but still several-fold higher than the average annual inflows during 1990–94 (approximately $18.2 billion per annum). Brazil ($30.3 billion in FDI inflows in 2000 alone) has continued to be the main recipient of FDI in the region, but small countries such as Trinidad and Tobago (especially in the energy sector), the Dominican Republic (tourism), and Costa Rica (manufacturing for export) have also been successful in attracting significant volumes of FDI (Naciones Unidas 2001, 53).

Table 8.1 shows the distribution of net FDI flows into Latin America and the Caribbean by subregion for 1997–2000. While the larger countries in the region—the South American countries plus Mexico, members of the Latin American Integration Association (Asociación Latinoamericana de Integración, ALADI)—attracted the bulk of incoming FDI, the smaller economies of the Caribbean basin were quite successful as well. Thus, net FDI into the Caribbean basin nations (except financial centers) amounted to $4.2 billion in 1997 and $6.1 billion in 1998, declining to $5.4 billion in 1999 and $4.5 billion in 2000. The best performing countries in the subregion in at-

Table 8.1 Net FDI Flows to Latin America and the Caribbean, by Subregion
(in Billions of U.S. Dollars)

	1997		1998		1999		2000	
	Value	Percent	Value	Percent	Value	Percent	Value	Percent
ALADI[a]	61.1	87.5	66.0	84.1	85.6	91.5	67.2	90.6
Caribbean basin (except financial centers)[b]	4.2	6.0	6.1	7.8	5.4	5.8	4.5	6.1
Caribbean basin (financial centers)[c]	4.5	6.4	6.4	8.2	2.6	2.8	2.5	3.4
TOTAL	69.8	100.0	78.5	100.0	93.6	100.0	74.2	100.0

Source: Economic Commission for Latin America and the Caribbean, *Foreign Investment in Latin America and the Caribbean—2000* (Santiago, Chile: CEPAL, 2001), p. 39.

Notes: Asociación Latinoamericana de Integración—Argentina, Bolivia, Brazil, Chile, Colombia, Ecuador, Mexico, Paraguay, Peru, Uruguay and Venezuela. b. Costa Rica, El Salvador, Guatemala, Honduras, Nicaragua, Anguilla, Antigua and Barbuda, Aruba, Barbados, Belize, Cuba, Dominica, Grenada, Guyana, Haiti, Jamaica, Montserrat, Dominican Republic, St. Kitts and Nevis, St. Lucia, St. Vincent and the Grenadines, Suriname and Trinidad and Tobago. c. Netherlands Antilles, Bahamas, Bermuda, Cayman Islands, Virgin Islands, and Panama.

tracting FDI in 1999 were the Dominican Republic (net FDI inflows of $1.3 billion), Costa Rica ($669 million), Trinidad and Tobago ($633 million), and Jamaica ($524 million) (Naciones Unidas 2001, 52).

The United Nations Conference on Trade and Development (UNCTAD 2001) estimates the stock of FDI in Latin America and the Caribbean at the end of 2000 at $613.1 billion, of which $377 billion (61.5 percent) was located in South America; $97.2 billion (15.9 percent), in Mexico; and $138.9 billion (22.7 percent), in Central America and the Caribbean. Within the Central American and Caribbean countries not considered as financial centers, the largest concentration of FDI stocks in 2000 were in Trinidad and Tobago ($7 billion), Costa Rica ($5.2 billion), the Dominican Republic ($5.2 billion), Guatemala ($3.4 billion), and Jamaica ($3.3 billion).

Cuba's Balance of Payments

Socialist Cuba began to publish balance of payments (BOP) statistics in the 1990s. Earlier, in the 1980s, Cuba published BOP statistics only for its hard currency foreign accounts in reports issued by the Cuban National Bank to support renegotiation of the island's hard currency debt.[3] These partial BOP statistics are of very limited value since hard currency transactions accounted for a relatively small share of Cuba's overall external economic relations during the 1980s.

The shift in Cuba's external economic relations in the 1990s to the use of hard currencies eliminated the dichotomy in the external accounts (that is, separate hard currency and soft currency accounts). As mentioned earlier, the Cuban National Bank has begun to make public overall BOP statistics in pesos or U.S. dollars (since the official exchange rate is one peso equals one U.S. dollar). These statistics have been published in a major study of the Cuban economy conducted by UNECLAC (Naciones Unidas 1997, 2000) and in reports by the Cuban National Bank and its successor, the Cuban Central Bank.[4]

Table 8.2 presents Cuban BOP statistics for selected years from 1989 to 2000 from the mentioned UNECLAC report and official Cuban statistical sources. The information contained in this table clearly shows the collapse of the external sector of the Cuban economy brought about by the breakdown of economic relations with the former Soviet Union and the Eastern European socialist countries. In 1989—perhaps the last year of "normal" economic relations with these countries—Cuban exports of goods amounted to 5.4 billion pesos and imports to 8.1 billion pesos, with an overall deficit in the current account of 2.7 billion pesos. However, by 1993 exports of goods had shrunk to 1.1 billion pesos (a decline of nearly 80 percent from 1989), imports to under 2.0 billion pesos (a decline of about 75 percent from 1989), and the current ac-

Table 8.2 Cuban Balance of Payments
(in Millions of Pesos)

	1989	1993	1994	1995	1997	1998	1999	2000
Current account balance	–3001	–388	–260	–518	–437	–392	–462	–687
Trade balance (goods and services)	–2615	–381	–308	–639	–746	–757	–747	–837
Goods	–2732	–900	–971	–1484	–2265	–2689	–2909	-3174
Exports	5392	1137	1381	1507	1823	1540	1456	1692
Imports	8124	2037	2353	2992	4088	4229	4365	4865
Services (net)	117	519	664	845	1519	1932	2163	2337
Current transfers (net)	–48	255	470	646	792	813	799	842
Factor services	–338	–262	–422	–525	–483	–449	–514	–693
Capital account balance	4122	404	262	596	457	409	485	717
Change in reserves	–1121	–16	–2	–79	–21	–17	–23	–29

Source: 1989–93, Naciones Unidas (1997; 2000, table A-15); 1994–2000, ONE (2000, 128).
Note: *Estimate.

count deficit to 390 million pesos (a decline of 87 percent from 1989). The sharp drops in exports and imports meant that Cuba was not able to purchase raw materials and capital goods required to maintain a high level of economic activity.

The behavior of the capital account is more telling for our purposes. In 1989 Cuba drew in over 4.1 billion pesos in net capital flows, which more than offset the current account deficit and permitted Cuba to accumulate financial reserves of over 1.1 billion pesos. But by 1993 the net flow of foreign capital had fallen to 404 million pesos (a decline of 90.2 percent); in 1994 the net flow of foreign capital fell even lower, to 262 million pesos. It then peaked at 717 million pesos in 2000, still only 17 percent of its level in 1989. While there are no statistics on the composition of capital flows during the crucial period of 1989–91, when economic relations with the former Soviet Union and the socialist countries of Eastern Europe broke down, the bulk of the capital flows in 1989 (and even in 1990 and 1991) probably resulted from credits from the former socialist bloc, as Cuba's access to credit from Western countries was already severely restricted because of the country's difficulties in servicing the hard currency debt accumulated in the 1970s and early 1980s.

To summarize, in 1989 Cuba incurred a deficit in the current account of at least 3 billion pesos. This is a conservative estimate since exports of Cuban sugar to the Soviet Union until about 1990–91 were priced well above world market prices—in 1989 about 3.3 times as high as the world market price, according to a scholar (who also estimates the subsidy in U.S. dollars transferred from the Soviet Union to Cuba related to sugar sales at $2.2 billion in that year, and about $1.9 billion after adjusting for differentials in nickel and oil pricing) (Mesa-Lago 1993, 142–144; Pérez-López 1991, 1992). Thus, if Cuban sugar and nickel exports to the Soviet Union and imports of Soviet oil had been priced at world market prices, Cuba's trade deficit in 1989 would have been higher by about $1.9 billion. This suggests that foreign capital flows in the range of 3 to 5 billion pesos (or U.S. dollars) per annum were necessary to sustain the 1989 level of imports and economic activity.

Cuban FDI Flows and Stocks

As discussed above, quantitative information on Cuban FDI is scarce and inconsistent. In October 1991, Julio García Oliveras, chairman of the Cuban Chamber of Commerce, reported that negotiations were ongoing regarding potential investments of $1.2 billion (Business International Corporation 1992, 24). Vice President Carlos Lage stated that by the end of that year, joint ventures would have provided Cuba with $1.5 billion in FDI stated (Havana Tele Rebelde Network 1994). According to Cuban officials, FDI reached more than $2.1 billion by the end of 1995 (Havana Radio 1995) and $2.2 billion by the end of 1997. Cuban authorities stated that a total of $5 billion was invested in Cuba from 1988—when FDI was first permitted—through 2000 (Spadoni 2001, 21).

Cuban Balance of Payment Statistics. Cuban BOP statistics began to break out of FDI flows within the capital account in 1993. Column 2 of table 8.3 presents Cuban FDI flows, in millions of pesos, for 1993 through 2000. Column 3 cumulates the annual investment flows to estimate the stock of foreign investment. These FDI stock estimates probably underestimate overall FDI stock since they do not include FDI flows in 1991 and 1992. Thus, according to the FDI flow data for 1993–2000, the stock of FDI in Cuba at the end of 2000 was 1.9 billion pesos (or U.S. dollars). It is puzzling, then, that a Cuban scholar has written that (presumably referring to the end of 2000) FDI was in the range of $1,558 million (Pérez Villanueva 2001), suggesting that FDI flows in 1991 and 1992 were either zero or were captured by the statistics reported for subsequent years. Based on the BOP data, average annual flows of FDI from 1993 to 2000 can be calculated to be approximately 240 million pesos (190 million pesos per annum for 1991–2000, assuming flows for 1991 and 1992 were captured in the data for subsequent years).

Table 8.3 Foreign Direct Investment in Cuba from BOP Statistics
(in Millions of Pesos)

	1993	1994	1995	1996	1997	1998	1999	2000
Value (Flow)	54.0	563.4	4.7	82.1	442.0	206.6	178.2	399.9
Cumulative (Stock)	54.0	617.4	622.1	704.2	1146.2	1352.8	1531.0	1930.9

Source: Banco Nacional de Cuba (1996) and ONE (2000).

Table 8.4 Foreign Direct Investment in Cuba
(in Millions of U.S. dollars)

	1991	1992	1993	1994	1995	1996	1997	1998	1999	2000
Value (Flow)	10	7	3	14	9	12	13	15	9	13
Cumulative (Stock)	12	19	22	36	45	57	70	85	94	107

Source: Banco Nacional de Cuba (1996) and ONE (2000).

To put the FDI data in perspective, Cuban BOP statistics in the same Cuban National Bank and Cuban Central Bank reports show that Cuba's net unrequited transfers[5]—consisting mostly of private remittances to Cuban citizens from relatives and friends abroad[6]—amounted to 262.9 million pesos in 1993; 470.2 million in 1994; 646.2 million in 1995; 743.7 million in 1996; 791.7 million in 1997; 813 million in 1998; 798.9 million in 1999; and 842.4 million in 2000; for a cumulative 1993–98 total of 5,369 million pesos, or an average of 671 million pesos per annum. Thus, the ratio of average net transfers to FDI from 1993 to 2000 was about 2.8 to 1.

United Nations Statistics. Two UN agencies produce major annual studies of FDI: UNCTAD produces the annual World Investment Report, which contains global FDI flows and stocks statistics and analysis, and ECLAC produces the annual La inversión extranjera en América Latina y el Caribe, which concentrates on FDI flows and analysis for the countries of the Western Hemisphere (except the United States and Canada). The figures they report for Cuban FDI flows and stocks in U.S. dollars (table 8.4) differ drastically from those reported by Cuban officials or obtained from official Cuban BOP statistics.[7] Thus, FDI stocks of $107 million through 2000 would place Cuba at the very bottom in attracting FDI in the Latin American and Caribbean region.

Information from Other Sources. Two other estimates of the stock of Cuban FDI are also available. The U.S.-Cuba Trade and Economic Council, a private organization based in New York, collects and collates "announced" and "committed/delivered" FDI into Cuba from the media, other public sources, discussions with individual company representatives, Cuba-based enterprise managers, Cuban government officials, and government officials in other countries. According to this source, as of 20 March 1999, announced FDI in Cuba since 1990 amounted to $6.119 billion, while committed/delivered FDI amounted to $1.767 billion (UN Conference on Trade and Development 2001). Second, a U.S. Department of State official reported that FDI in Cuba from 1990 through December 1998 amounted to $1.7 billion, with another $1.6 billion in firm commitments (Hamilton 1999). There are no more recent estimates of FDI stocks from either of these sources.

Table 8.5 Foreign Investment in Cuba, 1999
(in Millions of U.S. Dollars)

Country	Announced	Committed/ Delivered	Announced as a % of Committed/Delivered
Australia	500.0	0.0	0.0
Austria	0.5	0.1	20.0
Brazil	150.0	20.0	13.3
Canada	1807.0	600.0	33.2
Chile	69.0	30.0	43.5
China	10.0	5.0	50.0
Dominican Republic	5.0	1.0	20.0
France	100.0	50.0	50.0
Germany	10.0	2.0	20.0
Greece	2.0	0.5	25.0
Honduras	7.0	1.0	14.3
Israel	22.0	7.0	31.8
Italy	397.0	387.0	97.5
Jamaica	2.0	1.0	50.0
Japan	2.0	0.5	25.0
Mexico	1806.0	450.0	24.9
The Netherlands	300.0	40.0	13.3
Panama	2.0	0.5	25.0
Portugal	15.0	10.0	66.7
Russian Federation	25.0	2.0	8.0
South Africa	400.0	5.0	1.3
Spain	350.0	100.3	28.7
Sweden	10.0	1.0	10.0
United Kingdom	75.0	50.0	66.7
Uruguay	0.5	0.3	60.0
Venezuela	50.0	3.0	6.0
TOTAL	6119.0	1767.2	28.9

Source: U.S.-Cuba Trade and Economic Council, http://www.cubatrade.org/foreign.html.

Note: The above figures "represent the overall amounts of announced, committed, and delivered investments since 1990 by private sector companies and government controlled companies from various countries to enterprises within the Republic of Cuba as of 20 March 1999. Information, which may or may not be in the public domain, compiled through the media, other public sources, individual discussions with company representatives, non-Republic of Cuba government officials, and Republic of Cuba-based enterprise managers and government officials."

FDI by Country of Origin. There are no official statistics on FDI flows or stocks by country of origin. The U.S.-Cuba Trade and Economic Council statistics on announced and committed/delivered FDI by country of origin from 1990 through 20 March 1999 are given in table 8.5. Based on these statistics, Canada ($600 million), Mexico ($450 million), Italy ($387 million), and Spain ($100.3 million) are the leading sources of committed/delivered FDI in Cuba through the first quarter of 1999; France and the United Kingdom ($50 million each) and the Netherlands ($40 million) were also significant sources of FDI. In all, according to table 8.5, businesspersons from twenty-six countries had announced their intention to invest in Cuba, and investors from twenty-five countries had actually committed or delivered such investment.

Another way to examine FDI by country of origin is through the number of joint ventures consummated. As of the end of 1997, a total of 317 joint ventures with foreign investors had been established (Pérez Villanueva 1998). Six countries—Spain (62), Canada (59), Italy (34), France (16), the United Kingdom (15), and Mexico (13)—accounted for 199 joint ventures, or 62.8 percent of the total number of joint ventures (table 8.6). According to another source, the total number of joint ventures by 1998 had risen to 345, of which 70 were with investors from Spain, 66 from Canada, 52 from Italy, 15 from the United Kingdom, and 14 from France (Peters 1999, 9). At the end of 2000, the number of joint ventures had reportedly risen to 392 (Pérez Villanueva 2001), but statistics on the distribution of the joint ventures by country of origin of the foreign partner are not available.

FDI by Economic Sector. There are no official statistics on FDI flows or stocks by economic sector. The mentioned statement by a U.S. Department of State official indicated that out of the $1.7 billion invested in Cuba from 1990 through December 1998, $650 million were in telecommunications (38.2 percent), $350 million in mining (20.6 percent), and $200 million in tourism (11.8 percent).

The distribution of joint ventures by ministry of the Cuban government—which can be used as a proxy for the economic sectors that have been most successful in attracting foreign investment—is given in table 8.7. According to the table, 93 joint ventures were associated with basic industry (including mining), 54 with tourism, 31 with light industry, 24 with the food industry, 16 with construction, and 16 with agriculture. These sectors accounted for 234 joint ventures, or 73.8 percent of the total number of joint ventures established through 1997. According to another source, by 1998 there were 88 joint ventures in basic industry (including mining, oil exploration, and

Table 8.6 Joint Ventures by Country of Origin of Foreign Investor

Country	1988	1989	1991	1992	1993	1994	1995	1996	1997	Total
Total	1	1	12	25	40	64	51	54	69	317
Spain	1		2	5	7	10	14	10	13	62
Canada			1	8	6	20	7	9	8	59
Italy				1	5	4	6	5	13	34
France				3	6		3	2	2	16
United Kingdom					1	2	2	5	5	15
Mexico			3	1	1	4	2	1	1	13

Source: Pérez Villanueva (1998).

Table 8.7 Joint Ventures by Ministry Associated with the Cuban Investor

Ministry	1988	1989	1991	1992	1993	1994	1995	1996	1997	Total
Basic industry (incl. mining)			6	9	17	24	9	11	17	93
Tourism	1			2	7	10	5	12	17	54
Light industry				1	3	4	10	2	11	31
Food industry				1	5	3	5	7	3	24
Construction				1	2	11	1		1	16
Agriculture				2		2	3	5	4	16
TOTAL	1	1	12	25	40	64	51	54	69	317

Source: Pérez Villanueva (1998).

heavy industry), 58 in tourism, 30 in light industry, 20 in food processing, and 17 in agriculture (Peters 1999, 9).

Joint ventures with foreign investors already play a significant role in certain sectors of the Cuban economy. Thus, according to Cuban sources, foreign-invested joint ventures accounted for the following shares of economic activity, presumably at the end of 1997 (Pérez Villanueva 1998):

- 100 percent of oil exploration
- 100 percent of metallic mining
- 100 percent of the production of lubricants
- 100 percent of telephone services (wire and cellular)
- 100 percent of the production of soap, perfumes, personal hygiene products, and industrial cleaners
- 100 percent of export of rum
- 70 percent of production of citrus fruits, juices, and concentrates
- 50 percent of production of nickel
- 50 percent of production of cement
- 10 percent of all rooms suitable for international tourism plus an additional 39 percent operated by joint ventures through hotel management contracts

Investing in Cuba: Issues and Challenges

There is already an extensive literature that has identified political, legal, and economic obstacles to FDI in Cuba (See Suchlicki and Jorge 1994; Lessmann 1994; Pérez-Lopez 1994, 1995, 1996–97, 1998; Werlau 1996, 1997). Rather than covering this same ground, this section concentrates on a few issues that appear to be among the most influential in the behavior of FDI flows to the island and that present significant challenges to Cuban authorities in the years ahead.

Ultimately, investors base their decision to invest in a foreign country on an assessment of economic and political factors—the elusive "investment climate"—compared to potential risk. In 1999, at the same time that the Cuban government was seeking investment in more than one hundred projects in nearly all sectors and geographic areas of the country (Scarpaci 1999),[8] Canadian company Sherritt International had been unable to find suitable projects to invest the $474 million it had raised for investment in Cuba and indicated it might place those funds elsewhere (de Córdoba and Vitzhum 1999).[9]

Uncertainty about the Cuban Government's Commitment to FDI

During potential investors' visits to Cuba and at international fora, Cuban officials invariably express the government's commitment to FDI. For example, speaking at a roundtable sponsored by *The Economist* in February 1999, National Assembly President Ricardo Alarcón reassured participants that Cuba was ready to broaden the role of foreign investment in the nation's economic development strategy. An adviser to the minister for foreign investment and economic cooperation told a group of U.S. businesspersons at the third U.S.-Cuba Business Summit in Cancún in May 1999 that their investments in the island would be guaranteed "today and by the successor government" to Fidel Castro's regime ("Dan garantías a los inversionistas" 1999).

Despite these reassuring statements, other pronouncements by officials and deeds by the Cuban government concern some investors. For example, vice president and economic czar Carlos Lage stated in March 1999 that "foreign investment is an important element of the development that we must further, but it is complementary. The main effort is being done by the government with its resources" ("Lage on Joint Ventures" 1999). Lage further expressed that with the ongoing economic recovery being experienced, "now the government could be in a position to take on projects and leave the creation of the mixed enterprises with foreign capital to those cases in which it is 'really justified'" ("Economy-Cuba" 1999). Echoing Lage's views, the minister for foreign investment and economic cooperation Ibrahim Ferradaz stated in May 1999 that Cuba remained committed to foreign investment as "a complement" to its own efforts to achieve economic recovery and that the Cuban government would now be "more selective" in choosing FDI partners.[10] Finally, Fidel Castro stated also in May 1999 that Cuba would not be "sold" to foreign investors and that some sectors of the economy were off-limits to FDI (Cawthorne 1999).

Pursuant to Article 2(b) of Law No. 77, the authorization by the Executive Committee of the Council of Ministers or by a government commission appointed by the Council of Ministers necessary for a foreign investment to operate in Cuba is given "for a specified period of time." Meanwhile, Article 4(1) permits the extension of the authorization to operate provided a request to do so in proper form is filed in a timely manner. Should the extension not be granted, Article 4(2) calls for the liquidation of the enterprise and for the foreign investor to receive the appropriate share of the proceeds. Raúl Valdés Vivó (1998), rector of the school for cadres of the Cuban Communist Party, in an article published in early 1998 justifying the opening to foreign capital, stresses that foreign investments in Cuba have "contractual time limits."

The lack of permanence of foreign investment, and the purely discretionary nature of the extension process, favor investors with a very short time horizon (for example, speculators) or those only willing to make relatively small investments. Fragmentary information on existing FDI seems to support these two points. According to a Cuban analyst, only nine joint ventures were dissolved in 1995–97, compared to more than fifty before 1995; the analyst attributes the relatively low number of dissolutions in 1995–97 to improvements in the "quality of the investments" (Pérez Villanueva 1998, 13). And 75 percent of the joint ventures established through 1997 reportedly involved capital investment under $5 million (Fernández-Mayo and Ross 1998, 7).

There are numerous examples of business deals dissolved by the Cuban government to the detriment of the interests of foreign investors:

The pension fund of ENDESA, the Spanish electric company, through several agreements with Cuban enterprises, planned to invest $100 million to build hotels in Cayo Coco and Varadero. According to the Spanish investor, the Cuban government failed to perform on its contractual obligations. The ENDESA pension fund is seeking compensation from the Cuban government for nonperformance in proceedings before the International Chamber of Commerce in Paris (Fábregas i Guillén 1998, 36).

A Spanish entrepreneur who operated the restaurant La Tasca Española in the Marina Hemingway, near Havana, was allegedly forced out by the government and his investment was liquidated. The entrepreneur claims that the restaurant was very successful and the government's decision to shut him down was arbitrary (Fernández González 1996, 75–81).

The Spanish company Ibercusa entered into a joint venture agreement with a Cuban enterprise to build the Hotel Cohiba in Havana. Disputes between the parties led to delays in the construction of the hotel and the dissolution of the joint venture. The hotel was eventually completed and is operated through a joint venture involving another Spanish company (Pérez-López 1994, 199).

A German-Canadian investor claims to have lost over $1 million in a joint venture to manufacture lightweight concrete extrusions. After being authorized to set up the joint venture, the foreign entrepreneur was allegedly denied access to his plant and equipment (Tamayo 1999).

A Spanish investor who had invested in a computer company in Havana claims he was forced out of business by a top government official who started a rival business (Tamayo 1999).

Canadian company FirstKey Project Technologies had its authorization to modernize an existing electric power plant and build a new generator—a project valued at $500 million—revoked by the Cuban government. The government claimed that FirstKey had failed to obtain the necessary financing to carry out the project. The Canadian investor reportedly incurred a loss of $9 million (de Córdoba and Vitzhum 1999).

Government Constraints on the Operation of Enterprises

There are numerous government constraints on the operation of foreign-invested enterprises in Cuba. These constraints reflect, in part, the ambiguity of the Cuban government toward FDI and the reluctant acceptance of FDI as a "necessary evil" to overcome the economic crisis. Valdés Vivó (1998) is more blunt, referring to joint ventures with foreign investors as associations "which we would have preferred not to make."

First, foreign investments must be individually screened and approved by the Cuban government. As discussed above, in an effort to streamline the approval process, Law No. 77 (Article 21) made it possible for certain investments to be approved by a government commission appointed for this purpose by the Executive Committee of the Council of Ministers. But the Executive Committee of the Council of Ministers retains approval authority for investments that (1) are valued at over $10 million; (2) are wholly foreign owned; (3) involve public services; (4) involve a foreign investor who is wholly or partially a state-owned corporation; (5) exploit a Cuban natural resource; (6) entail the transfer of Cuban state assets or property rights of the Cuban state; and (7) relate to military enterprises. Law No. 77 (Article 23) establishes a sixty-day time period for the government to allow or disallow an investment.

The investment approval process is complex, time consuming, and uncertain. As Vice President Carlos Lage in March 1999 stated: "Foreigners must be well informed from the beginning that their relations with Cuba are different from those established with other countries, where negotiations are held directly with the owner. Here, the owner is the state, it is the people; therefore since the one negotiating is not the owner, analysis, consultations, and approval from a higher authority must be made. It is more complex, requires more time, and will continue to be like that." This highly discretionary decision-making process also creates opportunities for favoritism and administrative corruption.

Second, some sectors of the economy are closed to foreign investment. Although Law No. 77 (Article 10) explicitly declares out of bounds for FDI only health and education services and national defense (other than commercial enterprises of the armed forces), there are other limitations on foreign investment:

Minister for Foreign Investment and Economic Cooperation Ferradaz stated in May 1999 that Cuba's strategy is to promote FDI, consistent with current law, "in all fields in which foreign investment could provide access to new technologies, new markets or new sources of financing." Ferradaz also expressed the government's "absolute refusal" to accept investments in sugar production, stating that "Cuba already knows how to make sugar" (Cawthorne 1999).

In a speech in which he indicated an openness to FDI, President Castro stated that no area of the economy was "untouchable" to foreign investment. He quickly clarified, however, that "some (things) are untouchable; the distribution system is untouchable and land is also untouchable ("Castro fija límites" 1999).

Third, after a flurry of activity in 1993–94, Cuba's economic reform process has essentially come to a halt. Structural reforms that would revamp state enterprises, permit the operation of small businesses, liberalize the labor market, and begin to create markets for intermediate goods have been shelved. In the view of a Spanish investor, "until the system changes and private initiative is allowed to operate without so many constraints, the economy will not prosper" ("Los temores de los españoles" 1999).

Enterprises' Inability to Manage Human Resources

Law No. 77 and Resolution No. 3/96 of the Ministry of Labor and Social Security set the parameters for the relationship between foreign-invested enterprises in Cuba and their workers. The bottom line is that the Cuban state reserves for itself many of the human resource functions typically conducted by management in commercial environments in order to maximize productivity and profitability: recruiting, hiring, firing, recognizing workers for a job well done.

Article 33 of Law No. 77 states unequivocally that Cuban citizens or permanent residents working in foreign-invested enterprises will be employed by an "entity" of the Cuban government so designated by the Ministry for Foreign Investment and Economic Cooperation and authorized by the Ministry of Labor and Social Security. (The designated employment entity is most often ACOREC, S.A. [Agencia de Contratación a Representaciones Comerciales, S.A., or Contracting Agency for Commercial Offices], although CUBALSE, S.A. [Empresa de Servicios al Cuerpo Diplomático, S.A., or Services Agency for the Diplomatic Corps], may sometimes serve as the designated entity.) For greater clarity, Article 34 states that (1) the employment relationship is between the worker and the entity (not the foreign-invested enterprise); (2) the entity is responsible for paying the worker's salary; (3) the entity is responsible for replacing workers who fail to perform; and (4) worker grievances are raised with the entity, although the foreign-invested enterprise is ultimately financially responsible for costs associated with settlement of grievances.

Resolution No. 3/96 of the Ministry of Labor and Social Security, issued on 27 March 1996, establishes regulations for workers of foreign-invested companies operating in Cuba. The resolution elaborates on Article 33 of Law No. 77, which states that workers of foreign-invested companies are formally hired by an "entity" of the Cuban government designated by the Ministry for Foreign Investment and Economic Cooperation and authorized by the Ministry of Labor and Social Security. This entity, in turn, contracts with foreign-invested enterprises for labor services. Further, the foreign-invested enterprise pays the entity for the labor services in convertible currency while the entity pays Cuban workers their salaries and benefits in domestic currency (pesos).

Article 7 of Resolution 3/96 sets forth the following regarding the relationship between foreign-invested enterprises and the "entity":

> the foreign-invested enterprise submits to the entity its labor needs, including occupations, number of workers, desired labor force characteristics, and delivery schedule *(períodos de entrega);*
>
> the entity recruits and selects workers from among those who meet the requirements set out by the foreign-invested enterprise;
>
> enterprises can return *(devolver)* workers to the entity during the probationary period (30 to 180 days) and obtain a replacement;
>
> after the probationary period is over, enterprises can still return and seek replacement of workers for the following reasons: (1) failure to perform the job for which they were hired; (2) serious violations of discipline; (3) physical disability; (4) imprisonment exceeding six months; and (5) "improper conduct, whether or not illegal, that affects the prestige each worker should enjoy," as set out in suitability *(idoneidad)* criteria in the resolution (see the appendix).

That is, an entity of the Cuban government controls all aspects of an enterprise's human resources, with the role of management of a foreign-invested enterprise relegated to receiving workers preselected by the entity and sending them back to the entity if they fail to perform.

The fact that the entity selects the workers of foreign-invested enterprises means that the former can screen applicants and send to the enterprise workers of its choice. Currently, employment in foreign-invested enterprises is highly coveted among Cuban workers, since these jobs tend to bring workers in contact with the hard currency sector of the economy and therefore create the possibility for obtaining scarce hard currency (for example, tips), even if the salary is paid in domestic currency (see below). The entity can favor certain classes of workers who may be politically closer to the government than others. For example, retired members of the armed forces are allegedly overrepresented among the workers of foreign-invested enterprises, particularly in the tourism industry. Among the complaints of a group of Mexican investors in tourism was the requirement that they hire Cuban Communist Party members and retired personnel of the armed forces "who are not always the most qualified for the jobs they hold" (Zúñiga 1999). According to Pax Christi Netherlands, a Dutch NGO, the Cuban government entity selects workers for employment by foreign-invested enterprises "on the basis of their loyalty to the Party, not capacity," in violation of Convention 111 of the International Labor Organization, which guarantees the right to nondiscrimination in appointment (Pax Christi Netherlands 1999, 23).[11]

Resolution No. 3/96 also sets out criteria for dismissing workers, including for conduct "that affects the prestige that every worker of the enterprise should possess" (Article 15.d) and considered to violate worker "suitability" *(idoneidad)* standards spelled out in an annex to the resolution. The "suitability" requirements give the entity the power to screen out workers for political correctness. These suitability requirements are very similar to those promulgated in 1990 for workers in joint ventures in the tourism sector, which placed much heavier emphasis on personal qualities and behavior than on the performance of a job assignment for workers in this industry compared to the requirements in the Cuban labor code.[12] It should be noted, however, that the entity's screening mechanism may not be ultimately successful in weeding out workers whose political views disagree with those of the government. According to a U.S. scholar who interviewed workers of foreign-invested enterprises in Cuba, "while it is clear that a black mark of any kind on one's record is likely to disqualify a Cuban from a sought-after job, it bears noting that in interviews conducted . . . employees of joint ventures who had successfully passed through this screening process reflected the full range of opinion on Cuban government policy" (Peters 1999).

Finally, it bears mentioning that because there is no employment relationship between workers and foreign-invested enterprises, workers cannot bargain with representatives of the workplaces where they labor. That is, Cuban workers employed in foreign-invested enterprises are prevented from bargaining directly with their employers over conditions of their work.

Inability to Pay Workers in Convertible Currency

Although foreign-invested enterprises pay the Cuban entity in convertible currency for the total compensation (that is, salary plus benefits and social security contributions) of workers, the workers in turn draw their salaries from the entity in domestic currency. The Cuban government uses the official exchange rate—one U.S. dollar equivalent to one peso—for effecting these currency exchanges. The reality is that the exchange rate of the U.S. dollar in Cuba has been about twenty pesos for one U.S. dollar; this is the rate that prevails in exchange houses operated by the Cuban government. At the 20:1 exchange rate, the Cuban government appropriates 95 percent of the salaries of the approximately sixty thousand Cuban workers employed by foreign-invested enterprises.[13] This practice allegedly violates the principle of integrity of salary contained in the Cuban labor code as well as Articles 5 and 6 of International Labor Organization Convention 95 regarding protection of a worker's salary.[14]

Salary is one of the key factors that motivates workers. A worker who is adequately compensated, at a level sufficient to meet the needs of his or her family, can concentrate during work hours in increasing productivity and firm profits. Alternatively, a worker who is not earning sufficiently to satisfy these needs will be distracted and will devote time and energy to make ends meet, detracting from productivity. Inadequate remuneration may be associated with behavior inconsistent with high productivity: absenteeism; tardiness; pilfering of finished products, raw materials, or recyclable wastes; unauthorized used of equipment or property.

Managers of foreign-invested enterprises know that their workers' salaries in pesos are woefully inadequate to meet their basic needs. Under certain circumstances, managers of some foreign-invested enterprises have been known to supplement the earnings of workers by providing a small stipend in hard currency, a basket *(jaba)* of goods that are available only in hard currency stores, free lunches or a meal allowance, or free transportation. Following are examples of the application of these practices—which technically may be illegal but seem to be condoned (Peters 1999, 6–8):

A cleaning woman at a hotel in Varadero earns a monthly salary of 267 pesos, a *jaba,* a four-dollar cash supplement, and a share of tips that usually amounts to ten dollars (the fourteen dollars in hard currency is worth 280 pesos, more than the domestic currency salary and the average Cuban salary of 217 pesos per month).

A junior manager for a Canadian company earns three hundred pesos plus one hundred dollars per month.

A sales representative for an industrial equipment manufacturer earns three hundred pesos plus a side payment of three hundred dollars per month.

Table 8.8 Monthly Employment Cost of Cuban Workers in Foreign-Invested Companies, 1995 *(in U.S. Dollars)*

Category	Basic Salary	Vacation Pay (9.09%)	Payroll Taxes (25%)	ACOREC Commission (10%)	Total
Manager	520.14	47.28	141.85	56.74	766.01
International sales specialist	358.02	32.54	97.64	39.06	527.26
Sales assistant	259.39	23.58	70.74	28.30	382.01
Engineer	439.08	39.91	119.75	47.90	646.64
Executive secretary	231.00	20.99	62.99	25.19	340.17
Computer specialist	378.28	34.39	103.17	41.27	557.11
Automobile driver	143.00	12.99	38.99	15.59	210.57

Source: Information obtained from a 17 February 1995 bill sent by ACOREC, S.A., to the office of a foreign-invested company operating in Cuba, as reproduced in Fábregas i Guillén (1998, 130).

An executive in Havana pays his sixty employees a supplement of about sixty dollars per month in the form of a three-dollar-per-day lunch stipend.

Workers at an all-inclusive resort in Varadero receive a forty-dollar pay supplement each month.

Workers at the Moa nickel plant operated as a joint venture between Canada's Sherritt International and the Cuban government are paid a monthly supplement in convertible currency that ranges from 10 to 22 percent of the peso wage (for example, a three hundred-peso-per-month salary would be accompanied by a supplement of thirty to sixty-six dollars).

Convertible currency supplements—whether in cash or in kind—are useful tools to motivate workers and increase productivity. However, the ability of managers to make these supplements sufficiently large to meet the basic needs of their workers is limited because of the relatively high payments that foreign-invested enterprises already make to the Cuban state through the domestic labor entity.

Table 8.8 illustrates monthly employment costs—in U.S. dollars—for Cuban workers in selected occupations as billed by ACOREC, S.A., in February 1995 to a foreign-invested company operating in Cuba. Column 1 presents the basic monthly salary of the worker; the worker's take-home pay is based on the amount reported in this column less taxes and other deductions. ACOREC also collects from the employer each month one-twelfth of the basic salary (9.09 percent of the basic salary), which is set aside to pay for the one-month paid vacation all workers receive annually (column 2). ACOREC also collects a payroll tax, equivalent to 25 percent of the basic salary augmented by the contribution to vacation pay, intended to pay for social security and other programs (column 3). In addition, ACOREC charges enterprises a monthly commission for its services, calculated as 10 percent of the basic salary plus pro rata vacation pay (column 4). Finally, column 5 reports the total monthly employment cost payable by the foreign-invested enterprise to ACOREC, S.A.

To illustrate, an engineer hired by ACOREC, S.A., to work in a foreign-invested enterprise earned a basic salary of $439.08 (table 8.8, fourth row). The employer was also responsible for a contribution in deferred compensation of $39.91 to cover the worker's one-month vacation, for an adjusted monthly salary of $478.99. In addition, the foreign-invested enterprise contributed 25 percent of the adjusted salary to the Cuban state to cover social security and other employee benefits ($119.75) and 10 percent to ACOREC, S.A., for its services ($47.90). Thus, the total monthly cost to the foreign-invested enterprise of employing an engineer was $646.64. Meanwhile, the Cuban worker's monthly take-home pay was somewhat less than the basic salary (depending on taxes and other deductions) payable in domestic currency, or under 439 pesos per month. At the current 20:1 peso per U.S. dollar exchange rate, the monthly take-home pay of the Cuban engineer was the equivalent of under $22, or 3.4 percent of the total outlay incurred by the foreign-invested enterprise, for his or her services.

The hard currency revenue flowing to the Cuban state as a result of the employment of roughly sixty thousand Cuban workers by foreign-invested enterprises under the current confiscatory salary regime is significant. For example, taking the monthly employment costs of a sales assistant from table 8.8 ($382.01) as representative of the cost of Cuban workers employed by foreign-invested enterprises, the Cuban government collected over $22.9 million per month, or about $275 million per annum. This latter figure exceeded annual FDI flows into the island during 1993–98 (about $225 million).

U.S. Sanctions

Foreign investors operating in Cuba and producing goods that enter international commerce are subject to U.S. laws that prohibit the importation of Cuban goods. Because the U.S. import ban covers not only whole articles but also articles that might contain parts or materials produced in Cuba, it can affect multinational companies that trade extensively with the United States and have joint ventures in Cuba.

In March 1996 the United States enacted the Helms-Burton Act.[15] Two sections of the act are particularly relevant to current or prospective foreign investors in Cuba:

Title III of the act makes persons who knowingly and intentionally traffic in properties expropriated from U.S. nationals by the Cuban government after 1 January 1959 without compensation subject to private civil damage suits in U.S. Federal District Courts. The act defines *trafficking* very broadly. For example, a trafficker is a person who knowingly and intentionally (1) sells, transfers, distributes, dispenses, brokers, manages, or otherwise disposes of confiscated property, or purchases, leases, receives, possesses, obtains control of, manages, uses, or otherwise acquires or holds an interest in confiscated property; (2) engages in commercial activity using or otherwise benefiting from confiscated property; or (3) causes, directs, participates in, or profits from trafficking by another person or otherwise engages in trafficking through another person without the authorization of any U.S. national who holds a claim to the property.

Title IV directs the U.S. secretary of state to deny a visa to, and the attorney general to exclude from the United States, aliens (including their spouses, minor children, or agents) involved in the confiscation of property, or the trafficking in confiscated property, owned by a U.S. national.

It bears recalling that there are 5,911 unresolved American claims against Cuban nationalizations certified by the U.S. government valued at $1.8 billion (1960 value). The current value of these claims is around $6 billion, taking into consideration interest at 6 percent per annum. In addition, there are much larger claims for nationalizations of assets owned by Cuban citizens who have immigrated to the United States since 1959 and have acquired U.S. citizenship.

Thus, foreign investments that use assets confiscated by the Cuban government and whose ownership is claimed by U.S. nationals are vulnerable to sanctions under the Helms-Burton Act. According to the minister for foreign investment and economic cooperation, "around half a dozen" of the joint ventures with foreign investors active in mid-1996 were operating with properties expropriated from U.S. citizens ("Foreign Investment Minister" 1996). According to press reports, some of these foreign investors, and the assets subject to claims by U.S. nationals with which they are operating or have considered operating, include Mexican Grupo Domos' operations, with the assets of the former Cuban Telephone Company, a subsidiary of multinational corporation ITT; Sherritt International's nickel and cobalt mining operations at Moa Bay, with assets owned by Freeport-MacMoRan, Inc.; Unilever's joint venture to produce soap, detergent, and other personal hygiene products using assets claimed by Procter & Gamble; and CEMEX's proposed joint venture to operate a cement plant at Mariel claimed by Lone Star Industries.

To date, Title III of the Helms-Burton Act has not been applied against any foreign investor in Cuba. U.S. Presidents Clinton and Bush have repeatedly exercised a six-month waiver authority under the law to postpone the ability of U.S. citizens to initiate suits against third party nationals. They have then used the hiatus to negotiate agreements with trading partners, such as the "European Union–United States Memorandum of Understanding Concerning the Helms-Burton Act and the U.S. Iran and Libya Sanctions Act," concluded in April 1997, that commits the European Union to take steps to advance democracy in Cuba. Title IV has been applied, however, with the U.S. Department of State reportedly sending letters notifying denial of entry into the United States to executives and family members of Sherritt International of Canada, Grupo Domos, and CEMEX of Mexico, Grupo BM of Israel, and a Panamanian firm selling automobiles in Cuba. According to a U.S. Department of State official, by March 1999 three determinations of trafficking under Title IV of the Helms-Burton Act had been made and fifteen executives and their family members had been denied entry into the United States (Larson 1999).

Cuban officials have subtly made the case that the Helms-Burton Act has been ineffective in stemming FDI flows into Cuba. In March 1999, Minister for Foreign Investment and Economic Cooperation Ferradaz reported that 20 new joint ventures with foreign investors had already been established in 1999, and over 100 foreign investment projects were under consideration. At the end of 1998, according to Ferradaz, 340 joint ventures with foreign investors were in operation, of which 57 were established in 1998 ("Se acelera en 1999" 1999). Minister Ferradaz's response to a journalist's question regarding the effect of the Helms-Burton Act on FDI was this:

> The Helms-Burton Law . . . was approved three years ago with the very objective of stopping the foreign investment process in the island. It has not met this objective, as the foreign investment process has not stopped. Out of the more than 360 joint ventures with foreign investment that are operating in Cuba today, more than 50 percent were established after the passage of the Helms-Burton Law.
>
> This should not lead us to underestimate its effects. How many more investors would have invested with us today if it were not for that Law? It is very difficult to say. How many will take out their investments while the law is in force? This is also very difficult to predict.
>
> The effects of the Helms-Burton Law are with us. The law makes the conditions for us to obtain financing more difficult and, without a doubt, does not allow some entrepreneurs to do business with Cuba, but it does not prevent business activity. (Veloz 1999)

Conclusion

Socialist Cuba has had some success in attracting FDI in the 1990s. The Law on Foreign Investment of September 1995 defined more clearly the legal framework for foreign investment in the island. The roughly 1.9 billion pesos in FDI from 1993 to 1998 (based on official Cuban BOP statistics), an average of 240 million pesos per annum, has undoubtedly helped Cuba in managing an otherwise very difficult BOP situation. These FDI flows are relatively small when compared with the massive financial needs of the country, however.

In the 1990s FDI has flowed into Latin American and Caribbean countries at a very rapid pace. Even in 1998 and 1999, two years marked by slower world economic growth associated with the Asian financial crisis, Latin America and the Caribbean attracted record levels of FDI. By comparison, Cuba's performance in attracting FDI has been lackluster. There are numerous reasons that may be responsible for this performance. Among them are (1) uncertainty about the Cuban government's commitment to FDI; (2) government constraints on the operation of enterprises; (3) the inability of foreign-invested enterprises to manage their human resources; (4) the inability to pay workers in convertible currency; and (5) the threat of U.S. sanctions. Adequately addressing these issues will require fundamental political and economic changes designed to move Cuba in the direction of democracy and a free market orientation.

Appendix 8.1 Norms of Conduct for Cuban Workers Employed by International Economic Associations

Behave in accord with the interests of our society.

Faithfully comply with our laws and demand their strict fulfillment.

Maintain social conduct that will make them recipients of respect and confidence of other Cuban citizens, no engaging in any ostentatious behavior or obtaining personal perquisites and maintaining a lifestyle in accord with our society.

Reject and combat negligent and irresponsible behavior or personal practices that run counter to the economic and social objectives of the work they perform.

Maintain objectivity, respect, and good manners in the conduct of their work and in their relations with any person in their work.

Ensure that the best interests of our people prevail in all of their acts and decisions.

Maintain scrupulous discretion over matters that come to their attention and reveal them only to persons with a need to know.

Behave in such a manner that the enterprise where they work meets its objectives with the greatest efficiency.

Use material, financial, and human resources under their control in the most rational way possible, benefiting the nation and the enterprise, and only for the purpose for which such resources were assigned, and never for personal or family use or for other purposes.

Not accept or request from subordinates or from persons with whom they come in contact, payments, gifts, perquisites, or special favors that might have a negative effect on the work and personal conduct that our cadres and workers should exhibit, and might compromise the healthy spirit of collaboration that should exist between labor and management.

Source: "Resolución No. 3/96" (1996, 272).

Notes

1. The rationale for this policy of minimum reporting on FDI, as articulated by Vice President Carlos Lage, is "the pressure which everyone who comes to invest in Cuba is subjected to [by the United States]," in order to discourage FDI in Cuba (Lage 1992).

2. The formal name of the Helms-Burton Act is the Cuban Liberty and Democratic Solidarity (LIBERTAD) Act of 1996, Public Law No. 104–14 (1996).

3. Banco Nacional de Cuba, *Economic Report*, February 1982 (Havana), and similar reports issued in March 1984 and February 1985. Beginning in December 1982 and through about mid-1990, the Cuban Na-

tional Bank also issued a *Quarterly Economic Report* and its Spanish version, *Informe económico trimestral*, with the same types of data as the annual reports. The Cuban National Bank resumed publication of annual reports in the mid-1990s. With the reform of the Cuban financial system in the late 1990s, the central banking functions have been assigned to the Banco Central de Cuba (BCC); BCC has taken over the publication of the annual reports.

4. Banco Nacional de Cuba, *Economic Report 1994*, August 1995, and *Informe económico 1995*, May 1996; Banco Central de Cuba, *Informe económico 1997*, May 1998, and subsequent issues.

5. In the BOP methodology of the International Monetary Fund, unrequited transfers are "transactions stemming from the noncommercial considerations, such as family ties or legal obligations, that induce a producer or owner of real resources and financial items to part with them without any return in those same forms" (International Monetary Fund 1977, 71). Unrequited transfers can be of an official nature (for example, foreign grants or aid in kind for which no payment is required) or of a private nature (for example, remittances from individuals).

6. According to UNECLAC, transfers received by Cuba are predominantly private and take the form of cash remittances (Naciones Unidas 1997, 172).

7. According to UNECLAC, the FDI flows data used in the report originate from the International Monetary Fund (IMF) and are prepared (1) following the methodology developed by that organization for BOP statistics and (2) relying on information provided to the IMF by central banks. UNECLAC notes that national FDI statistics often differ from those developed by the IMF because the former are complied on the basis of surveys of foreign investors and rely on different criteria on FDI than that used by the IMF. E-mail correspondence between the author and UNECLAC, Santiago, Chile, 13–14 September 1999.

8. Among the new areas that Cuba has targeted for foreign investment are building materials, cultural projects, publishing and media, and information technology.

9. By way of explanation, Sherritt CEO Ian Delaney was quoted as saying, "There's a limit to the rate you can invest in Cuba" (de Córdoba and Vitzhum 1999).

10. The Cuban press announced on 28 August 1999 that Ferradaz had been named minister of tourism, replacing Osmany Cienfuegos. Ferradaz was replaced as minister for foreign investment and economic cooperation by Marta Lomas Morales, the former first vice minister.

11. The issue of Cuban discrimination of persons on political grounds in education, training, and employment has been the subject of continuing complaints and reviews since 1989 by the Committee of Experts on the Application of Conventions and Recommendations (CEACR) of the International Labor Organization. For detailed information on the complaints and the observations of the CEACR, see the ILO electronic database, ILOLEX, at http://www.ilo.org.

12. "Resolución No. 15/90 del Comité Estatal de Trabajo y Seguridad Social," *Gaceta Oficial*, 15 September 1990. For an analysis of the labor regime for the international tourism sector and its comparison with the Cuban Labor Code, see Pérez-López (1992–93, 221–79).

13. The estimate of sixty thousand workers in foreign-invested enterprises in 1997–98 is from Peters (1999, 9). Dídac Fábregas i Guillén (1998, 59) reports fifty thousand workers employed by foreign-invested enterprises but presumably refers to an earlier period. There is also a more recent estimate of 160,000 workers employed directly and indirectly by foreign-invested enterprises, but this figure is not used here since it is not clear how indirect employment has been defined. See Nogueras (1998).

14. Efrén Córdova, "Régimen laboral," in *40 años de revolución: El legado de Castro*, edited by Efrén Córdova (Miami: Ediciones Universal, 1999), 167. See also Alberto Luzárraga, "Cuba socialista—La nulidad de los contratos de inversión extranjera por causa ilícita—Defraudar al trabajador," at http://www.amigospais-guaracabuya.org. In July 1999, the Comité Cubano Pro-Derechos Humanos and the Federación Sindical de Plantas Eléctricas, Gas y Agua, two Miami-based organizations, filed suit before the circuit court of the state of Florida against more than twenty foreign companies with investments in Cuba, alleging that these companies colluded with the Cuban government to violate human rights of Cuban citizens, including the indirect contracting of Cuban workers whereby the worker realizes only a small frac-

tion of the total payment for his or her services made by the foreign investor to the Cuban government. The plaintiffs requested injunctive relief plus compensation for the workers who had not received the full amount of their salaries. See Rui Ferreira, "Demanda a inversionistas por violar derechos humanos," *El Nuevo Herald*, 25 June 1999. The text of the lawsuit is available at http://www.cubanet.org/ref/dis/demanda.

15. The discussion of the Helms-Burton Act in this section draws from Jorge Pérez-López and Matías Travieso-Díaz, "The Helms-Burton Law and Its Antidotes: A Classic Standoff?" *Southwestern University Journal of Law and Trade in the Americas*, forthcoming.

Bibliography

Banco Nacional de Cuba. 1982. *Economic Report*. Havana, Cuba.

______. 1995. *Economic Report 1994*. Havana, Cuba.

______. 1996. *Informe económico 1995*. Havana, Cuba.

Burguet Rodríguez, René. 1995. *Ley de la inversión extranjera en Cub*. Madrid: Consultoría Jurídica Internacional.

Business International Corporation. 1992. *Developing Business Strategies for Cuba*. New York: Business International Corporation.

"Castro fija límites a la política de inversiones." 1999. *El Nuevo Herald*, 19 May.

Cawthorne, Andrew. 1999. "La Habana se ha hecho más selectiva en la búsqueda de inversionistas." *El Nuevo Herald*, 15 May.

"Cuban Liberty and Democratic Solidarity (LIBERTAD) Act of 1996" (commonly known as the Helms-Burton Act). Public Law No. 104–114.

"Dan garantías a los inversionistas de EU 'más allá de Fidel Castro.'" 1999. *El Nuevo Herald*, 24 May.

de Córdoba, José, and Carlta Vitzhum. 1999. "For Jilted Engineers from Canada, Cuba Was Not a Cheap Date." *Wall Street Journal*, 28 June.

"Economy-Cuba: Foreign Investment Now at $4 Billion." 1999. Inter Press Service (Havana), 17 March.

Fábregas i Guillén, Dídac. 1998. *La ley de la inversión extranjera y la situación económica actual de Cuba*. Barcelona: Viena, S.L.

Fernández González, José. 1996. *Cuba: Del socialismo al Fascismo—Un Español dentro de la revolución Cubana, 1980–1996*. Puerto Rico.

Fernández-Mayo, María Antonia, and James E. Ross. 1998. *Cuba: Foreign Agribusiness Financing and Investment*. International Working Paper IW-98-7. Gainesville: University of Florida.

"Foreign Investment and Cuba." 2000. At http://www.cubatrade.org/foreign.html.

"Foreign Investment Minister on Helms-Burton Law." 1996. *El País* (Madrid), 15 June 1996 (as reproduced in *FBIS-LAT-96-119*, 19 June 1996).

Hamilton, John R. 1999. "Cuba: Economic Transition and U.S. Policy." Remarks prepared for delivery by the principal deputy assistant secretary, Bureau of Western Hemisphere Affairs, U.S. Department of State, 25 March.

Havana Radio. 1995. "Support for Economic Changes." Reproduced in FBIS-LAT-*95-137*, 18 July 1995, Havana, Cuba.

Havana Tele Rebelde Network. 1994. "Carlos Lage Addresses Conference 21 November." Reproduced in *FBIS-LAT-94-229-S*, 29 November 1994. "Ley No. 77—Ley de las inversiones extranjeras." 1995. *Gaceta Oficial*, 6 September, 5–12.

International Monetary Fund. 1977. *Balance of Payments Manual*. 4th ed. Washington: International Monetary Fund.

Lage, Carlos. 1992. "Carlos Lage Comments on the Economy." Havana Tele Rebelde and Cuba Vision as reproduced in *FBIS-LAT-92-219*, 12 November 1992, p. 9.

"Lage on Joint Ventures, Foreign Investment in Cuba." 1999. *Prensa Latina* (Havana), 16 March.

Larson, Alan P. 1999. "Advancing Human Rights and Property Rights in Cuba: The Role of Multilateral

Coalitions." Remarks prepared by the assistant secretary of state for economic and business affairs, delivered to the U.S.-Cuba Business Council Conference, Coral Gables, 9 March.

Lee, Susana. 1999. "Ratifica Alarcón disposición de Cuba a desarrollar la inversión extranjera." *Granma* (online edition), 25 February.

Lessmann, Robert. 1994. *Empresas mixtas en Cub.* Caracas: Nueva Sociedad.

"Ley No. 80—Ley de reafirmación de la dignidad y soberanía Cubanas." 1996. *Gaceta Oficial,* 24 December, 299–301.

"Ley No. 88—Ley de Protección de la Independencia Nacional y la Economía de Cuba." 1999. *Diario las Américas,* 23 March. Adopted by the National Assembly in February 1999.

"Los temores de los españoles." 1999. *El Nuevo Herald,* 4 June. Luzárraga, Alberto. 2000. "Cuba socialista—La nulidad de los contratos de inversión extranjera por causa ilícita—Defraudar al trabajador." At http://www.amigospais-guaracabuya.org.

Mesa-Lago, Carmelo. 1993. "The Economic Effects on Cuba of the Downfall of Socialism in the USSR and Eastern Europe." In *Cuba after the Cold War,* edited by Carmelo Mesa-Lago. Pittsburgh: University of Pittsburgh Press.

Naciones Unidas, Comisión Económica para América Latina y el Caribe. 1997 and 2000. *La economía Cubana: Reformas estructurales y desempeño en los noventa.* Mexico, D.F.: Fondo de Cultura Económica.

______. 2001. *Foreign Investment in Latin America and the Caribbean 2000.* Santiago, Chile: CEPAL.

Nogueras, Olance. 1998. "Empleados sufren 'explotación extrema.'" *El Nuevo Herald,* 13 December.

Oficina Nacional de Estadisticas (ONE). 2001. *Anuario estadístico de Cuba, 2000.* Havana, Cuba: ONE.

Ossman, Ghassan. 1996. "Recent Developments Relating to the Role of the Public Administration in Regulating Investment in Cuba." *Journal of International Banking Law* 11, no. 10 (October): 415–23.

Pax Christi Netherlands. 1999. *Cuba: A Year after the Pope*. Utrecht: Pax Christi Netherlands.

Pérez-López, Jorge F. 1991. *The Economics of Cuban Sugar*. Pittsburgh: University of Pittsburgh Press.

______. 1992. "Cuba's Transition to Market-Based Energy Prices." *Energy Journal* 13, no. 4:17–40.

______. 1992–93. "Cuba's Thrust to Attract Foreign Investment: A Special Labor Regime for Joint Ventures in International Tourism." *Inter-American Law Review* 24, no. 2 (winter): 221–79.

______. 1994. "Islands of Capitalism in an Ocean of Socialism: Joint Ventures in Cuba's Development Strategy." In *Cuba at a Crossroads,* edited by Jorge F. Pérez-López, 190–219. Gainesville: University Press of Florida.

______. 1995. "Odd Couples: Joint Ventures between Foreign Capitalists and Cuban Socialists." North-South Agenda Paper No. 16. Coral Gables: University of Miami.

______. 1996–97. "Foreign Investment in Socialist Cuba: Significance and Prospects." *Studies in Comparative International Development* 31, no. 4 (winter): 3–28.

______. 1998. "Foreign Direct Investment in the Cuban Economy: A Critical Look." Paper presented at the international symposium "Reintegration into World Society: Cuba in International Perspective," Queens College, SUNY, 28 September.

Pérez-López, Jorge F., and Matías Travieso-Díaz. 2000. "The Helms-Burton Law and Its Antidotes: A Classic Standoff?" *Southwestern University Journal of Law and Trade in the Americas* 12, no. 1:95–155.

Pérez Villanueva, Omar Everleny. 1998. "La inversión extranjera directa en Cuba: Peculiaridades." Mimeograph.

______. 2001. *La inversión extranjera directa en Cuba: Evolución y perspectiva*. Paper presented at the 2001 Meeting of the Latin American Studies Association, Washington, D.C., September.

Peters, Philip. 1999. *A Different Kind of Workplace: Foreign Investment in Cuba.* Arlington, Va.: Alexis de Tocqueville Institution.

Resolución económica: V Congreso del Partido Comunista de Cuba. 1997. Havana: Editora Política.

"Resolución No. 3/96, Ministerio de Trabajo y Seguridad Social, Reglamento sobre el regimen laboral en la inversión extranjera." 1996. *Gaceta Oficial,* 24 May, 266–72.

"Resolución No. 15/90 del Comité Estatal de Trabajo y Seguridad Social." 1990. *Gaceta Oficial,* September.

Rui Ferreira. 1999. "Demanda a inversionistas por violar derechos humanos." *El Nuevo Herald,* 25 June. The text of the lawsuit is available at http://www.cubanet.org/ref/dis/demanda.
Scarpaci, Joseph L. 1999. "Government Trying to Attract Investment in Growing Number of Fields." *Cuba News* 7, no. 3 (March): 6.
"Se acelera en 1999 la inversión extranjera." 1999. *El Nuevo Herald,* 28 March.
Spadoni, Paolo. 2001. "The Impact of the Helms-Burton Legislation on Foreign Investment in Cuba." Vol. 11, *Cuba in Transition.* Washington: Association for the Study of the Cuban Economy.
Suchlicki, Jaime, and Antonio Jorge, eds. 1994. *Investing in Cuba: Problems and Prospects.* New Brunswick: Transaction Publishers.
Tamayo, Juan O. 1999. "Crackdowns, Restrictions Sour Investors on Cuba." *Miami Herald,* 10 June.
UN Conference on Trade and Development. 2001. *World Investment Report, 2000.* New York: United Nations.
UN Economic Commission for Latin America and the Caribbean (UNECLAC). 2001. *Foreign Investment in Latin America and the Caribbean, 2000.* Santiago, Chile: CEPAL.
Valdés Vivó, Raúl. 1998. "Why Cuba Says No to Privatization." *Workers World,* 15 January, at http://www.workers.org/ww/1998/cuba0115.html.
Vega Vega, Juan. 1997. *Cuba: Inversiones extranjeras a partir de 1995.* Madrid: Ediciones Endymion.
Veloz, Marta. 1999. "La inversión extranjera no se ha detenido." *Opciones en el Web,* 18 April, at http://www.opciones.cubaweb.cu.
Werlau, María C. 1996, "Foreign Investment in Cuba: The Limits of Commercial Engagement." Vol. 6, *Cuba in Transition,* 456–95. Washington: Association for the Study of the Cuban Economy.
______. 1997. "Update on Foreign Investment in Cuba, 1996–97." Vol. 7, *Cuba in Transition,* 72–98. Washington: Association for the Study of the Cuban Economy.
______. 1998. "Update on Foreign Investment in Cuba 1997–98 and Focus on the Energy Sector." Vol. 8, *Cuba in Transition,* 202–12. Washington: Association for the Study of the Cuban Economy.
Zúñiga, Jesús. 1999. "Cadena hotelera mexicana retiraría inversión en Cuba." *CPI* (Havana), 3 September, at http://www.cubanet.org/desdecuba.html.

CHAPTER 9

The Cuban Software Industry

Luis Casacó

This work focuses on an emerging industry in Cuba, namely the software development industry. It is formed by a number of software firms, most of which are associated with the Information Technology Group of the Informatics and Communication Ministry, while a few others are spread out among the rest of the ministries. Something important to highlight is the presence of some foreign firms that are either associated with Cuban counterparts or are established in Cuba's free trade zones.

History, Evolution, and Development

Historical evidence shows that the first data processing equipment was introduced into Cuba in the 1920s. Ten years later, IBM set its regional offices in Havana, from which it managed all regional businesses for the next thirty years.

At the beginning of 1960 two first-generation American mainframe computers, the UNIVAC and the RAMAC, were acquired by the Cuban government. In 1963 the ELLIOT 803-B, a second-generation British computer, was acquired and destined to the National Center for Scientific Research (CNIC). The entrance of this computer marked the beginning of the study of computer science as a professional discipline in Cuba. Also in 1963 the first National Data Processing Enterprise was created. It specialized in data processing services and equipment maintenance. In 1968, two SEA-4000 second-generation computers were acquired in France and were employed in the processing of all data gathered during the population census of 1970. All of the IRIS series (third-generation computers) that entered Cuba were acquired in France around this time as well.

The first prototype of a Cuban minicomputer, the CID-201, was designed in 1969. This early model was continuously developed in the 1970s, evolving into a whole series of third-generation machines known as the series CID-201 A, CID-201 B, and CID-300/10. As a result of the advancement in computer production and design, Cuba signed an agreement with the former socialist countries to facilitate the development of electronic computer machines. This agreement was instrumental in helping Cuba to become an active member of the Computer Inter-governmental Commission.

Software Activities during the 1970s

Software was considered a supporting activity to the economy and not a profitable one in its own right. Looking back, we can say that a rigid framework was established around computer-related activities. There were departments of automated management systems at all ministries. Official institutions had centers for the design of automated systems, which were enterprises, budgetary units, or strategic units. And computing centers, which consisted of computer-equipped offices, supported all of the accounting activities for firms and official ministries.

National Institute for Automated Systems and Computer Technology (INSAC)

On 30 November 1976 INSAC was created. Among its main functions were designing, leading, executing, and controlling policies related to the development of automated systems and computing techniques. The institute was also responsible for the installation and technical maintenance of computer systems; design of new computing centers; supply of new equipment and spare parts; production of electronic calculators and minicomputers; design and deployment of automated systems for managing technological processes; and promotion of research and development as a main activity among its enterprises.

The 1980s: Microcomputers Enter the Stage

Once microprocessors became powerful enough to support an electronic architecture such as the PC, the computer world changed very quickly. Microcomputers invaded all markets around the world. These developments were felt in Cuba as well. The most important event in this period came with the creation of the modern and well-equipped factory Copextel, which began to assemble the first Cuban microcomputer: the LTEL 24, an IBM-compatible PC.

In 1985 there were just two desktop computers in the Havana Institute of Technology (ISPJAE), the most important technical university in Cuba. A year later, there were computer labs in each of its departments and programs, plus a large computer center. It was the first time computers were being used by all of the institute's five thousand students and professors.

In the 1980s research centers and computer services firms appeared all over Cuba. At the same time, some factories grouped into a business corporation, eventually leading to the creation of the Group of Electronics of the Steel, Mechanics, and Electronics Ministry.

Among the most outstanding companies and institutes created in this period were the research and development centers of EICISOFT, ICID, Neuroscience (CNIC), ICIMAF, and BURO SAD-PT; the services firms of Servitec, Fondo de Software, and Infomed; technology plants such as Pinar del Rio's Hi-Tech Plant of Microchips and Electronics; and Copextel, a producing/exporting corporation of electronics and hardware.

The 1990s

After the collapse of the Soviet bloc, many of the firms within or linked to the electronic and computer industry were forced to restructure their business philosophy and management. As a consequence of the economic crisis, some firms changed their business portfolio and tried to adapt to a new environment. At the same time, the National Assembly passed legislation allowing foreign firms not only to invest in Cuba but also to retrieve their investment and repatriate their profits in the moment they decided to. In this period of readaptation, the first all-Cuban software companies were created, most of them linked to the only sector exhibiting some recovery after the crisis—tourism. They offered software solutions and support to both the hotels and the distribution and supply companies. Other software firms, especially those research and development centers created in the previous decade and linked to the health services and biotechnology remained unaltered in their missions in spite of the hard times they faced.

Cuba had revealed a hidden yet powerful skill: the ability to write excellent software applications. With skilled professionals in research, medicine, biotechnology, and neuroscience, Cuba generated several technology firms:

Softel, informatic solutions: http://www.softel.cu
Softcal, computer software design: http://www.softcal.cu
GET, electronic group for tourism: http://www.cubaweb.cu/teledatos/
ESI Network, a nationwide network of service firms
Centersoft, software trading: http://www.centersoft.cu
Neuronica, S.A., a joint venture dedicated to neuroscience and learning disabilities: http://www.neuronic-sa.com

Internet and E-commerce

Connectivity

Cuba's first connectivity to an international network began in 1991 with a UUCP link between the Center for Automated Interchange of Information of the Cuban Academy of Sciences (CENIAI) and Web/NIRV, an association for progressive communications affiliates in Toronto, Canada. By 1995 there were four networks with international UUCP links: CENIAI; CIGB, the Center for Genetic Engineering and Biotechnology; TinoRed, a network for nongovernmental organizations; and an X.25-based tourism network. International e-mail traffic was more than sixty thousand bytes per month, and more than 2,600 Cubans were using email. Cuba had many internal LANs, UUCP, and PPP links over telephone and X.25 connections, IP intranets, but no major international IP link.

In 1996 Cuba was officially connected to the World Wide Web. CENIAI, a Cuban state-owned firm, set a 64 kbs/sec bandwidth channel with Sprint, an American communication and ISP company. In this way, CENIAI became the first ISP in Cuba, allowing Internet access to Cuban-based firms, both foreign and national, offical institutions, and agencies on the island. This monopoly lasted only a few years until new ISPs entered the market, totalizing four first-level ISPs with a national coverage, and thus became CENIAI competitors: Teledatos, ColombusNet, and the former ETECSA's ISP, now ENET. Since then, other international channels have opened up with Europe and Canada.

E-commerce

Cuba's geographical position and lack of modern and efficient means of transportation, electronic payment systems, and communication systems represent a large impediment to e-commerce activities. To make things even more complicated, the Cuban Ministry of Foreign Investment and Economic Cooperation (MINVEC) restricts which economic sectors are approved for investment, and usually foreign investment is welcomed only in select business sectors that do not include retail sales. Obviously, by restricting foreign investment Cuba is missing out on the rapidly expanding e-commerce market. A look at Latin America shows how e-commerce revenues have grown steadily, from $109 million in 1999 to $580 million in 2000. Currently, a governmental e-commerce commission is attempting to clear regulatory hurdles to domestic business-to-business transactions and exports.

Cuban e-commerce started with Cubaweb (www.cubaweb.cu), a tourism Web site attracting foreign visitors and investment partners to Cuba. Cubaweb also expanded to Cuba's first e-commerce site by selling Cuban music CDs abroad. Payments were routed through a Canadian service, Internet Secure, Inc. (www.internetsecure.com), to avoid American embargo restrictions.

Most Cuban e-commerce Web sites are outward oriented, such as those for lodging, car rental, travel, and exporters of Cuban products. In fact, many sites now offer customers the ability to buy gifts for relatives and friends in Cuba just by visiting virtual stores such as CubaGiftStore (www.cubagiftstore.com), of DimensionW, and Precios Fijos (www.preciosfijos.com), of ICC Corp; customers can send money to Cuba through Quick Cash (http://quickcash.cubaweb.cu/ing/login.asp), Duales (www.duales.com), or Cash2Cuba (www.cash2cuba.com), and they can instantly call someone using Calls2Cuba (www.calls2cuba.com).

In the area of business-to-business sales, the most relevant initiatives are those of Tecun (http://tecun.cimex.cu), a computer hardware vendor of CIMEX Corporation, and Centro Comercial Web (www.ccw.cu), a vertical e-marketplace, now in exclusive use by Divep, a spare parts vendor.

When it comes to Cuban Internet portals, however, the list is quite extensive. Following are the most significant:

Cubanacan.cu, a portal of Cubanacan Corporation: www.cubanacan.cu
Cuba-Nic, a division of CITMATEL: www.nic.cu
Cuba's Chamber of Commerce: www.camaracuba.cu
CubaWeb: www.cubaweb.cu
Infomed, a telematic network of the Public Health Ministry: www.sld.cu
Islagrande.cu, of ColombusNet: www.islagrande.cu
Portal de Cuba: www.cuba.cu
Transnet, a specialized network of the transportation ministry: www.transnet.cu

Hardware Manufacturing

Cuba's hardware industry was initially concentrated in approximately one dozen plants under the auspices of INSAC. Between 1970 and 1980, the Cuban hardware industry developed a variety of products that were used internally but were mainly exported to member countries of the Council for Mutual Economic Assistance (COMECON). About three hundred minicomputers as well as thousands of asynchronous terminals were produced in this period.

The dissolution of the Soviet Union devastated the Cuban hardware industry. Prior to the Soviet collapse, Cuban industrial planners had developed a capacity expansion plan to increase output. Because the industry relied on export guarantees from COMECON nations, there was not much that could be done when the former Soviet

Union and its preferential trading arrangements with Cuba collapsed. Cuban industrial planners then changed their strategy and devoted themselves to luring foreign investment with the promise of inexpensive, well-educated Cuban labor.

Today, none of the major global hardware companies conduct business in Cuba. Although it has some limited production of hardware, exports are minimal, and Cuba is not recognized as a regional player in any hardware niche. It can be safely said that Cuban pundits see software development, not hardware, as the future of information technology in the country.

Software Manufacturing: "SWOT Analysis"

The following strengths, weaknesses, opportunities, and threats (SWOT) analysis may be helpful in analyzing the main features of the Cuban information technology industry:

Strengths

The Cuban population is one of the most educated among developing nations
Labor costs are lower than for most software developing countries
Cuba is already recognized as a regional leader in biotechnology
The Cuban government is fostering FDI

Weaknesses

Inadequate domestic IT/telecommunications infrastructure
Price and availability of Internet technology and services
Minimal IT growth in the domestic marketplace

Opportunities

Poor IT infrastructure provides growth opportunities for wireless technologies
Market penetration of PCs in the home and business sectors is very low

Threats

High piracy rates/lack of value ascribed to software development
Cuba's inability to attract foreign aid and FDI
International political sanctions

IT Labor Market

Cuba has one of the best-educated workforces in the Caribbean and Latin America. All Cuban citizens are provided with a free education, from elementary school through university training. Accordingly, Cuba boasts one of the highest literacy rates in the Caribbean and Latin American region. Using a definition of literacy as individuals over age fifteen who can read and write, 95.7 percent of Cubans are literate. At the same time, Cuba has the most highly educated population in the Caribbean and Latin American region. Cuba has forty-seven universities, each with dedicated IT departments. For each one hundred inhabitants, there are five citizens with a college degree and more than twelve technicians. It is estimated that there are thirty thousand people linked to computer/software activities.

The average wage is 280 cuban pesos in state-owned firms, nearly U.S.$10.77 (26 Cuban pesos = U.S.$1) for IT professionals; however, in free trade zones, wages range from U.S.$100 to U.S.$300 monthly, plus the tax levied to these firms by the concessionaire. These taxes are sometimes fivefold the "plus" these foreign firms usually pay to their Cuban employees.

National Software Development Initiatives

Within the informatics sector, the Cuban government's industrial policy is to make Cuba a software engineering and development center. Cuba has several key potential advantages. First, Cuba currently has an oversupply of university graduates with few IT opportunities beyond state-sponsored organizations. International organizations can obtain inexpensive development and programming labor through the Cuban IT workforce. Joint venture or FDI projects will provide a technology transfer into Cuba while giving Cuba international exposure in the global software industry. Most important, FDI ventures would require minimal initial capital requirements, making Cuban opportunities more lucrative.

The Cuban government plans to develop this programmer base in university IT departments and hone their skills with development groups in universities and in research and development centers such as the Laboratory of Artificial Intelligence and the Institute of Cybernetics, Mathematics, and Physics. A ground-level youth initiative has been launched through the Communist Youth Union, which has opened more than 170 computer clubs islandwide, with more than 1,250 microcomputers, 290 printers, and 160 modems. In 2000 the Informatics and Communication Ministry was created by a merger of the National Institute for Automated Systems and Computer Technology (INSAC) and the former Ministry of Communication. One of the main missions of this new organization is the promotion of Cuba as an IT Society.

The latest addition to Cuba's IT development plan is the Computer Science University (Universidad de las Ciencias de la Informatica), opened in 2002. Located in the former radio-electronic surveillance Russian base of Lourdes, the university has been supported by the ICM and the High Education Ministry.

Opportunities in Cuban Software Manufacturing

Joint ventures with Cuba allow foreign companies to penetrate the Latin and Caribbean market. Cuba does have a potential advantage in creating Spanish software. Most software products for the office, home, and educational sector in Latin America are currently produced in English. Should Cuba develop a variety of Spanish application software packages, it may obtain a significant advantage.

Outsourcing Services

Although Cuba's IT population is small, the country has been focusing on expanding its computer science and engineering programs. Two Cuban high-tech companies (Centersoft Corporation and Datacimex, the software division of Cimex Corporation), have paired up with two Canadian software companies (Sentai Software Corporation and Indcom Trading Company) to create an international software consortium called CubaSoft Solutions Inc. (www.cubasoft.com). This enterprise aims to recruit Cuban IT talent to Canadian software companies while undertaking IT development projects for both Cuban and Canadian companies.

Statistics

Paradoxically, in the era of information and technology, researchers in Cuba face inmense obstacles while searching for information. Cubanic (www.nic.cu), a division of CITMATEL, not only has control over the ".cu" domain registration but also gathers and delivers all cuban-related information over the Internet. Such delivery, however, seldom occurs. Therefore, the figures presented in table 9.1 stem from an unofficial source in the ICM, and all belong to those firms associated within the ITG of this ministry in 2001. There are software developer firms and hardware suppliers

Table 9.1 Estimated Value of Output, Cuban Informatics Industry, 1996–2001

Currency	1996	1997	1998	1999	2000	2001
Cuban peso sales	8,642.3	16,439.9	21,955.5	25,502.3		61,599.3
U.S. dollar sales, domestic market	1,970.4	3,211.8	4,484.6	8,554.7	11,190.9	37,744.8
U.S. dollar sales, exports	931.6	4,484.6	3,878.9	2,788.4	2,909.6	9,023.8
Total sales in U.S. dollars	2,902.0	3,878.9	8,363.5	11,343.1	14,100.5	46,768.6

Source: Informatics and Communications Ministry

Note: The total sales in U.S. dollars figures entirely exclude the sales in Cuban pesos due to the difficulty of knowing a realistic exchange rate for the conversion.

scattered among the rest of ministries and in free trade zones from which neither economic nor financial information is available.

Some conclusions arise from these figures. A significant expansion in both the domestic market and in exporting activities may be observed. The maximum growth rates occurred in 2000 and 2001 in both domestic marketplace and in exports (141.54 percent in CUP, 237.28 percent in USD-F and 210.14 percent in USD-E). Although the trend is clearly upward, it is impossible to know whether the growth is caused by hardware or software production.

Conclusion

It is important to underline the expertise in software development Cuba has accrued through years of research in fields such as medicine and biotechnology, which can be translated into the welfare and recovery of the national economy. However, it is not clear whether combining highly skilled workers with low wages is a comparative advantage at all. Fiscal policies such as a gradual liberalization of the IT labor market, especially in free trade zones and joint ventures, must be implemented to entice potential investors to take advantage of Cuba's highly qualified labor force. At the same time, the Cuban economy will benefit from technology transfer and launching to global markets. There is no doubt that Cuba has the potential to become a global player in its own right. Focus and goodwill are what is needed.

References

Bomkamp, Dana, and Maria Soler. 2000. *Information Technology in Cuba.* Washington, D.C.: American University.

Cuba Economic News at http://www.cubabiz.com/.

International Trade Center. 2001. "The Key to Ecommerce: A Guideline for Small and Medium-Size Exporters." At http://www.intracen.org.

Lage, Carlos. 1998. "Como acceder a Internet en Cuba?" Speech given at Internet seminar, 17 June 1996, Editora Política, Havana, Cuba.

Lapper, Richard. 2000. "For Now, a Story of Mixed Fortunes." FinancialTimes.com, 1 November, at http://www.financialtimes.com/.

"Los joven clubs, una entidad de nuevo tipo en la comunidad." 1999. *Analisis de coyuntura,* no. 7 (July).

Pedroso Gutierrez, Orlando. 1982. "Introducción y desarrollo de las tecnicas de computacion en Cuba: Situación actual y perspectivas." *CID Magazine: Electronics and Dataprocessing in Cuba* 1, no. 4.

UN Development Programme (UNDP). 1997. *Human Development Report 1997.* New York: Oxford University Press.

Van Straaten, Tess. 1998. "Cuba a Prolific Source of IT Staff, Projects." *Ottawa Citizen,* 30 November.

PART V

Labor and Society

CHAPTER 10

The Macroeconomics of Social Security Finance

María Cristina Sabourin Jovel

After the triumph of the Cuban revolution, taxes, prices, and fiscal budget did not play important roles in the overall coordination in the Cuban economy. In fact, the 998th and 1,213th laws of 1962 and 1967 significantly reduced their importance. Since then, taxation and the budgetary system have been subordinated to other economic policies.

In Cuba, the state is not only the main taxpayer, but it is also the economic agent that spends the most. There is no balance between different sources of revenues within the tax system. Not until 1977 was the importance of the economic analysis and monitoring of the fiscal budget legally established. Finally, in 1981, with decree-law 44, government revenues and the government's fiscal budget were explicitly considered. Still, Cuban taxation was mainly a transfer of resources between different government accounts, closely monitored by the corresponding authorities.

The preexisting fiscal imbalance was in fact amplified by the economic crisis of the nineties commonly known as the Special Period in Time of Peace, when Cuba lost its special partnership with the former Soviet Union and the socialist system. After 1990, a sharp decrease was observed in the real GDP up to 34.8 percent in relation to 1989. The GDP has not yet recovered its 1989 levels.

Budget revenues since 1991 have been fairly unstable and moved around 62 percent of GDP. More significant for this analysis is the fact that government revenues seriously decreased during the Special Period in Time of Peace. A discrete recovery occurred in 1994 because of a new approach to financial policy and changes in the relationship between enterprises. In 1998 government revenues reached 1989 levels. Fiscal expenditures, on the other hand, were stable during the 1990s economic crisis following government intention of not using social programs in the adjustment process. As a result, the budget imbalance reached up to 36 percent of GDP in 1993. This deficit was financed by printing money. Achieving the financial health of the public sector is fundamental in the Cuba's current struggle to maintain past social achievements and raise efficiency in the allocation of the scarce resources.

Cuba is currently involved in reforming its tax system and recovering its fiscal health. In fact, the government budget deficit has been steadily decreasing since 1993. First, a discrete decrease in fiscal expenditures occurred due to changes in the demographic structure of Cuban society and the 1990s economic crisis. Second, tax revenues have increased due to the following measures: drastic reduction in deficit of public enterprises since 1994, decrease in government subsidies to unprofitable public enterprises, encouragement of public sector sales, and price increase of nonessential goods. All these measures play a significant role in a balanced budget. Transfers to unprofitable public enterprises are a major factor in this struggle. However, as a rule the importance of a financially balanced social security system has been ignored.

This chapter presents a diagnosis of the Cuban social security regimen, with particular emphasis on the analysis of its financial balance and economic sustainability within the budget system from a macroeconomic perspective. For that purpose, the focus here will be on the relation between its programmatic variables and the main macroeconomic aggregates, not on its actuarial equilibrium.

Cuba has a social security system with universal coverage that redistributes adequate benefits with respect to wage levels. This system is confronted with serious financial and actuarial disequilibrium, which calls for an immediate reform. A fundamental part of the existing deficit is actuarial in nature. In addition, the aging of the Cuban population and the significant reduction in the fertility rate point toward further increase in the old-age dependency ratio. On the other hand, the Cuban social security system initially covered only a fraction of the working population, but over the past forty years the coverage has been widely extended. The Cuban social security system could not have maintained such levels of benefits without significant government transfers. Since 1989 the Cuban social security deficit has represented more than 60 percent of revenues. This system should have doubled its revenues in 1992 in order to meet its requirements. The fact that multiple benefits are freely granted to the Cuban population without consideration of its financial effect is also contributing to this upward trend. A balanced social security system would greatly contribute to the financial health of the public sector.

Cuba's Public Sector

The importance of the public sector in economic development is particularly significant for a country where public enterprises account for the majority of the country's production. Cuba has a large public sector, where the state controls investment decisions to try to ensure both economic and social growth.

The Cuban government has local and central levels of power. Currently, Cuba has thirty-two organizations of central administration, including twenty-seven ministries. Local administration includes municipal and provincial levels, as well as all subordinated enterprises and administrative entities. The Cuban government budget includes an estimate of all financial expenditures and revenues for the specific year, as well as a reserve fund for unexpected expenditures. It is approved annually by the National Assembly of People's Power, and it is formulated, administrated, and controlled by the Ministry of Finances and Prices, taking into account provincial and municipal needs in terms of economic and social development. Revenues and expenditures appear separately in it, and their imbalance is not considered. The state totally assumes the resulting deficit. Central, local, and social security resources are accounted for in separate budgets. The central budget expenditures are directed toward economic, social, scientific, and cultural development at the national level, as well as defense, police, internal order, and justice departments. The provincial budget includes the revenues and expenditures of the provincial and municipal levels of the People's Power Organization. The social security budget is independent of the aforementioned budget.

Since 1992 many institutional reforms have been established, including new laws for foreign investment and the financial system, liberalization of agricultural production and its commercialization, revitalization of self-employment, legalization of possession of foreign currency by Cuban citizens, introduction of a government-controlled dual market, and the shrinkage of government administration structure.[1]

Cuba's Social Security System

Since 1980 the Cuban social security system has consisted of a social security regime, a social assistance regime, and five special regimens for the self-employed, artists, agriculture workers, armed forces, and internal order personnel. This system protects all individuals in need, as well as workers and their families. Its benefits include monetary, free in-kind services, and community and work programs. Special laws are in place for maternity protection, surviving dependants, and total and partial disability. Medical assistance is provided free of charge to all Cubans. (See the appendix.) The analysis in this chapter focuses on the old-age pension system.

Cuba has a pay-as-you-go system with universal coverage financed with payroll taxes and general revenues. Since 1992 employers have been contributing 14 percent of their total payroll to the government budget for social security,[2] which is insufficient to cover the system's outlays. This contribution rate is set each year in the budget law, and it is used to finance retirement and disability pensions, as well as compensations for maternity leave, unemployment, accidents, and illness. The equilibrium level in the current system is between 14 and 22 percent. There are no explicit workers' contributions.

The financial equilibrium in the Cuban social security system, contrary to pay-as-you-go systems elsewhere, is highly dependent on fiscal transfers. The fiscal budget totally finances any social security deficits.

Social security contributions decreased in 1990–92 and 1993–94 as a result of a sharp fall in the general wage level, which depends on the number of workers in the formal and informal economy and self-employment, as well as the level of monthly wages.[3] All these variables were seriously affected by the economic crisis of the 1990s. The increase in social security contributions in 1993 was mainly the result of an expanded contribution rate to the social security regime from 8 percent to 12 percent, and not of economic recovery of the Cuban economy. A special worker's contribution has been established in principal in the new tax law. Still, taxable base and tax rates have not been determined yet, mainly for political reasons, as well as for the "subsistence" character of Cuban wages and salaries.

Fiscal Expenditures and the Social Security System

Since 1959 social security expenditures have increased rapidly. In fact, in 1958 they represented 6 percent of the GDP, which quickly increased to 12.2 percent in 1971. From 1975 to 1980 these expenditures oscillated around 9 percent to 10 percent of the GDP. An analysis of government expenditures in table 10.1 reveals a structural change in the 1990s. The transformation in the relative importance of social security, education, and health care expenditures, as a percentage of the GDP, result from changes in economic and social strategies and demographics variables. As the age structure changes, the needs in terms of social expenditures also change.[4]

As shown in table 10.1, social security spending is currently the most significant expenditure of budgetary activity. The high growth rate of the social security system expenditures is due fundamentally to the system's generosity, the growing rate of beneficiaries, and the increasing life expectancy after retirement age. Spending in the form of transfers to unprofitable public enterprises is currently ranked second among government expenditures, accounting for 11 percent of total fiscal spending. It is important, however, to notice that this segment of the budget is experiencing a diminishing trend because measures have been taken in order to raise the efficiency of the public business sector.

On the other hand, the large sums that were invested in education to cope with the baby-boom generation are no longer necessary, as the population growth rate in the zero-to-fourteen age range drastically declines.[5] Therefore, the sums needed in matter of preschool, elementary, and secondary education, which account for over 80 percent of total spending in education, are now lower. However, the recent reform in the wage policy of this sector has put an upward pressure on the education expenditures.

Expenditures on health show a recent discrete upward trend, due to the increase in wages, emphasis on preventive medicine, reduction in hospitalization time, improvement in hospital services, and organizational efficiency, along with a lack of medical supplies, have somewhat balanced this increase in wages.

Social security expenditures have not been affected, at least in nominal terms, during the current economic crisis. Contrary to what occurs in most Latin American countries, Cuban social security spending behaves contra-cyclically. This implies that alongside the growing importance of social spending, there is a strong tendency toward imbalance, which affects basic macroeconomic equilibrium and delays recovery. In cases of instability in fiscal balance, it is very common to use social spending as an adjustment factor. This indicates that more priority is usually given to fiscal adjustment than to the compensation of income. This did not happen in Cuba.

An increase in social security spending up to 9.6 percent of the GDP occurred 1993, which resulted from the diminishing GDP since 1991 and the systematic increase in social security system outlays. If one were to include health care spending, this figure would reach 12 percent of the GDP. The Cuban social security system, with a mature, universal, generous system, represents a growing burden for the Cuban economy.[6] The weight of 7 percent of GDP tends to be very heavy.

Fiscal Revenues and the Social Security System

Budget revenues sharply diminished from 1990 onward, showing some recovery starting in 1994, as shown in table 10.2. This recovery can partially be explained by the efforts undertaken toward a balanced budget, such as encouraging public sector sales and price increases in selected nonessential goods.

The Cuban economic crisis reduced the total value of wage payments, which led to the reduction of social security contributions during 1990–94. As mentioned, the increase in 1993 is mostly due to an expanded contribution rate (from 8 percent to 12 percent), rather than revival of the wage volume. Note that the social security revenues are closely related to the behavior and restructuring of the labor force, which includes the number of active workers, their productivity, and the number of workers in the informal and independent sectors, all of which are reflected in the total volume of wages.

Analyzing the structure of fiscal revenues, it becomes evident that social security contribution is insufficient to cover current commitments of the regime. Again, these

Table 10.1 Fiscal Expenditures in Major Social Programs
(in Millions of Cuban Pesos, Current Prices)

Expenditures Items	1989	1990	1991	1992	1993	1994	1995	1996	1997	1998	1999	2000	2001
Fiscal expenditures (FE)	13,904	15,482	14,714	15,048	14,566	14,178	13,809	12,692	12,622	13,062	13,149	14,195	14,505
FE growth rate (%)		11.3	–5.0	2.3	–3.2	–2.7	–2.6	–8.1	–0.2	2.9	2.7	11.1	–2.7
SSS expenditures (SSE)	1,093	1,164	1,225	1,348	1,452	1,532	1,594	1,653	1,636	1,705	1,786	1,800	1,845
SSE growth rate (%)		6.5	5.2	10.0	7.7	5.5	4.0	3.7	–1.0	3.1	4.8	0.8	2.5
SSE/FE (%)	7.9	7.5	8.3	9.0	10.0	10.8	11.5	13.0	12.9	13.1	13.3	12.1	12.7
Education expenditures (EdE)	1,651	1,616	1,504	1,488	1,385	1,334	1,359	1,430	1,454	1,510	1,830	2,125	2,360
EdE/FE (%)	11.9	10.4	10.2	9.9	9.5	9.4	9.8	11.3	11.5	11.6	13.6	14.2	16.3
Health care expenditures (HCE)	904	925	925	977	1,077	1,061	1,108	1,210	1,265	1,344	1,553	1,732	1,815
HCE/FE (%)	6.5	6.0	6.3	6.5	7.4	7.5	8.0	9.5	10.0	10.3	11.6	11.6	12.5
Welfare program expenditures (WE)						94	119	146	135	145	158	187	200
WE/FE (%)						0.7	0.9	1.2	8.3	1.1	8.8	10.4	10.8
SSE+HCE+WE+Ede	3,648	3,705	3,654	3,813	3,914	4,021	4,180	4,439	4,490	4,704	5,327	5,844	6,220
(SSE+HCE+WE)/FE (%)	26.2	23.9	24.8	25.3	26.9	28.4	30.3	35.0	35.5	36.0	39.7	39.2	42.9
Fiscal Transfer to enterprises (FTr)	2,653.2	2,975.3	3,882	4,889	5,434	3,447	1,803	1,400	1,350	1,139	770	588	280
FTr/FE (%)	19.1	19.2	26.4	32.5	37.3	24.3	13.1	11.0	10.7	8.7	5.7	3.9	1.9

Sources: Informe del Banco Nacional (1994, 1995); MFP (1989–2001); ONE (1985–2000); Ministerio de Economia (1991–2000).

Table 10.2 Fiscal Revenues Structure and Social Security System
(in Millions of Cuban Pesos)

	1989	1990	1991	1992	1993	1994	1995	1996	1997	1998	1999	2000
Total Fiscal Revenues (FR)	12,509	13,524	10,949	10,179	9,516	12,757	13,043	12,243	12,204	12,502	13,419	14,915
SSS contribution (SSC)	663	692	666	673	925	880	898	972	1,071	1,025	1,115.4	1,181.2
SSC/FR (%)	5.3	5.1	6.1	6.6	9.7	6.9	6.9	8.0	8.7	8.2	8.3	7.91
Sales tax* (ST)	5,138	5,017	3,979	3,736	3,310	5,097	5,684	5,164	4,876	5,076	5,786	6,131
ST/FR (%)	41.1	37.1	36.3	36.7	34.8	40.0	43.6	42.6	40.0	40.6	43.1	41.1
Tax on public services	409.2	425.6	417.2	367.5	301	498	481	434	454	467	550	602
TPS/FR (%)	3.3	3.1	3.8	3.6	3.2	3.9	3.7	3.5	3.7	3.7	4.1	4.0
Contribution on profits (CP)	1,887.9	1,404.3	1,066.4	1,193.2	1,399.9	1,864.6	1,556.5	2,156	2,684	1,908	1,515	1,553
CP/FR (%)	15.1	10.4	9.7	11.7	14.7	14.6	11.9	17.8	21.5	15.3	11.3	10.4

*Sales tax includes old circulation tax.
Sources: Informe del Banco (1994, 1995); MFP (1989–2001); ONE (1985–2000); Ministerio de Economía (1991–2000).

outlays increase substantially if one includes expenditures on health. The expenditures-revenues imbalance in this sector becomes larger. Furthermore, their difference is totally covered by the government budget to the detriment of its fiscal health.

Since the mid-seventies, there has been a gradual increase of the social security system deficit. This structural problem has been present since the system's inception. In fact, the deficit of social security represented almost half of the revenues of the system in 1980. The growth rate of expenditures is superior to that of revenues at all times.

Table 10.3 illustrates that the social security deficit diminished only momentarily in 1992 after the increase of the contribution rate. At the present time, as much as 40 percent of this system's expenditures were being covered by the fiscal budget, leaving Cuba with an enormous budget deficit, affecting the amount of resources dedicated to other social programs.

The social security deficit represents close to 5 percent of total budget spending, which is significantly high in comparison to other areas. Moreover, in 1996 social security deficit reached almost 3 percent of GDP, which represents a greater percentage than the fiscal deficit itself. In fact, almost 6 percent of budget revenues are directed solely to cover the social security deficit.

The social security deficit was less than the public enterprises deficit up to 1994, when the latter decreased drastically.[7] A transformation occurred in the structure of the fiscal deficit such that social security became the most important component of the budget. In 1996 the deficit of this system was larger than the fiscal deficit, as shown in table 10.3. This resulted from an unfavorable evolution of total wage volume, GDP, the aging of the population, and the drastic reduction of the fiscal deficit.

Table 10.3 Fiscal Deficit Structure in Cuba
(in Millions of Cuban Pesos)

	1986	1989	1990	1991	1992	1993	1994	1995	1996	1997	1998	1999	2000	2001
SSS expenditures (SSE)	896	1,093	1,164	1,225	1,348	1,452	1,532	1,594	1,653	1,636	1,705	1,786	1,786	1,845
SSE growth rate (%)		22.0	6.5	5.2	10.0	7.7	5.5	4.0	3.7	–1.0	3.1	4.8	0.8	2.5
SSS revenues (SSR)	601	663	692	666	673	925	880	898	972	1,070	1,025	1,115	1,181	1,240
SSR growth rate (%)		10.3	4.3	–3.6	0.9	37.5	–4.8	2.0	8.2	10.1	5.5	8.7	5.9	5.0
SSS deficit (SSSDef)	295	430	473	559	676	527	652	696	681	565	680	670.3	604.4	610.5
SSR/SSE (%)	67.1	60.7	59.4	54.4	49.9	63.7	57.5	56.3	58.8	65.4	60.1	62.4	66.1	67.2
SSSDef/SSR (%)	49.1	64.8	68.3	83.9	100.4	57.0	74.1	77.5	70.1	52.8	66.3	60.1	51.2	49.2
Fiscal deficit and SSS														
Fiscal deficit (FDef)		1,403	1,958	3,764	4,869	5,051	1,421	766	569	570.7	560	611.7	745	672.2
SSSDef/FDef (%)		30.6	24.1	14.8	13.9	10.4	45.9	90.9	119.7	123.1	121.4	109.5	81.1	90.8

Sources: Informe del Banco Nacional (1994, 1995); MFP (1989–2001); ONE (1985–2000); Ministerio de Economía (1991–2000).

In fact, Cuba is devoting between 8 percent and 13 percent of fiscal budget expenditures to cover the costs of the social security regime.

For any social security system confronted with a high dependency rate, constant benefits, and contributions, as is Cuba's, pensions can only be maintained if real wages are capable of compensating for the changes in the worker-pensioner relation. A growth in real wages, which in turn implies growth in productive jobs, is necessary in Cuba, given the tenuous worker-pensioner ratio. Such growth has not occurred in the period under study.

Conclusion

An analysis of the Cuban social security system reveals a serious financial and actuarial imbalance, which has an adverse effect in key macroeconomic variables. The validity of universal social security policy is undeniable from a social perspective. However, under the current conditions, such a policy is not sustainable in the long run.

Currently, the social security deficit accounts for 2.2 percent of the GDP, which represents a heavy burden for Cuba. There is a great controversy over which type of financing should be used. No consensus exists on this issue. A simple simulation model shows a serious actuarial and financial imbalance in the Cuban social security system. If Cuban birth rates remain low and life expectancy remains high, the expected level of contributions from the working population twenty years from now will be drastically lower than the expected future system's obligations.

Given that productivity has declined and that the birth rate and life longevity have increased, if the current contribution is kept constant, benefits will necessarily decrease. On the other hand, if benefits are kept constant, the contribution rate must increase. There is a necessity of alternative ways of financing for this system. The long run viability of this system depends on whether or not this regime would be connected with capital markets, aiming at the capitalization of its funds, independently from the financing system used. However, the introduction of capital markets is not viable in the short run.

The financial viability of the social security system poses a serious economic and political dilemma. Any proposed solution must involve a careful balancing out of the efficiency-equity trade off. In order to ensure the future viability of this system, the retirement age should be adjusted upward, gradually increasing up to sixty (for women) and sixty-five for men, and perhaps incentives to postpone retirement should be introduced.

A gradual introduction of tighter eligibility standards must be considered, as well as an increase in employers' contributions up to 25 percent or 30 percent, in order to have a small surplus with the objective of creating a reserve fund for contingencies and of easing the burden on the budget. This reserve fund could be invested in low-risk international markets given the lack of domestic financial markets.

The Cuban government is not in a position to introduce a general employees' contribution, but this may be possible for workers with high incomes, specifically the ones working in joint ventures, tourism, and any other sector where they earn foreign currency. A fully funded system is not viable in the short run given the lack of adequate financial institutions. However, it is feasible to establish a system of multiple pillars, or one of its variants, with a second tier that complements the reformed pension public system.

Appendix: Main Characteristics of the Cuban Social Security System

Program Specific
Mature system
Ordinary retirement age: fifty-five for women and sixty for men
Twenty-five years of service for standard eligibility
Benefits independent on contribution levels
Adequate benefits in relation to wages (in nominal terms)
No reserve fund
Average nominal retirement pension 2000: $117.81
Average nominal wage 2000: $234.00
Social security deficit represented 2.19 percent of the GDP and 89.9 percent of the fiscal deficit in 2000
Equilibrium contribution rate: higher than 22 percent since 1996; this rate is expected to be 33 percent in 2010.
Demographic
Change in the age structure of the Cuban population
High life expectancy at birth: seventy-five years in 2001
High percentage of elderly population (14.3 percent of total population in 2000, in 2015 expected value of 18.5 percent, in 2030, 31 percent)
Increasing life expectancy after retirement: 26 years for women (22 after 60 years) and 19.5 years for men
Low annual rate of population growth: 3.3 in 2000; negative rates are expected for 2030
Low birth rates: 12.8 per thousand of inhabitants in 2000
Fertility rate has been below the natural replacement rate since 1978 (0.76 in 2000)
High old-age dependency ratio: 3.1 workers per pensioners in 2000

Notes

To Lázaro Villegas Heredia for his advice, comments, infinite dedication, support, and understanding. To my professors Frances Woolley, Archibald Ritter, Carlos Monasterio, and Ricardo Paes de Barros for introducing me to the fascinating world of market economics. Thank you for all your support and encouragement.

1. Supermarkets, cafeterias, restaurants, and many other services are now available for Cuban citizens as long as they pay in American dollars.

2. The rates are 12 percent for long-term assistance and 2 percent for short-term assistance

3. In Cuba, wages are calculated monthly, not hourly.

4. As the birth rate has fallen, the average woman has had fewer than two children, while her life span has increased.

5. For 1960–90 the population growth rate was 0.03 percent.

6. Contributions are generous with respect to salaries, in nominal terms.

7. Public enterprises deficit: deficit that results from the fiscal subsidies to public enterprises' net of profits contributions.

References

Alonso, J., R. Donate-Armada, and A. Lago. 1994. "A First Approximation Design of the Social Safety Net for a Democratic Cuba." *Cuba in Transition* 4.

Anuario demográfico Cuba. 1995.

Anuarios demográfico mundial. 1994.

Banco Nacional de Cuba, Informe. 1994, 1995. La Habana, Cuba.

Bonilla Garcia, Alejandro, and Alfredo H. Conte-Grand. 1998. "Pensiones en América Latina: Dos décadas de reforma." OIT.

Buttari, Juan. 1999. "The Labor Market and Retirement Pensions in Cuba during the Transition: Reflection on the Social Safety Net Experience of Former Socialist Economies."

Comisión Económica de America Latina (CEPAL). 1994a. *Panorama social de América Latina.* Mexico, D.F.: CEPAL.

______. 1994b. *Transformación económica de América Latina y el Caribe.* Mexico, D.F.: CEPAL.

______. 1997. *Reformas estructurales y desempeño en los noventa.* Mexico D.F.: CEPAL.

De Paula Gutiérrez, Francisco. 1994. "Qué nos indican los indicadores económicos?" *INCAE* 2.

Dirmoser, Dietmar, and Jaime Estay. 1997. "Economía y reforma económica en Cuba." *Nueva sociedad.*

Donate-Armada, Ricardo. 1994. "Cuban Social Security: A Preliminary Actuarial Analysis of Law #24 of Social Security. *Cuba in Transition* 4.

UN Economic Commission for Latin America and the Caribbean (UNECLAC). 1997. *The Cuban Economy in the Nineties: Structural Reform and Economic Performance.* Mexico, D.F.: UNECLAC.

Gallagher, Mark. 1999. "Some Ideas for Taxation during Cuba's Transition." *Cuba in Transition* 9.

Ghandi, Ved P., and Mihaljek Dubravko. 1992. "Scope for Reform of Socialist Tax System." In *Fiscal Policies in Economies in Transition,* edited by Vito Tanzi.

IMF. 1999. "Taxation in Latin America: Structural Trends and Impact on Administration." Working paper.

Informe Banco Nacional. 1994. Havana, Cuba.

______. 1995. Havana, Cuba.

Kotlikoff, Laurence J. 2000. "The Right and Wrong Ways to Reform Pensions in Russia."

Leiva, Aldo M. 2000. "Cuban Labor Law: Issues and Challenges." *Cuba in Transition* 10.

Manual de Cuentas Nacionales. 3d ed. ONU.

Mesa-Lago, Carmelo. 1996. "La seguridad social y la pobreza en Cuba." In *La seguridad social en América Latina: Seis experiencias diferentes.* CIEDLA.

______. 1997. *Modelos alternativos de la reforma de la seguridad social en América Latina: Comparación y evaluación.* Riedrich Ebert Stiftung.

______. 1998. "The Cuban Economy in 1997–98: Performance and Policies." *Cuba in Transition* 8.

______. 2000a. *Desarrollo social, reforma del estado y de la seguridad social, al umbral del siglo XXI.* Serie políticas socials. Mexico, D.F.: CEPAL.

______. 2000b. *Estudio comparativo de los costos fiscals en la transición de ocho reformas de pensiones in América Latina.* Serie financiamiento del desarrollo 93. Mexico, D.F.: CEPAL.

Ministerio de Economía. 1991–2000.

Ministerio de Finanzas y Precios (MFP). 1989–2001. *Presupuesto del estado.*

Ministerio de Trabajo y Seguridad Social. 2000. "La Seguridad Social en Cuba: boletín estadístico."

Oficina Nacional de Estadística (ONE). 1985–2000. *Anuarios estadísticos de Cuba.*

Perez, Lorenzo. 1998. "The Pension System of Cuba: The Current Situation and Implications of International Pension Reform Experiences for Addressing Cuba's Problem." *Cuba in Transition* 8.

Pérez-López, Jorge. 1992. *The Cuban State Budget: Concepts and Measurements.* Miami: University of Miami, Research Institute for Cuban Studies.

Quintana, Didio. 1995. *La seguridad social y la distribución de los ingresos en Cuba: Un enfoque para la situación actual.*

Roqué, Diego R. 1998. "Actuarial Model of the Impact of Linking Economic Variables to a Life Survival Function." *Cuba in Transition.*

Sabourin, María Cristina. 1996. "El régimen de seguridad social en Cuba." IPEA, IBGE.

Uthoff, Andras. "Reformas a los sistemas de pensiones en América Latina y el Caribe." Mexico, D.F.: CEPAL.

World Bank. 1994. *Averting the Old Age Crisis: Policies to Protect the Old and Promote Growth.* Washington, DC.

CHAPTER 11

Corruption and the Cuban Transition

Jorge F. Pérez-López

Corruption, the misuse of public property for private gain, is as old as government itself. Kautilya, chief minister to the king in ancient India, wrote in the fourth century B.C. in his *Arthasastra*: "Just as it is impossible not to take the honey (or the poison) that finds itself at the tip of the tongue, so it is impossible for a government servant not to eat up at least a bit of the King's revenue. Just as fish moving under water cannot possibly be found out either as drinking or not drinking water, so government servants employed in the government cannot be found out (while) taking money (for themselves)" (quoted in Bardhan 1997, 1320).

Other references to corruption in ancient times abound. Klitgaard (1988, 7), for example, refers to the writing some 2,300 years ago of the Brahman prime minister of Chandragupta listing at least forty ways of embezzling money from the government; to the practice in ancient China of giving an extra allowance to government officials called Yang-lien, meaning "nourish incorruptness" (the practice apparently often failed to prevent corruption); to Abdul Rahman Ibn Khaldun's writings in the fourteenth century asserting that the root of corruption was "the passion for luxurious living within the ruling group"; and to Plato's discussion of bribery in *The Laws:* "The servants of the nation are to render their services without any taking of presents. . . . To form your judgment and then abide by it is no easy task, and it's a man's surest course to give loyal obedience to the law which commands, 'Do no service for a present.'"

The 1990s have witnessed what Moisés Naím (1995) calls a global "corruption eruption": allegations of systematic and generalized corruption brought down several heads of state, cabinet ministers, and legislators. These allegations of corruption have touched every region of the world, regardless of cultural background, economic system, or level of development. In Brazil and Venezuela, democratically elected presidents were impeached following accusations of corruption. Three ministers in India were accused of corruption and resigned in disgrace. A Japanese prime minister resigned following charges that he had mismanaged public funds. And an Italian prime minister was toppled after being targeted by a corruption investigation conducted by a group of prosecutors subsequently investigated for similar improprieties (Rico and Salas 1996, 39; Naím 1995, 246; see also Johnston 1997 and Celarier 1996). In March 1999, the twenty-member European Commission, including President Jacques Santer, resigned en masse, stung by a report of independent experts that accused the commissioners of chronic cronyism and corruption (Whitney 1999).

Has there been a quantum increase in corruption around the world? Why the increased attention focused on corruption? The inherent difficulties in measuring the degree of corruption—either at a point in time or over time—make it impossible to assert unequivocally that corruption is more prevalent today than in the past. Tanzi's (1998, 560–64) tentative conclusion seems reasonable: the current interest in corruption probably reflects an increase in the scope of the phenomenon—because of an increase in recent decades in the role of the government in national economies, the growth of international trade and business that has created more situations for the payments of "commissions" (bribes), and privatization of state-owned property—and not just a greater awareness of an age-old problem.

What is clear, however, is that corruption has been recognized as a development issue. Moreover, there is a willingness on the part of public officials in developing countries to discuss openly the problem of corruption and its effects. Reportedly, in a survey of more than 150 high-ranking public officials and key members of civil society from more than sixty developing countries, the respondents ranked public sector corruption as the most severe impediment to development and growth in their countries (Gray and Kaufmann 1998, 7). Corruption has also been recognized by the World Bank and the International Monetary Fund (IMF) as an impediment to development. Thus, the IMF's Guidelines on Governance reflect the consensus within that organization on the importance of good governance, including the avoidance of corrupt practices, for economic efficiency and growth (IMF 1997).

This chapter is a preliminary exploration of issues surrounding corruption in Cuba's transition to a market economy. The emphasis is on economic-related corruption issues, as opposed to those that are more focused on the political realm, although all forms of corruption issues are related.

The Economics of Corruption

The potential for corruption exists whenever a public official has discretionary power over distribution to the private sector of a benefit or a cost (Rose-Ackerman

1997, 31). Private individuals or firms are willing to pay bribes to obtain these benefits or avoid costs.

National, state, and local governments buy and sell goods, distribute subsidies, organize privatization of firms, and provide concessions. Individuals or firms may pay off government officials to be included in the list of bidders for a project, to be selected as the winning bidder, or to charge a higher price or deliver goods or services of lower quality than contracted. They may also pay bribes to obtain goods sold by the state at lower prices or subject to more convenient delivery schedules, to obtain access to credit or to foreign exchange, or to obtain a subsidy. Privatization of government-owned enterprises is conceptually similar to tendering for a large infrastructure project, and therefore it creates the same potential for corruption.

National, state, and local governments also enforce rules and regulations, levy taxes, and enforce criminal laws. In performing these functions, governments can impose costs selectively and therefore affect the competitive position of firms in an industry. Individuals or firms may pay to get a favorable interpretation of rules and regulations, pay lower taxes (for example, through a lower tax assessment) or import duties (for example, through misclassification of imports or their undervaluation) or avoid application of criminal law (for example, through payoffs of inspectors to overlook violations).

Government officials often have a monopoly of information that is very valuable to outsiders. Private individuals or firms may pay government officials to obtain information on the bids of competitors, on the location of a highway or public works project, or on the confidential economic condition of a firm to be privatized.

Finally, individuals and firms often pay bribes to influence the timing of government actions. In most instances, individuals and firms pay bribes to avoid government delays in taking action, whether to expedite payment from the government more quickly for goods sold or for services rendered, such as the installation of telephone service or the issuance of one of the many licenses required to operate a business. In other instances, bribes may be paid to delay an action that may be favorable to a competitor until the payer of the bribe can bolster his or her bid.[1]

The Determinants of Corruption All other things being equal, the size and structure of the state determine the demand for corrupt services—that is, the supply of bribes. Klitgaard (1988, 75) has summarized the "basic ingredients of corruption" as follows:

Corruption = Monopoly + Discretion – Accountability

That is, the level of corruption depends on the degree of monopoly exercised by the state over the supply of a given good or service, of discretion enjoyed by a government agency in making resource allocation decisions, and of accountability of the government (or its agents) to others.

Monopoly. The size of the government, and the types of activity in which it engages, are important indicators of potential government monopoly and of the degree of corruption. There is a positive correlation between the size of a government—as measured by its share of GDP—and the level of expected corruption: the larger the share of GDP it gets its hands on, the larger the corruption that will likely emerge. A large government share of GDP is consistent with high levels of regulation and implies a large bureaucracy and a high level of red tape and opportunity for malfeasance (LaPalombara 1994, 338).

As important as the size of the government are the types of activity in which government engages: a government that operates monopolistic state-owned enterprises or limits competition through excessive regulation or trade restrictions creates economic rents and therefore opportunities for corrupt rent-seeking behavior.[2] Empirical research has shown that there is a positive correlation between corruption and the share of state-owned enterprises in nonagricultural GDP, and a negative correlation between corruption and the openness of economies measured by trade shares (Elliott 1997, 182–83).

Discretion. The larger the discretionary power of government officials, the larger the supply of benefits that may be subject to bribes. For example, government officials may be able to extract payoffs from a contractor by introducing delays in payments (that could be expedited with a bribe) or by adding regulatory hurdles not in the original contract. They can also implement regulations inconsistently, extracting payments for clarity, and they can channel public resources to projects more prone to corruption (for example, large infrastructure construction projects, military procurement) than others even though the contribution of the former to national welfare may be lower than that of others. In privatization processes or in instances of natural resource concessions (for example, a concession to mine a certain ore, the ability to build a resort hotel in a particular beach or tourist attraction), government officials might be able to manipulate decision making to favor a particular bidder who may be willing to pay a bribe to obtain the newly privatized firm or concession (Rose-Ackerman 1997, 39).

Accountability. The accountability of the state (and its agents) to the public affects the degree of government monopoly and discretion and therefore the level of corruption. At one extreme, total absence of accountability over the state's actions (or inaction) means that the state's monopoly power and discretion are unchecked and there is high potential for corruption. Positive public accountability—in the form of transparency in government operations, including procurement activities, accounting and auditing standards, grievance and appeal procedures, media scrutiny—inhibits monopoly, discretion, and corruption.

The Economic Effects of Corruption

Empirical work on the economic effects of corruption has been limited by measurement problems. In a seminal study, Mauro (1995) used indices of corruption, red tape, and the efficiency of the judicial system for about seventy countries compiled by a private investment rating agency to identify the channels through which corruption and other institutional factors affected economic growth and to quantify the magnitude of these effects. He found a statistically significant negative association between corruption and investment, as well as between corruption and growth.[3] In a subsequent study including ninety-four countries, Mauro (1977) found a reduction of corruption of 2.38 points on his 10-point corruption scale would increase a country's annual investment by 4 percent of GDP and would increase annual growth of GDP per capita by 0.5 percent.

Surveys of theoretical and empirical studies of the economic effects of corruption (for example, Mauro 1997a, 1997b; Gray and Kaufmann 1998) suggest the following:

1. Corruption that requires businessmen to pay an up-front bribe to start a business or to be subject to payments of part of the proceeds of the investment by corrupt officials acts as a tax that diminishes the incentives to invest (Wei 1997). Thus, this form of corruption lowers investment and retards economic growth significantly. However, because bribes differ from taxes in one crucial way—namely, unlike taxation, corruption is usually illegal and must be kept secret—corruption is more distortionary than taxation, creating opportunities for government officials to change the mix of economic activity toward those that can result in bribes (Sheifler and Vishny 1993, 611–612).

2. To the extent that taking bribes is more lucrative than carrying out productive work, talent will be misallocated, with the more talented and better educated persons choosing to take jobs where bribes can be obtained rather than engaging in productive work. This misallocation of human resources has adverse consequences for the country's growth rate.

3. Corruption in the form of the diversion of aid from abroad can lead foreign countries to reduce future aid flows, with a consequent adverse impact on the balance of payments and the overall growth rate.

4. Corruption in the form of tax evasion reduces government revenue and leads to

ever-higher taxes on the limited number of firms that do comply with the rules. Higher tax rates, in turn, push firms to go underground (into the informal sector), reducing the number of tax-paying firms even more. The overall decline in government revenues limits the ability of the state to provide essential services, including the rule of law.

5. Corruption in government contracting can lead to lower quality of goods and services procured by the state. This may result, for example, in transportation disruptions or flooding of certain areas if low quality construction services are used in infrastructure projects (for example, bridges, dams) that subsequently fail. Supply stretching, another form of corrupt practice that lowers the quality of a product distributed by the state (for example, adulteration of fertilizer or pesticides purchased by the state and distributed to farmers), can lower production yields or fail to curb destructive pests, with a negative impact on agricultural production (Alam 1990, 91).

6. Corruption may distort the composition of government expenditures in favor of expenditures that are apt for bribe seeking (for example, large infrastructure projects, military weapons procurement) and away from other forms of expenditures (for example, salaries of teachers) that might have a more positive effect on public welfare and contribute to long-term economic growth. Tanzi and Davoodi (1997) found that political or "grand" corruption is often tied to capital projects, especially in weak or underdeveloped controlling or auditing institutions. Corruption distorts the decision-making process connected with public investment projects; it is likely to increase the number of projects undertaken in a country and to change their design by enlarging their size and complexity. The corruption-induced increase in public investment comes at the expense of productivity, and the net result is that public investment ends up having a negative impact on growth.

7. Corruption generally undermines the state's legitimacy and leads to instability. Instability, in turn, has an adverse impact on the investment climate and private investment.

Corruption and Transitions

Well-functioning public management systems, accountable organizations, a strong legal framework, an independent judiciary, and a vigilant civil society protect a country against corruption (World Bank 1997, 39). These institutions tend to be very weak or missing altogether in countries undergoing a transition to market economies. This is particularly so in former centrally planned economies, which makes them highly vulnerable to corruption. Moreover, changes that accompany the transition can exacerbate the potential for corruption.

Corruption and the Centrally Planned Economies

One of the key features of socialist, centrally planned economies (CPEs) is "the virtually all-encompassing public sector," which includes not only the realm of high-level government officials but also the dealings of shop clerks (Heidenheimer et al. 1989, 443). Under this system, "there is no distinction between public and private purses, and government officials simply 'appropriate' state assets" (Rose-Ackerman 1997, 33).

In the idealized socialist CPE, the totality of production facilities of the nation would be under state ownership. In practice, the degree of state ownership across CPEs has varied, but a common feature of each has been state control over the preponderance of productive facilities, with the exception of agriculture.

Public ownership of productive facilities results in a lack of identifiable ownership and widespread misuse and theft of state resources. As an analyst of the Soviet system stated with regard to that country, but probably applicable to other CPEs as well, "most reliable sources agreed that theft of socialist (state) property is as widespread as state property itself" (Feldbrugge 1989, 318). Individuals in these societies tended to use state property as their own, with very little stigma attached to it.

The high degree of state ownership also means that relatively little private activity has been allowed. CPEs have myriad state regulations waiting to be broken by enterprising individuals with the connivance of corrupt government officials. The combination of the sheer size of the public sector, and the web of regulations that circumscribe private activity, create opportunities for illegal behavior and for the use of state property for private gain.

Socialist systems, such as the ones that were in power in the former Soviet Union and Eastern Europe and currently in the People's Republic of China and Cuba, present a complex interplay of governmental and economic institutions, ideologies, and traditional political cultures that make them particularly prone to corruption (Heidenheimer et al. 1989:443–44). The overwhelming size of the public sector means that the state employs an inordinately large number of workers. Therefore, the potential for corruption is very large. Central planning of hundreds of production enterprises, thousands of retail outlets, and tens of thousands of individual products and services requires a huge bureaucratic apparatus. At every turn, production and distribution decisions are regulated by inflexible plans and allocations procedures; enterprise managers often have little choice but to use illicit influence to get around planning strictures to obtain labor or raw materials. The ruling party itself is often the locus of corruption, as the top leadership is normally immune to exposés and reprisals from below and can engage in self-serving behavior.

In a study of corruption in communist societies, Holmes (1993, 77) used the following definition of corruption: "Actions or non-action—by an individual or a small group of individuals occupying (an) official (party and/or state and/or legal and/or military and/or socially responsible) elected or appointed position(s)—that are perceived, at least by some criteria, to be improper or illegitimate in the particular sense of being seen simultaneously against the collective (societal) interest and in the official's (officials') individual (self-regarding) interests." Based on this definition, Holmes developed a taxonomy of twenty different forms of corruption in communist countries (see appendix 11.1). It should be noted that two or more forms of corruption may be involved in a single act; for example, an official may forge a document in return for a bribe, or an official may refuse to investigate criminal activity carried out by a crony. The very extensive and personalized power in the hands of government officials in socialist societies translated into wide discretion to act in a corrupt manner: taking bribes, getting cuts or kickbacks, extorting graft. Exploitation of the power of an office for personal gain was enhanced by the dictatorial and secretive nature of the regime and mutual solidarity of members of the political elite (Grossman 1979, 845).

One form of corruption that seems to have reached exceptionally high levels in CPEs is the system of perquisites and favors attendant to the ruling class or political elite, what one analyst has called the new class (Djilas 1957) and others the *nomenklatura* (for example, Voslensky 1984). Djilas (1957, 152) described the new class of rulers of the Soviet Union as "those who have special privileges and economic preferences because of the administrative monopoly they hold." According to Voslensky (1984, 75), the nomenklatura was (1) a list of key positions with the government, appointments to which are made by the higher authority of the Communist Party; and (2) a list of persons appointed to these positions or held in reserve for them. This group of government officials was fiercely protective of its status and privileges and suspicious of actions that might erode its position. As Djilas (1957, 65) put it:

> The new class instinctively feels that national goods are, in fact, its property, and that even the terms "socialist," "social," and "state" property denote a general fiction. The new class also feels that any breach of its totalitarian authority might imperil its ownership. Consequently, the new class opposes any type of freedom, ostensibly for the purpose of preserving "socialist" ownership. Criticism of the new class's monopolistic administration of property generates the fear of a possible loss of power. The new class is sensitive to those criticisms and demands depending on the extent to which they expose the manner in which it rules and holds power.

The privileged class of the former Soviet Union was able to draw on the resources of the state and to treat socialist property as its own: salary supplements, the best housing, special food allocations, access to restaurants, stores, and other facilities, vacation country villas, or *dachas*. It also participated heavily in the system of taking bribes in return for doing favors such as appointments of persons to prestigious posts, protection, promoting people up the bureaucratic ladder, and using influence to stop the government from taking actions (Pérez-López 1995, 24–25).

The Transition from Central Planning

As Naím (1995, 251) points out, a corollary to Klitgaard's stylized corruption equation is that the deepening of democratization should have corruption-curbing effects. Why, then, is there a perception that corruption is rampant in countries transitioning from authoritarian, centrally planned regimes to democratic, market economies?

One explanation for this phenomenon is that in the absence of strong institutions, democracy and free markets provide more—and more visible—opportunities for corruption than those present under authoritarian rule. Under authoritarian rule, corruption can be more institutionalized, controlled, and predictable. Naím argues that a well-organized dictatorship can provide "one-stop shopping" for corruption services, where the right amount of money given to the right official will take care of all needed interventions. Under this system, bribe takers under the control of the authority (either the authoritarian leader or a political party) collude and keep their actions out of the public's view. Under a democratic system, in contrast, the central government's control over the providers of bribery services is diluted, and corrupt officials compete for bribes, resulting in a process more visible to the public than under authoritarianism.

Particularly during the early stages of transition—as the "old" national institutions of authoritarianism are being torn down and decentralization, privatization, and the opening of these economies to international participation are taking place while new institutions promoting good governance have not yet taken hold—there are opportunities for corruption to explode. As Glynn et al. (1997, 10) put it: "Corruption in these emerging markets is doubly pernicious. First, it compromises the efficacy and efficiency of economic activity, making the transition to free market democracy more difficult. Second, and equally important, corruption distorts public perceptions of how—and how well—a proper market economy works. Under such circumstances it becomes all too easy for economically beleaguered publics to confuse democratization with the corruption and criminalization of the economy—creating fertile soil for an authoritarian backlash and engendering potentially hostile international behavior by these states in turn."

It is probably fair to argue, however, that democratic regimes, over the long run, engender more powerful antibodies against corruption than authoritarian systems, under which political liberties are stifled (11).

Decentralization. The relaxation of the state's economic monopoly creates novel opportunities for rent-seeking by government officials. For example, the economic opening brought about by perestroika in the former Soviet Union that legalized some secondary markets translated into an increase in corruption and black market activity, as government officials diverted scarce (and low-priced) goods from the distribution system and into secondary markets where they could gain rents from resale (Schuknecht 1990). Deregulation of areas formerly under the exclusive control of the state create opportunities for fraud until a regulatory structure is established.

Privatization. Privatization, the transfer of state-owned property to private owners, provides manifold opportunities for rent-seeking and misconduct by government officials. The experience of reforming countries of the former Soviet Union and Eastern Europe undergoing massive privatization has been of an increase in corruption, leading analysts to question whether corruption is the inevitable price to pay for privatization (Kaufmann and Siegelbaum 1997, 421).

Opening to International Participation. The opening of the economy to international participation—through increased international trade and investment—creates opportunities for corruption particularly in the form of commissions for issuing import and export permits and authorizations or allocating foreign exchange or for misclassifying goods to obtain more favorable tariff treatment. The approval process for foreign investment, particularly if it requires a multitude of discretionary permits, is fertile ground for corruption.

Corruption and Transitions from Central Planning

Examples of corruption in former socialist, centrally planned economies during transition to market economies abound. In the early 1990s, corruption was rampant in Romania: bribes were common for making reservations in hotels, renting real estate, or getting a grave in a cemetery. Hungary was affected by severe smuggling, counterfeiting, and tax cheating. Describing priorities for 1995, a Vietnamese Communist Party leader told a Cuban journalist that "we must also give special attention to new issues emerging from the process of changing to a market economy, including fund embezzlement, squandering, and, above all, corruption, illegal commerce, and other crimes and social vices" (Pérez-López 1997, 181).

In China, corruption became a major concern in the 1990s. Many bureaucrats in agencies such as the bureaus of finance, foreign trade, industries, material supplies, commerce, and construction projects and land approvals accepted bribes. Government officials took advantage of China's ambiguous economic system—neither completely centrally planned nor completely market—to abuse their position and power and speculated in raw materials and finished products through the dual pricing system. Among many corrupt practices, government officials "sold" valuable parcels of land to well-connected businesses at bargain prices (Hao and Johnston 1995; Johnston and Hao 1995).

In Russia, the process of *privatizatsia* ("privatization") was nicknamed *prikhvatizatsia* ("grabitization") to highlight the high degree of corruption that it involved; it has been estimated that 61 percent of Russia's new rich were former Soviet managers who made their own the industries they managed during privatization (Naím 1995, 253). With the loosening of the restraining hand of the KGB, the Soviet Union's once-illegal shadow economy came into its own as the *mafiya* (Malia 1995). Capitalizing on corrupt officials, organized crime in Russia—the mafiya—has acquired large holdings of state assets through criminal and violent methods and has broadened its reach to over two dozen countries, including the United States, Canada, and Sweden.

Corruption in Socialist Cuba

Since the early 1960s the Cuban state has controlled an overwhelming share of the nation's productive resources. In 1968, the Cuban state already controlled 100 percent of industry, construction, transportation, retail trade, wholesale and foreign trade, banking, and education; only in agriculture—70 percent under state control—was there a sizable private sector presence. By 1988 the state's share of agriculture had risen to 92 percent (Rodríguez 1990, 61). Although precise comparisons are difficult to make, available information suggests that in Cuba the state's share of ownership of productive resources was as significant, if not more so, than in other CPEs, including the former Soviet Union, East Germany, and Czechoslovakia, as well as socialist Hungary and Poland.

Similarly, the Cuban economy also has been subject to Soviet-style central planning since the early 1960s. In 1961 a central planning board (Junta Central de Planificación, JUCEPLAN) was created and charged with formulating annual and long-range plans. A network of central ministries and agencies was created, or the mandate of existing ministries modified, to take charge of the various economic sectors, mostly in the form of state monopolies dealing with foreign trade, finance, labor, and banking. State enterprises producing the same type of good were merged into trusts *(consolidados)*, each controlled by a central ministry. Centralization took a quantum leap in 1962 when the government imposed strict controls on prices, put in place a commodity rationing system, and set quotas on the output of private farmers that the latter had to sell to the state (Acopio) at predetermined prices.

Corruption through to the End of the 1980s

There is, of course, very little information on the breadth and depth of corruption in Cuba.[4] It stands to reason, however, that corruption on the island would follow closely the patterns in other socialist, centrally planned economies whose ideology and political and economic systems Cuba emulated. Illegal economic activities associated with corruption for which some concrete evidence is available are black market operations, misuse of office, and special perquisites extracted by the Cuban nomenklatura. To be sure, other forms of corrupt behavior—for example, bribes to influence government decisions such as installing a telephone or exchanging homes *(permutas)*—were probably also rampant, but they are more difficult to document.

Black Markets. Black markets for consumer goods began in Cuba in 1962 when commodity rationing was instituted. Despite periodic crackdowns and heavy sentences imposed on black marketeers, these illegal markets have remained an important source of consumer and industrial goods and services. Because prices in the black market are substantially higher than in official markets, there is a significant incentive for black marketeers to ply their trade and for corrupt government officials to provide goods to supply this market.

The Cuban state's overwhelming control over the economy translates into black markets in nearly all areas of economic activity. Thus, not only are there black markets for food and consumer goods—items ostensibly covered by the rationing system—but also for construction materials for home repairs and spare parts for appliances and motor vehicles. Misappropriation of government resources (via theft, diversion of goods, shortchanging of customers) has traditionally been one of the main sources of goods entering black markets.

Misuse of Government Office. The extremely high concentration of resources in the state, and the centralized nature of the decision-making system, place a great deal of power in the hands of government officials and hence create ample opportunities for corruption. In addition to corrupt behavior in return for bribes, corruption in socialist Cuba takes the form of using power to obtain access to other things, degenerating in a generalized "I'll scratch your back if you'll scratch mine" system that rewards those who are friendly with government officials and is generally referred to as *sociolismo*, a take-off on *socio* (buddy) and *socialismo*. General prosecutor of the republic Ramón de la Cruz Ochoa told a journalist in 1991 that Cuba's corruption problem was "*sociolismo organizado*, sometimes used to solve enterprise problems and other times to solve personal problems. These corrupt practices tend to build on each other and bring about a lack of respect for rules and laws" (Carrasco 1991, 27).

Privileges and Abuses of Power by the Ruling Elite. As in the former Soviet Union and other socialist countries, Cuba has a system of special privileges for the nomenklatura, whose members are referred to on the island as *pinchos, pinchos grandes,* or *mayimbes*. These perquisites, which are not available to the public and are reserved only for government officials, include total or partial exemption from the rationing system, the ability to obtain imported food and other consumer goods, good housing (including vacation homes), use of government vehicles, access to special hospitals and imported medications, admission to special schools for their children (the so-called *hijos de papá*), and the ability to travel abroad, to name a few.[5]

Corruption in the 1990s

The economic crisis that enveloped socialist Cuba in the 1990s has brought about changes in the form and visibility of corruption. Some of the economic policies implemented during this period—particularly since 1993—that opened up some space for the private sector in the absence of well-developed property rights and legal institutions have also created new opportunities for corruption. The legalization of the use of foreign currencies and the enthusiastic pursuit of foreign investment in order to ease very serious balance of payment problems, have been among the policies most directly responsible for the government's concern that corruption is rampant and a threat to the socialist system.

Misappropriation of Public Goods. Pursuant to legislation adopted in September 1993, Cuba authorized self-employment in more than one hundred occupations subject to certain restrictions and fees; an additional eighteen occupations were added in October 1993. Despite the restrictions—university graduates and managers were not allowed to be self-employed, health and education services were outside of the scope of occupations authorized for self-employment, self-employed individuals cannot hire paid helpers—self-employment increased rapidly, reaching nearly 209,000 workers in December 1995.

Particularly impressive was the growth of home restaurants, the so-called *paladares,* that sprung up throughout the island: an estimated one thousand to two thousand such outlets in the city of Havana alone and four thousand nationwide (Pérez-López 1995, 182).

Since markets for raw materials are very limited, Cuban self-employed workers generally obtain their equipment and raw materials from the black market, which in turn is largely fed by theft from the state sector:

> Cuba has no wholesale distributors. The Cuban government has not opened up supply markets. Intermediaries are not only illegal, but unwanted. . . . When Jorge [a self-employed shoe-

maker] is asked about where he has been buying the little equipment he uses to work, he answers coyly, "little by little I have been collecting it," but his smile seems to say, "Why are you asking such a dumb question?" And it is, in fact, a silly question. Everybody knows that there are no free markets for any of the instruments used by Jorge; nor are there supplies for most of the products the artisans make. They either take them from their workplaces (in other words, steal them) or they buy them in the black market. Where do the products in the black market come from? From other workers who do the same thing. Everyone has to steal in Cuba for survival (Jatar-Hausmann 1999, 108–9).

Spontaneous Privatization. Although the Cuban leadership has stated unequivocally that it will not stray from the path of socialism, and privatization is out of the question, the latter is in fact already occurring through a method that is "the very essence of corruption, being the outright theft of public assets by politicians and/or enterprise directors associated with the *nomenklatura*" (Kaufmann and Siegelbaum 1996, 439).[6]

Spontaneous privatization refers to the appropriation of state property by members of the nomenklatura through the paper reorganization of state-owned enterprises into private corporations of which the nomenklatura members are owners or directors. For Hungarian political scientist Agh (1993, 15), spontaneous privatization is a phenomenon that occurs at a time when state socialism has weakened but while there are still legal gaps and uncertainties in property regulations. In a period of uncertainty, "those possessing economic power carve out for themselves and their clients valuable pieces of the state-owned cake" (Sik 1992, 158).

By the end of 1992, sixty-three reportedly privatized entities called *sociedades anónimas* (known by the initials S.A.) were operating in Cuba (Gunn 1993, 13). Some of the leading S.A. and their main activities and holdings are given in appendix 11.2. Although some claim that these corporations are privately owned, they are in fact instruments of the Cuban state. Their "owners" have not purchased assets from the state nor have they contributed intellectual property, invested any savings, or incurred any risks. Instead, they are individuals loyal to the Cuban government who have been given control over state assets illegally in a manner reminiscent of the systematic theft of property by the Sandinistas in Nicaragua known as *la piñata*. These sociedades anónimas operate in the more dynamic sectors of the economy that generate hard currency and are capable of attracting foreign investment: tourism, foreign trade, biotechnology, commercial real estate, and financial services.

The "owners" and managers of the sociedades anónimas are predominantly high-level military officers and Cuban Communist Party officials (Alfonso 1999b, 1A). The rise of this "capitalist" class is full of ironies. Ramiro Valdés, one of the revolutionary leaders with the longest association with Fidel Castro and a feared former minister of the interior, is the head of the Grupo de la Electrónica, which controls the production, sale, and imports of electronic products and services and computer hardware and software.[7] Valdés reportedly lives in Cuba in luxury and travels frequently to Spain, where he stays in first-class hotels, dines in "five-fork" restaurants, and has purchased expensive properties, including a large farm in Asturias ("Un señorito" 1999).

Misuse of Office. The visible rise in corruption associated with bribe-taking and misuse of office, particularly associated with the international tourism industry and other sectors of the economy that operate with foreign currencies, has triggered steps within the Cuban government and the Cuban Communist Party to address the most obvious excesses. According to the Cuban press, the Cuban Communist Party conducted 1,159 investigations in 1998 of allegations of "diversion and misuse of state resources" (439 investigations), "lack of economic controls, irregularities and lax management" (247), and "social conduct unbecoming of a Party militant" (170). About 1,500 members of the Cuban Communist Party were sanctioned in 1998 for corruption (Rousseau 1999). Overall, in 1998 the Cuban Communist Party reportedly received 21,828 complaints regarding misappropriation of public goods, lack of management controls, abuse of power, and conduct unbecoming a party member; 77 percent of the complaints were at least partly justified (Tamayo 1999a).

Officials of several sociedades anónimas (among them Cubanacán, Cimex, Rumbos, and Cubalse), free trade zones and foreign businesses were reportedly implicated in corrupt activities and either arrested or fired in the first half of 1999 (Tamayo 1999b):

Several national and provincial-level executives of Rumbos, an agency that operates dollar-priced tourist tours and entertainment spectacles, golf courses, and cafeterias.[8]

The head of the hotel division of Cubanacán.

The manager of a large warehouse operated by Cubalse (Cuba al Servicio de Extranjeros), the firm that rents housing and sells dollar-priced goods, such as cars, furniture, office supplies, and foodstuffs, to foreigners living in Cuba.

The director of the Valle de Berroa free trade zone, operated by Cimex.

One foreign travel agency operating in Cuba and several of the firms located in free trade zones.

In what may be a related development on 28 August 1999, the Cuban media reported that Minister of Tourism Osmany Cienfuegos had been replaced by former Minister for Foreign Investment and Economic Cooperation Ibrahim Ferradaz ("Council of State" 1999).

The crackdown on corruption has also extended to other sectors of the economy. In one case, three top officials at the Hermanos Ameijeiras Hospital—run by the Cuban Communist Party, whose services are only available to party members and foreigners able to pay with hard currency—reportedly were fired or forced to resign because of allegations of corruption. Allegations of corruption have been floated with regard to the recent announcement that the long-term head of the Centro de Ingeniería Genética y Biotecnología, Dr. Manuel Limonta, had been replaced. Finally, a Canadian investor has stated that three Cuban officials who took a $200,000 bribe from a Canadian firm involved in an airport construction project had defected in Ottawa "to enjoy the fruits of their corruption" (Tamayo 1999b).

Controlling Corruption in the Cuban Transition

As discussed in the previous section, the limited economic liberalization policies introduced by the Cuban government in the 1990s have brought about marked changes in the nature of corruption. In addition to the more traditional forms of corruption associated with socialist, centrally planned economies, the opening of some space to nonstate economic activity has created new opportunities for corruption, which government officials have been quick to exploit. Whether there has been an overall increase in corruption in the 1990s or merely a shift to more visible forms of the same ill is difficult to assess. Cuban economist Marta Beatriz Roque Cabello (1997) argues that corruption in Cuba is generalized and that corruption is inherent in the island's socialist system. It is clear, however, that the corruption eruption that so worries Cuban leaders is a harbinger of what might occur with the implementation of broad-based policies to transform Cuba into a market economy unless explicit efforts are made in the design of transition strategies to reduce opportunities for corruption.

Reforms that limit state authority over economic processes are necessary, but not sufficient, to control corruption in transition processes. Corruption has continued to flourish in countries that have instituted such macroeconomic reforms because they have failed to carry out complementary microeconomic reforms at the sector level. Strong institutions are key to controlling corruption: a solid legal and judiciary framework, well-functioning public management systems, accountable organizations, and a vigilant civil society protect a country against corruption.[9]

Limiting State Authority

Policies that open up and liberalize the economy and promote competition limit state authority. These policies can be powerful tools in combating corruption. They include liberalization, privatization, and competitive procurement policies.

Liberalization. Some macroeconomic reforms and deregulation can contribute to the expansion of markets and reductions in rents. Lowering or eliminating tariffs, quotas, and other barriers to international trade as well as eliminating exchange rate restrictions, price controls, and unwarranted permit requirements strip government officials of the power to extract bribes. At the same time, removing such controls reduces transaction costs, eliminates bottlenecks, and fosters competition.

Privatization. Privatization removes the government from economic activities and reduces opportunities for corruption in sales, procurement, employment, and financing. In practice, privatization processes have proven to be vulnerable to corruption, as they can be manipulated by government officials to favor certain individuals or groups or even to benefit themselves. The most corrupt form of privatization is the outright theft of public assets that occurred in Eastern European countries shortly before their shift to market economies that has been euphemistically called "spontaneous privatization." To ensure the integrity of privatization, transparency measures must be an integral part of such processes. Privatization must also be accompanied with legal regulatory and commercial frameworks that promote competition and protect consumers and investors. In the absence of such frameworks, privatization merely shifts rent-seeking from governments to the private sector.

Competitive Procurement. Competitive government procurement removes the discretion of government officials from the selection of government suppliers and contractors by prescribing an open bidding process and laying out clear procedures and criteria for selection. Assistance from foreign donors often requires recipients to adopt competitive procurement procedures in order to avoid foreign funds being diverted from their rightful purpose and enriching government officials.

Strengthening the Legal Framework

A country's legal system—its laws and regulations, as well as the processes and institutions through which they are applied—is vital for controlling corruption, just as it is vital for resolving legal conflicts, enforcing property rights, and defining the limits of state power. Without enforcement, however, laws and regulations have no impact on reducing corruption and may foster general cynicism about reform efforts.

Enforcement of anticorruption legislation requires an efficient, predictable, and accountable judiciary. To hold public officials accountable to anticorruption laws, judiciaries need independence from the executive branch as well as institutional capacity. Strengthening judicial independence involves revising procedures for appointing, assigning, remunerating, and removing judges and prosecutors to insulate them from political influence. In some cases it might require the establishment of independent prosecutors to carry out investigations of senior officials. Strengthening the institutional capacity of the judiciary involves, among other things, modernizing the court system to facilitate swift and fair procedures through augmenting and upgrading staffs, improving legal training, and strengthening investigatory capabilities.

Reforming Public Management

A well-performing government inhibits corruption. A professional and well-motivated civil service, with selection and promotion based on merit rather than patronage, can serve as the foundation for good governance. A well-performing civil service resists petty corruption and provides the human resources for many of the institutions that protect integrity in the government: finance and personnel ministries, procurement boards, technical departments that issue permits and licenses, regulatory bodies, and internal and external audit departments. Adequate payment of civil servants and independence of the civil service from unwarranted political interference are two key issues.

Good financial management systems are powerful instruments for preventing, discovering, or facilitating the punishment of fraud and corruption. They reduce opportunities for corruption and increase the risk of detection, making corrupt behavior high risk. Such systems are critical in areas of government service that are particularly susceptible to corruption, such as tax and customs departments and government procurement and contract management systems.

Improving Accountability

Improving accountability entails efforts to improve both the detection and the sanctioning of corrupt acts. Better detection requires measures to improve transparency and oversight, while better sanctioning involves establishing criminal and administrative sanctions and improving electoral accountability. Among specific measures that improve transparency and oversight are freedom of information requirements, financial disclosure requirements, open budget processes, financial management systems and audit offices, independent auditors and ombudsmen, and special anticorruption agencies. Better sanctioning of corruption can be accomplished through vigorous legislative oversight, establishment of fraud hot lines, strong protections for whistleblowers, clear and meaningful sanctions, and free and fair elections that hold public officials accountable.

Energizing Civil Society

In addition to institutional reforms, successful efforts to fight corruption require societal reforms to change public attitudes toward formal political processes and to energize political will for change. Societal reforms generate new information about the costs and causes of corruption to stimulate demand for change and provide guidance on what to change. Societal reforms also foster structures to facilitate monitoring and advocacy by civil society. Without the mobilization of civil society, governments are unlikely to follow through on anticorruption reforms once they enter difficult political terrain. Among the ways in which civil society can be energized to engage in the fight against corruption are surveys of perceptions and attitudes toward corruption and ways to control it; public relations campaigns and workshops to educate the public on the costs of corruption and best practices to control it; investigative journalism that exposes egregious forms of corruption; civil advocacy organizations; and international agreements and conventions.

Appendix 11.1 Taxonomy of Corruption in Socialist Societies

Deliberate Dereliction of Duties, Inaction, and Obstruction

1. Turning a blind eye
2. Refusal to investigate/charge and/or obstructing an investigation
3. Avoidance of specific procedures

Improper Filling of Office—Patronage

4. Nepotism
5. Shared experiences (cronyism)
6. Shared interests

Deliberate Deception

7. False reporting—overstatement
8. False reporting—understatement
9. Deception of supplicants
10. Forging of documents

Other Interactive, Gain-Based Forms of Corruption

11. Accepting bribes
12. Offering bribes
13. Extortion
14. Blackmail

Possibly Noninteractive, Gain-Based Forms of Corruption

15. Not earning one's salary
16. Improper use of socialized property
17. Embezzlement
18. Speculation
19. Smuggling
20. Treason

Source: Adapted from Holmes (1993, 81–88).

Appendix 11.2 Principal Cuban *Sociedades Anónimas*

Grupo Gaviota S.A.

International tourism

Hotels, villas, marinas, rental automobiles, hunting preserves, and retail stores

Corporación Cubanacán S.A.

International tourism

Hotels, retail stores, a broad range of tourism services

Habaguanex S.A.

International tourism focused on the city of Havana

Hotels, restaurants, retail stores, and museums

Grupo Cimex S.A.

Export-import and retail trade, financial services

550 retail stores throughout the island (using hard currency only), warehousing facilities, cargo ships, domestic transportation equipment

Grupo de la Électrónica

Production and sale of electronic and computer equipment and computer services

Composed of several companies, including Copextel S.A., which manufactures and sells computer and electronic equipment, and Centersoft, which provides computer software and consulting services

Heber Biotec S.A.

Biotechnology products

Commercializes products manufactured by the Centro de Ingeniería Genética y Biotecnología

Real Inmobiliaria S.A.

Real estate (commercial and residential)

Havana Asset Management Limited

Investment management

Bravo S.A.

Processed meat products (ham, sausages, etc.) for sale to hard currency customers

Source: Adapted from Alfonso (1999b, 23A).

Notes

I am grateful to Roger Betancourt and Luis Salas for comments on an earlier version of this chapter; however, it presents only the personal views of the author.

1. Bardhan (1997, 1324) relates the anecdote of a New Delhi high official who reportedly told a friend: "If you want me to move a file [take an action] a little faster, I am not sure if I can help; but if you want me to stop a file, I can do it immediately."

2. Rents are payments to factors in excess of normal returns in competitive markets. The term *rent-seeking* to describe the behavior of corrupt government officials who take advantage of imperfectly competitive markets to seek bribes was pioneered by Krueger (1974).

3. Under some circumstances, corruption may not be inimical to economic development—for example, where there is an inept or understaffed bureaucracy or inefficient regulators, or where the rule of law is weak and there is no effective means of contract enforcement (Elliott 1997, 186). For an illustration of the latter in China, see Betancourt (1998, 162–64).

4. This section of the paper draws heavily from Pérez-López (1995, 1997).

5. The best treatment of this subject is the work by Clark, who has conducted several surveys of émigrés. Among his works, see Clark (1990, 1999).

6. For example, Vice President Carlos Lage (1999) stated in June 1999: "All of the policy changes that have occurred and will occur in the future are framed within our socialist system. They are aimed at relating more closely our economy to the world economy, while maintaining the dominant role of state ownership. Even though we are seeking foreign capital and are willing to accept a higher participation by foreign capital in our economy, in Cuba there isn't now and there will not be a policy of privatization."

7. Valdés participated in the 1953 attack on the Moncada Barracks; was a member of the expeditionary force that landed in Cuba in 1956 aboard the *Granma;* rose to the rank of *comandante,* the highest rank in the Rebel army; became military commander of the province of Matanzas in 1959; and was appointed head of intelligence (G2) in 1962.

8. Among the Rumbos executives dismissed for allegations of corruption is María Elena García, wife of former Minister of Foreign Relations Roberto Robaina (Alfonso 1999a).

9. This section borrows liberally from World Bank (1997) and USAID (1999).

References

Agh, Attila. 1993. "Europeanization through Privatization and Pluralization in Hungary." *Journal of Public Policy* 13, no. 1:1–35.

Alam, M. S. 1990. "Some Economic Costs of Corruption in LDCs." *Journal of Development Studies* 27, no. 1 (October): 89–97.

Alfonso, Pablo. 1999a. "Destituyen a la esposa de Robaina." *El Nuevo Herald,* 9 June.

_______. 1999b. "La piñata castrista," *El Nuevo Herald,* 13 June.

Bardhan, Pranab. 1997. "Corruption and Development: A Review." *Journal of Economic Literature* 35, no. 3 (September):1320–46.

Betancourt, Roger R. 1998. "A New Institutional Economics Perspective on Cuba's Reforms." In *Perspectives on Cuban Economic Reforms,* edited by Jorge F. Pérez-López and Matías Travieso-Díaz, 155–74. Tempe: Arizona State University Latin American Center.

Carrasco, Juana. 1991. "¿Hay corrupción en Cuba?" *Bohemia* 83, no. 6 (8 February): 26–30.

Celarier, Michelle. 1996. "Stealing the Family Silver." *Euromoney* (February): 64–66.

Clark, Juan. 1990. *Cuba: Mito y Realidad.* Miami: Saeta Ediciones.

_______. 1999. "Igualdad y privilegio en la revolución de Castro." In *40 años de revolución: El legado de Castro,* edited by Efrén Córdova, 219–52. Miami: Ediciones Universal.

"Council of State Removes Tourism Minister." 1999. *Granma,* 28 August, in *FBIS-LAT-1999–0828,* 28 August.

Djilas, Milovan. 1957. *The New Class.* New York: Praeger Publishers.

Elliott, Kimberly Ann. 1997. "Corruption as an International Policy Problem: Overview and Recommendations." In *Corruption and the Global Economy,* edited by Kimberly Ann Elliott, 175–233. Washington: Institute for International Economics.

Feldbrugge, F.J.M. 1989. "The Soviet Second Economy in a Political and Legal Perspective." In *The Underground Economies,* edited by Edgar L. Feige, 297–338. Cambridge: Cambridge University Press.

Glynn, Patrick, Stephen J. Kobrin, and Moisés Naím. 1997. "The Globalization of Corruption." In *Corruption and the Global Economy,* edited by Kimberly Ann Elliott, 7–30. Washington: Institute for International Economics.

Gray, Cheryl W., and Daniel Kaufmann. 1998. "Corruption and Development." *Finance and Development* (March): 7–10.

Grossman, Gregory. 1979. "Notes on the Illegal Private Economy and Corruption." In *The Soviet Economy in a Time of Change*, edited by the Joint Economic Committee, 834–55. Washington, D.C.: U.S. Government Printing Office.

Gunn, Gillian. 1993. *Cuba in Transition: Options for U.S. Policy*. New York: Twentieth Century Fund.

Hao, Yufan, and Michael Johnston. 1995. "Reform at the Crossroads: An Analysis of Chinese Corruption." *Asian Perspective* 19, no. 1 (spring–summer): 117–49.

Heidenheimer, Arnold J., Michael Johnston, and Victor J. Levine, eds. 1989. *Political Corruption: A Handbook*. New Brunswick: Transaction Publishers.

International Monetary Fund (IMF). 1997. "IMF Adopts Guidelines Regarding Governance Issues." *IMF Survey* 26, no. 15 (5 August): 233–38.

Jatar-Hausmann, Ana Julia. 1999. *The Cuban Way: Capitalism, Communism, and Confrontation*. West Hartford, Conn.: Kumarian Press.

Johnston, Michael. 1997. "Public Officials, Private Interests, and Sustainable Democracy: When Politics and Corruption Meet." In *Corruption and the Global Economy*, edited by Kimberly Ann Elliott, 61–82. Washington, D.C.: Institute for International Economics.

Johnston, Michael, and Yufan Hao. 1995. "China's Surge of Corruption." *Journal of Democracy* 6, no. 4 (October): 80–94.

Kaufmann, Daniel, and Paul Siegelbaum. 1997. "Privatization and Corruption in Transition Economies." *Journal of International Affairs* 50, no. 2 (winter): 419–58.

Klitgaard, Robert. 1988. *Controlling Corruption*. Berkeley: University of California Press.

Krueger, Anne O. 1974. "The Political Economy of the Rent-Seeking Society." *American Economic Review* 64, no. 3 (June): 291–303.

Lage, Carlos. 1999. "En Cuba no habrá privatización." *Opciones en el Web,* 13 June, at http://www.opciones.cubaweb.cu.

LaPalombara, Joseph. 1994. "Structural and Institutional Aspects of Corruption." *Social Research* 61, no. 2 (summer): 325–50.

Malia, Martin. 1995. "The Nomenklatura Capitalists." *New Republic* 212, no. 21 (22 May): 17–24.

Mauro, Paolo. 1995. "Corruption and Growth." *Quarterly Journal of Economics* 110, no. 3 (August): 681–712.

______. 1997a. "The Effects of Corruption on Growth, Investment and Government Expenditure: A Cross-Country Analysis." In *Corruption and the Global Economy,* edited by Kimberly Ann Elliott, 83–107. Washington, D.C.: Institute for International Economics.

______. 1997b. *Why Worry about Corruption?* Washington, D.C.: International Monetary Fund.

Naím, Moisés. 1995. "The Corruption Eruption." *Brown Journal of World Affairs* 2, no. 2 (summer): 31–60.

Pérez-López, Jorge F. 1995. *Cuba's Second Economy: From behind the Scenes to Center Stage*. New Brunswick, N.J.: Transaction Publishers.

______. 1997. "Cuba's Second Economy and the Market Transition." In *Toward a New Cuba? Legacies of a Revolution,* edited by Miguel Angel Centeno and Mauricio Font, 171–186. Boulder, Colo.: Lynne Rienner Publishers.

Rico, José Ma., and Luis Salas. 1996. *La corrupción pública en América Latina*. Miami: Center for the Administration of Justice, Florida International University.

Rodríguez, José Luis. 1990. *Estrategia del desarrollo económico en Cuba*. Havana, Cuba: Editorial de Ciencias Sociales.

Roque Cabello, Marta Beatriz. 1997. "Corrupción," 10 April, at http://www.cubasos.com/documentos/economy/corrupcion.htm.

Rose-Ackerman, Susan. 1975. "The Economics of Corruption." *Journal of Public Economics* 4:187–203.

______. 1997. "The Political Economy of Corruption." In *Corruption and the Global Economy*, edited by Kimberly Ann Elliott, 31–60. Washington, D.C.: Institute for International Economics.

______. 1999. *Corruption and Government: Causes, Consequences, and Reform*. New York: Cambridge University Press.

Rousseau, Denis. 1999. "Llueven los 'truenes' debido a la corrupción." *El Nuevo Herald,* 25 June.
Schuknecht, Ludger. 1990. "Rent-seeking and Perestroika." *Public Choice* 66:83–88.
Sheifler, Andrei, and Robert W. Vishny. 1993. "Corruption." *Quarterly Journal of Economics* 108, no. 3 (August): 599–617.
Sik, Endre. 1992. "From the Second to the Informal Economy." *Journal of Public Policy* 12, no. 2:153–75.
Tamayo, Juan O. 1999a. "Ofensiva contra la corrupción llega a altos jefes." *El Nuevo Herald,* 2 July.
______. 1999b. "Scandal in Cuba's Economy." *Miami Herald,* 8 June.
Tanzi, Vito. 1998. "Corruption around the World: Causes, Consequences, Scope, and Cures." *IMF Staff Papers* 45, no. 4 (December): 559–94.
Tanzi, Vito, and Hamid Davoodi. 1997. *Corruption, Public Investment, and Growth.* IMF Working Paper WP/97/139. Washington, D.C.: International Monetary Fund.
"Un señorito de la nueva clase en Cuba." 1999. *El Nuevo Herald,* 29 June.
U.S. Agency for International Development (USAID). 1999. *A Handbook on Fighting Corruption.* Washington, D.C.: Center for Democracy and Governance, USAID, at www.usaid.gov/topical/econ/integrity.
Voslensky, Michael. 1984. *Nomenklatura: The Soviet Ruling Class.* New York: Doubleday.
Wei, Shang-Jin. 1997. *How Taxing Is Corruption.* Working Paper 6030. Cambridge: National Bureau of Economic Research.
Whitney, Craig. 1999. "Group Running European Union Quits en Masse." *New York Times,* 16 March.
World Bank. 1997. *Helping Countries Combat Corruption.* Washington: World Bank.

CHAPTER 12

Human Resources and Development
What to Do after the Periodo Especial?

Francisco Léon

The Cuban economy is one of the best endowed with human resources in Latin America and the Caribbean. However, during the Special Period in Time of Peace (1990–2002) it also had the highest levels of unemployment and perhaps underemployment of the past four decades. After a deep recession and a process of severe structural adjustment, however, the economy began to recuperate somewhat during 1995–2000. In a possible favorable context, it would be desirable to make optimum use of human resources and to maintain a consistent and high level of employment in order to achieve sustained human development. In this chapter, some measures for improving the utilization of human resources are discussed in a long-term context.

Population, Human Resources, and Employment in Cuba, Latin America, and the Caribbean, 1980–2001

Population Dynamics and the Economic Cycle

Latin American and Caribbean countries are undergoing processes of demographic transition to low fertility and mortality rates, accompanied by reductions in the population under the age of fourteen, and increased participation of women in the workforce. These conditions increase the proportion of the population of working age and reduce overall demographic dependence levels. This in turn creates a situation favorable to economic development based on the intensive use of human resources and is advantageous in overcoming problems of inequity and poverty.

As is well known, the optimal demographic dependence situation is that in which the proportion of the nonworking age population (that is, youth) declines as a result of the reduction in fertility rates before the major increase in the proportion of the population of seniors.[1] This is the demographic window of opportunity. In Cuba's

Fig. 12.1 Population Seventy Years and Older
(as a Percentage of Total)

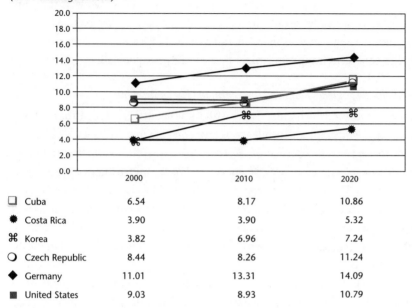

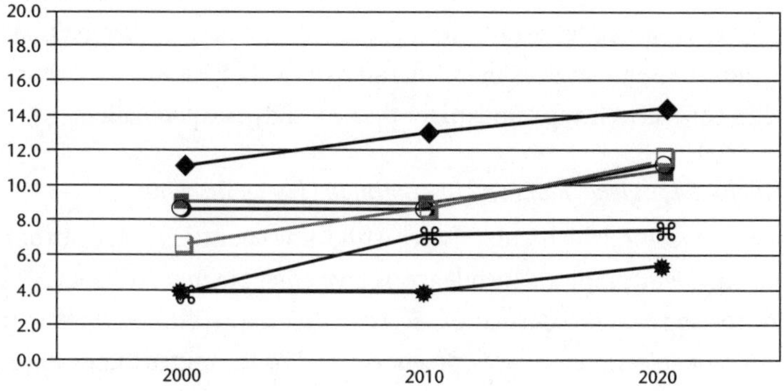

❑ Cuba	6.54	8.17	10.86
✸ Costa Rica	3.90	3.90	5.32
⌘ Korea	3.82	6.96	7.24
❍ Czech Republic	8.44	8.26	11.24
◆ Germany	11.01	13.31	14.09
■ United States	9.03	8.93	10.79

case, fertility rates declined gradually during the second and third decades of the revolutionary period, fell further from about 1989 to 1994 during the economic crisis, and then increased somewhat after 1995. Cuba's demographic transition from 1970 to 2000 thus proceeded rapidly, particularly with respect to the decline of the fertility rate and the corresponding lower proportion of the population under the age of fourteen.

The Cuban population's pattern of aging is an additional factor that contributes to the rapidity of their demographic transition and their migration to the exterior. The increase in life expectancy for people over the age of sixty-five is the result of development in general and health services in particular in recent decades. In the year 2020, Cuba's population of people over seventy years of age likely will be twice as large as Costa Rica's, 50 percent larger than Korea's, and similar to that of the United States. Only a few developed countries with early demographic transitions, such as Germany and some former socialist Central and Eastern European countries, will have greater proportions of seniors than Cuba, as is illustrated in figure 12.1.

Although some favorable and durable changes such as the increase of the fertility rate and the termination of net external migration may occur in the future, a high level of demographic dependence in the next twenty-five years requires a development process based on high employment levels and steadily improving productivity. Assuming that the labor force between the ages of twenty and sixty-five is fully employed, given its dependence rate, the income generated per worker in Cuba will have to be almost twice as large as that generated in Costa Rica and Mexico in order to finance an equivalent living standard for the over-sixty-five population.

Demographic Dependence Rates and Investment in Human Resources

A positive factor, which Cuba shares with some countries that confronted crisis with growing demographic dependence, is investment in human resources. This was the contributing factor to Germany's recovery after the Second World War and to the several decades of sustained development enjoyed by the United States and Southeast Asian countries. This factor is also common with Central and Eastern European countries, which share the transition to a centralized socialist economy with Cuba, as well as the challenge of transforming productive structures and modernizing the technology acquired within the former Soviet bloc in order to compete effectively in the international system.

Cuba's level of human resource development is high, owing to investment in health and education and professional development in particular. Nevertheless, Cuba will have to invest considerable amounts of its already scarce economic resources, not only to continue this development but also to maintain the capacity of human resources, which were originally highly qualified but which have been underutilized for a decade. Also, Cuba needs to cover the shortages in professions—accountants in newly reformed state enterprises, for example—which will be required in the economy of the future. At the same time, it needs to cater to the necessities of the new sectors that are taking on a central role in the economy, such as tourism.

Over the past two decades, the student population (five to twenty-five years old) has fallen by more than 30 percent in absolute terms. Its growth will likely be stagnant over the first decade of the 2000s. This event occurred during the economic crisis of 1991–95, reducing the state's capacity to provide educational facilities and increasing students' motivation to leave school early. The result has been a significant decrease in enrollment, especially from 1991–92 to 1997–98, as illustrated in figure 12.2, and at the higher levels of education—university and postsecondary technical education.

This reduction in the development of human resources at the secondary and tertiary levels has been different from that observed in other countries in Latin America and the Caribbean. In these countries, the crisis of the 1980s coincided with an increase of enrollment in secondary and tertiary levels of education (CEPAL 1998,

Fig. 12.2 Total Enrollment and Graduation by Level of Education.

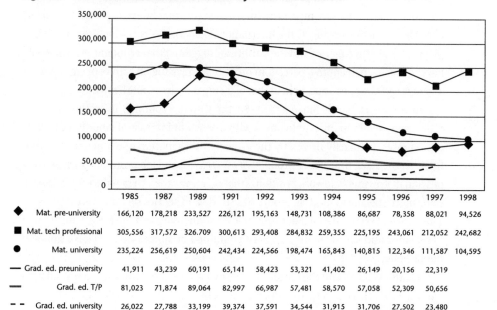

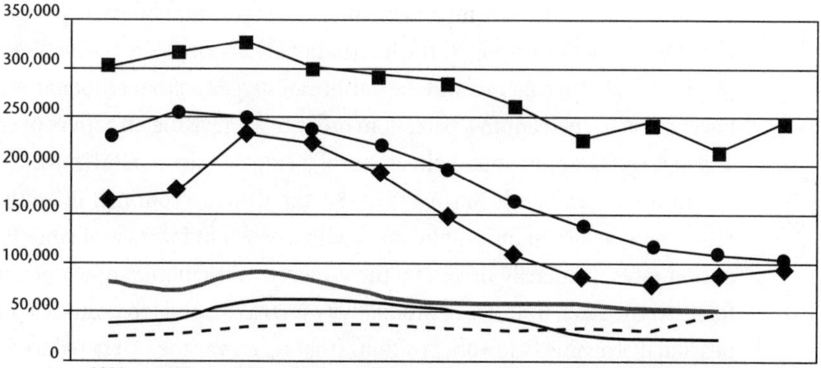

	1985	1987	1989	1991	1992	1993	1994	1995	1996	1997	1998
◆ Mat. pre-university	166,120	178,218	233,527	226,121	195,163	148,731	108,386	86,687	78,358	88,021	94,526
■ Mat. tech professional	305,556	317,572	326.709	300,613	293,408	284,832	259,355	225,195	243,061	212,052	242,682
● Mat. university	235,224	256,619	250,604	242,434	224,566	198,474	165,843	140,815	122,346	111,587	104,595
— Grad. ed. preuniversity	41,911	43,239	60,191	65,141	58,423	53,321	41,402	26,149	20,156	22,319	
Grad. ed. T/P	81,023	71,874	89,064	82,997	66,987	57,481	58,570	57,058	52,309	50,656	
- - Grad. ed. university	26,022	27,788	33,199	39,374	37,591	34,544	31,915	31,706	27,502	23,480	

1999a, 1999b). The fluctuations of enrollments by level and by sex in Cuba, except for professional and technical education, suggest that the decline has been the product of dynamic demographic pressures and changes in behavior of students and their families and not of a planned process.

Within this context, one can appreciate that human resources investment in Cuba during the decades of 1960–1990 has permitted the country to confront more effectively the economic crisis and the new conditions of international competition. However, in the 1990s a combination of demographic and economic factors reduced the national capacity to develop human resources at the secondary and tertiary levels, meaning that additional efforts in the short and medium term are needed. Only then will it become possible for Cuban workers to generate the income required to recover the levels of economic well-being lost during the crisis and to confront the evolution of their relationship of demographic dependence in the future (2000–2020).

Evolution of Demographic Dependence, the Labor Force, and Employment

When the majority of Latin American and Caribbean countries were beginning their transition to low fertility rates and diminishing rates of population growth during the 1970s, the regional studies available emphasized the incapacity of the economies to generate employment, the high levels of underemployment, the slow growth of paid employment, and an informal sector that often surpassed the formal one. The predictions made by the International Labour Organization Program of Employment of Latin America and the Caribbean suggested that economic growth would have to reach 5 percent to 8 percent in order to achieve the objectives of employment and of wage labor per household in the following decades (CEPAL 1989.)

On the other hand, during 1970–80 the Cuban economy, like other socialist economies, achieved full employment with a constant increase of labor force participation rates, primarily driven by the growing participation of women in the labor force. At the same time, labor productivity increased, and job positions, such as arduous and distressing fieldwork positions (that is, sugar cane), were reduced, while positions more specific to modern economies (trade and service sectors) were improved. The informal sector, defined in terms of low productivity and the marginalization of basic labor and social rights, had been contained or suppressed by legislation and public policy.

In Latin America and the Caribbean, the expansion of the working-age population and the labor force accelerated during the debt crisis of the 1980s. This expansion through the 1990s coincided with only partial economic recovery (generated by natural resources more than the intensive use of the labor force and human resources). However, during the debt crisis the labor force grew more rapidly than employment due mainly to the increase in the participation of women in the labor force because of inadequate earnings per household. However, the growth of the labor force was characterized by low levels of investment, low quality jobs, and increasing unemployment, in spite of the drastic fall of real wages in some countries. In the 1990s the recovery of investment has been insufficient, with a number of exceptions, to raise productivity and employment to incorporate the new labor force participants and those that desired to leave the low quality jobs that were previously created. The creation of employment and the human resource utilization continue to be challenges for Latin America, even for those countries that have succeeded in attracting important flows of foreign direct investment.

In Cuba, the employment record of the economy during the decade of the 1980s was not satisfactory, even though a debt problem with capitalist countries was largely avoided due to various forms of subsidization from the Soviet Union and the debt moratoria declared by the government in 1986. Since the early 1980s the available labor force permitted Cuba to provide several hundreds of thousands of skilled personnel, including members of the military, doctors, educators, and engineers to other developing countries.[2] Large numbers of industrial and less-skilled workers also worked in some socialist Central and Eastern European Republics and in the Soviet Union under government-to-government agreement. This temporary external migration of workers coincided with the approval of self-employment in such activities as housekeeping and automobile and domestic appliance repairs. Moreover, nearly 130,000 Cubans departed in 1980 in a "government sponsored or permitted exodus" to Peru, after entering in its Havana embassy, and to the United States from the port of Mariel.

At the beginning of the period of "rectifying errors and negative tendencies" in 1986 (that is to say the rearrangement of the model of centralized planning) the government officially acknowledged the underutilization of labor in the national economy. The rectification program included: personnel reduction in public companies and the civil service; the broadening of popular participation in the construction of housing; and a new way of organizing labor, the brigades, or "contingents," with higher remuneration, strong discipline, and assured inputs for effective operation.

The composition of the labor force also changed in the 1980s as professionals and technicians continued to rejuvenate and increase. At the same time, labor productivity apparently grew at an annual average rate of 6.3 percent during 1981–85, then diminished to an average of 2.4 percent to 2.6 percent in the 1986–89 period (Mesa-Lago 1991; Ferriol Muruaga 1998, 21–54). In the 1990s the impact of the economic crisis on the evolution of the labor force and of employment in Cuba has had important similarities as well as differences with the 1980s debt crisis in Latin America and the Caribbean. The similarities include the underutilization of labor, the expansion of the informal sector, the decrease of wage employment, and the increase of unemployment. Available statistics indicate a rate of 25 percent of labor underutilization in 1993 and of 34.1 percent in 1996—that is, without counting disguised underemployment, or the employment of workers in occupations far below the qualifications they possess (for example, nuclear engineers driving taxis). The informal sector grew rapidly during the economic meltdown of 1991–93, reaching about three hundred thousand workers. Thereafter, the size of the underground economy declined due to the legalization of self-employment occupations and the regulation of informal activities (González, 1993; 1995, 185–88). Employment in the state sector and in state/foreign owned enterprises (mixed enterprises) also diminished especially with the creation of the basic units of cooperative production in agriculture that employed 9 percent of the labor force in 1997.

Nevertheless, there are important differences between Cuba and the region regarding labor during their respective crises. First is the decline in labor force participation rates since 1991. In particular, the female labor force participation rate declined from 52.3 percent in 1990 to 44.7 percent in 1995, recovering its initial magnitude only in 2000 (CEPAL 1999a, table V.12) (see figs. 12.3 and 12.4). Another distressing factor is the increase in the number of young people that neither work nor study. This proportion rose from 27.7 percent in 1988 to 38.8 percent in 1998, while the rate of participation of people over the legal age of retirement (women fifty-five and over and men sixty and over) increased (Ferriol Muruaga 1993; Brundenius 2002).

It is difficult to compare the impact of the decline of real wages per household in Cuba with the evolution of labor participation rates in Latin America and the Caribbean, for in some cases, such as Bolivia, the decline in real wages surpassed 30 percent. According to the UN Economic Commission for Latin America and the Caribbean, in Cuba the deterioration of wages in real terms also exceeded 30 percent but took place while main sources of income became more diversified due to growing remittances from relatives in the exterior, informal sector activities, and migrant work. For that reason, declining income in some households was accompanied by rising incomes in others. One estimate indicates that the Gini index, a measure of income in equality, increased from 0.25 in 1989 to 0.38 in 1996–98 due to the unequal incidence of family remittances and the income differences between those in the dollar economy and those in the peso economy (Ferriol Muruaga 2001).

At the same time, there was a declining motivation to work, particularly in the state enterprises and the public services, which represented more than three-quarters of national employment. Furthermore, it is difficult, due to lack of information, to determine the number of Cuban residents licensed or under government assignment to work abroad. The government has tried to promote work outside of Cuba but only under government assignment.[3] For example, several thousand professionals, especially physicians, work in African, Caribbean, and Central American countries, and construction workers work in Spain and Portugal.

In summary, in Cuba during the Periodo Especial (1989–2002) the relationship between population, employment, and income has deteriorated. This deterioration has not only been in relation to the levels reached in the 1990s but also to the level necessary to sustain household incomes, especially those where the main source of income is social assistance and/or the payment of pensions to senior citizens. The country has utilized its human resources and its labor force even less effectively than in the 1963–89 periods (Madrid-Aris 1998). Lack of employment opportunities and low wages contributed to declining female participation (1994–97) and student early education desertion; and it was an obstacle to a generalized dismissal of a surplus, estimated in three to four hundred thousand, workers employed in the state sector. Finally, income and career differences in the dollar and peso economies and the lack of

Fig. 12.3 Male and Female Labor Force Participation Rates in Cuba, 1985–2000

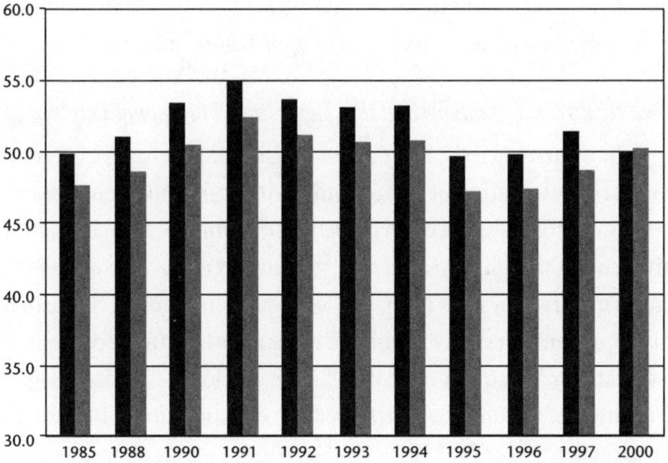

	1985	1988	1990	1991	1992	1993	1994	1995	1996	1997	2000
FT/ pop. 15–60	49.9	51	53.5	54.9	53.6	53.2	53.3	49.6	49.8	51.3	49.9
FT/ pop. 15–65	47.7	48.7	50.5	52.4	51.2	50.7	50.8	47.2	47.4	48.7	50.2

Fig. 12.4 Female Labor Force Participation Rates in Cuba, 1980–2000

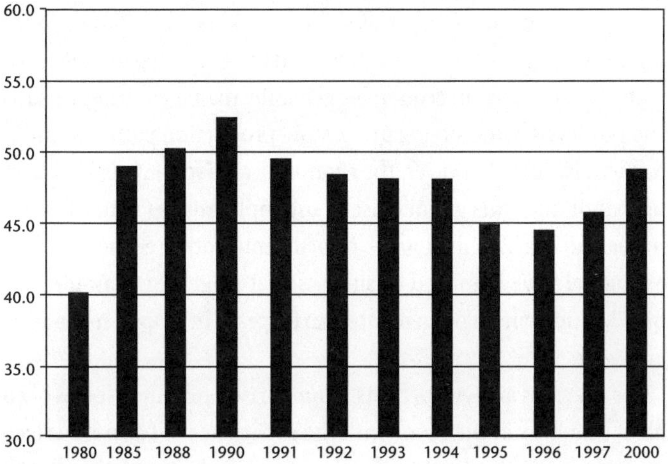

	1980	1985	1988	1990	1991	1992	1993	1994	1995	1996	1997	2000
FT/ pop. 20–55	40.2	49.1	50.2	52.3	49.6	48.4	48.2	48.2	44.9	44.7	45.8	49

employment opportunities in the latter generate a lack of education in formal education. As a result, many students have little interest in their studies and subsequently leave their universities or technical schools before graduation.

Productive Transformations and the Composition of Regional Employment

Cuba's current crisis, like the debt crisis in Latin America, requires a transformation of the foundation of its economy, with consequent change in employment patterns. In both cases, the main objective of economic transformation is international reinsertion through increased exports and successful import substitution. The devaluation of currencies has been, in most countries, one mechanism for implementing this approach. In essence, Cuba is a variant within this approach, which explains the devaluation of the quasi-official exchange rate for the peso, the legalization of the free circulation of the dollar, and the creation of export zones for industrial and commercial activities.

The initial assumption of these export-oriented models was that the comparative advantage of cheap labor would be the main force of development. Subsequently, governmental education policy placed greater emphasis on education for skilled and semiskilled workers than for higher level technicians. Subsequently, between 1993–94 and 1999–2000, the number of skilled workers who graduated increased (6,128 to 24,994) and that of technicians decreased (52,352 to 37,116) (ONE 2001).

The Latin American economies generally managed to adjust successfully, reorganizing production, modifying preexisting production patterns, and creating some low productivity jobs. However, the economic adjustment also led to some reduction of wage labor and thus an increase of unemployment (as in Chile in 1974–78 and Argentina and Brazil in the 1990s). Concurrently, other economies that opted for the export model have managed to surpass that stage (for example, Bolivia, Costa Rica, Chile, Mexico) and have generated an increase in employment as well as in the labor force.

The previous analysis permits a comparison of some aspects of employment in the Cuban economy in the 1990s with the experience of Latin American countries in the 1980s. However, the depth of the Cuban crisis, the problems of administration of the economy, and the exacerbation of inequity also explain some of the differences with those experiences. One could distinguish two subperiods in the Cuban case: the first, between the beginning of the crisis and the adoption of the adjustment program (1989–94), and the second, the implementation of that program (1994–2000). In the first period the labor force increased by about 10 percent from 1989 to 1991, increasing gradually after 1995–96 but by 2000 still not recovering to the 1991–94 level (see

Table 12.1 Employment by Sector, 1980–2000

	1980	1989	1991	1992	1993	1994	1995	1996	1997	1998	1999	2000
Agriculture	644.3	721.1	968.6	968.0	987.9	977.8	835.0	842.5	933.1	921.6	912.6	937.9
Industry	546.1	767.5	719.7	705.4	705.3	681.8	659.6	666.0	635.8	630.7	679.7	665.5
Construction	273.4	344.3	330.8	310.0	252.8	215.7	221.3	221.7	237.9	224.9	208.1	204.5
Commerce, restaurants, hotels	302.2	395.3	456.1	448.5	450.5	399.0	388.3	391.6	435.3	446.5	482.0	473.6
Transport and communication	193.2	235.9	249.0	231.6	216.5	200.1	204.6	208.0	188.8	199.9	181.1	194.9
Services, social and communal	598.6	835.7	1,006.0	1,010.2	1,050.1	1,220.0	1,194.6	1,207.5	1,157.0	1,212.6	1,222.9	1,258.4
Education, teaching staff	217.0	239.7	233.4	232.6	230.7	220.9						
Health	71.2	156.2	176.2	184.6	186.5	190.2						
TOTAL	2,599.9	3,666.3	3,888.2	3,826.4	3,815.1	3,839.5	3,591.0	3,626.7	3,705.2	3,753.6	3,821.3	3,843.0

Source: CEPAL (1989, 1996).

table 12.1). Total employment stabilized 1991–94 even though it expanded significantly in agriculture and personal services. In the second subperiod, the labor force declined sharply in 1994–95 (248,000 jobs) after the second adjustment package was implemented. Employment in industry and agriculture began to recover after 1995. From 1989 to 2000, service employment rose by an astounding 30 percent. On the other hand, the state sector employment share of total employment decreased from more than 90 percent to 77 percent. This decline has been most pronounced in education, decreasing from 233,400 to 195,917, while employment in health rose from 176,200 to 224,651 in the same period. Meanwhile, private and self-employment increased from less than 9 percent to more than 17 percent and accounted for most service sector growth (ONE 1989, 2001).

The evolution of employment in the first subperiod shows two principal movements. First, employment in agriculture increased to compensate for the fall of agricultural imports with increased use of labor in order to sustain food production and consumption and absorb labor from other sectors. Second, employment in services rose. In the second subperiod, however, new sources of income per household, notably remittances from relatives abroad, alleviated the pressure of entering the labor force and could, at the same time, control and diminish the growth of employment in services slightly. The evolution of employment has thus been driven mainly by the crisis itself and only marginally by the reorientation of the economy.

It is worth mentioning the impact that tourism has had in the growth of activities in commerce, restaurants, and hotels. Tourism has permitted the replacement of low quality occupations in other sectors and also probably supports thousands of workers in the illegal or submerged economy. At the same time, the industries that have begun to modernize, whether by means of foreign associations or in the state sector, have reduced and replaced personnel to improve labor productivity.

It is also crucial to highlight the inertia of the historical pattern of development that has dominated since 1970. This has involved investment in human resources and employment in the service sector, especially in health. Perhaps as a result of this, university enrollment in the field of medical sciences in 1991–92 and 1994–95 decreased less (around 10 percent) than enrollment in the fields of natural sciences and mathematics, while engineering (technical sciences) and economics declined by 40–60 percent. In 1996–97, the number of graduating doctors continued to be similar to 1990–91, declining after 1997. The share of medical sciences and education graduates as a proportion of total graduates still increased from 55 percent in 1993–94 to 65 percent in 1999–2000 (ONE 2001).

The measures adopted to adapt human resources development to the transformations of the economy in the medium and long term have been indecisive and marginal, which explains why the composition of university registration and graduation continues to concentrate around medical and pedagogical sciences. Enrollment and graduation in natural sciences and mathematics still seem inadequate for the expansion of modern sectors, such as biotechnology or electronics, and for the transformation of managerial administration and production. It does not seem logical, even if the export of health services assists development, to continue graduating more than six thousand doctors in a country that already has one doctor for every 170 inhabitants.

Recent Human Resource Policy Changes

A combination of factors induced the Cuban government to introduce important changes that have affected human resources and employment. The more important of these were partial economic recovery from 1995 to 1999; increased criticism of human capital and labor force use, particularly during the Periodo Especial; and a growing concern in the leadership for the political consequences of unrest or increasing interest in out-migration on the part of young people. The most important policy changes were (1) an increase in scholarships in high school, technical-professional, and higher education after 1998–99, with greater benefits for higher levels of education, resulting in increased enrollments by 4 percent in high schools, 15 percent in pre-universities, and 17 percent in technical and professional schools; and (2) increases in wages and increased incentives in pesos, dollars, and convertible pesos in the state sector, including education and health. In 2000, workers' premiums benefited 1.1 million with convertible pesos, 1.4 million with food, 2 million with shoes and clothes, and 700,000 with toiletry products (Rodriguez 2000). Additionally, workers under Cuban government service contracts in foreign countries were allowed to send up to U.S.$100 monthly to their families.

However, the economic downswing after 2000 has forced the government to reverse some of the above-mentioned policy changes. Particularly, beginning on 3 June 2002, prices in dollar stores were increased by 10–30 percent, thereby affecting all households using dollars from any source, as well as the 1.1 million workers receiving convertible pesos bonuses. And, at the end of August 2002, the drastic downsizing of the sugar sector eliminated one hundred thousand jobs from the sector, requiring a major retraining effort for about sixty thousand workers.

What to Do after the Periodo Especial?

The previous analysis demonstrates that if the Periodo Especial were to continue, it would be impossible to achieve significant growth in employment, productivity, and income in order to support an effective international reinsertion in the context of increasing demographic dependence. A new wave of reforms together with international negotiations on the external debt issue would be required in order to initiate sustainable development.[4]

Employment

One of the problems that persist with the Periodo Especial is insufficient generation of higher productivity employment in emerging and more attractive economic sectors. In light of international experience, this problem, more than the dynamic growth of each sector, concerns the relationship between sectors. The export sector does not necessarily have to be an important generator of direct employment if it can do so indirectly through linkages with other sectors. It is the ability to develop linkages with other sectors that is of most importance. In contrast to the 1970–90 era, the development strategy of the 1990s assigns top priority to tourism. However, that sector is an ineffective promoter of development due to the leakage of tourist expenditures into imports necessary to service the sector. This has led analysts to propose a strategy to develop agriculture and industrial production in order to produce domestic substitutes for such imports. Some advances have been made since the mid-1990s. According to the economic authorities in 2001, as much as 56 percent of products in the dollar stores and 66 percent of tourism inputs are of domestic origin (Varela Pérez 2001). However, most of those products also have a high import coefficient and employ mostly semiskilled workers.

Furthermore, in current circumstances (the U.S. Helms-Burton Act) it is not possible for the Cuban government to diversify the current pattern of tourism, such as providing shared condominium or apartment accommodations for temporary residents. Moreover, the volume of necessary investment in infrastructure (water and sewerage systems, highways, and public transportation) exceeds the capacity of the state and the current arrangements of joint state/foreign enterprises.

One useful method for reinforcing the linkage between tourism and agro-industrial production would be to diversify the existing range of products and raise the productivity of agricultural producers. A second option would be to increase tourist expenditures on goods and services, which utilizes trained personnel such as technicians, professionals, and entertainers. Providing health services to foreigners, which is in effect a service export, is also an attractive option. This approach would be the equivalent to adopting a European or a Mexican pattern in entertainment, a Spanish/Mexican arrangement in construction, and/or a Costa Rican variant in foreign old-age resident services.

Cuba may not have the architectural or archaeological attractions of Europe or Mexico, and perhaps it does not have a significant market differentiator with the rest of the Caribbean basin in terms of sun, sand, and surf. However, it does have a rich cultural and entertainment industry. In fact, Cuba is known the world over for several genres of music—traditional, jazz, salsa, ballads, classical, folk, and Afro-Cuban. The same can be said for dance, art, and sports. Moreover, the country has developed strong associations and links, both through trade and solidarity connections with the larger countries in the region, from Mexico to the U.S. It also has strong cultural ties with emerging economies, such as Venezuela, Central America, and Columbia.

Costa Rica's experience in the provision of longer-term care and medical attention for seniors might serve as a useful example for Cuba, as it possesses a number of existing advantages. First, it is near countries such as Canada and the United States in aging populations, which already generate health tourists for Mexico and Costa Rica. Second, precedents exist that could make health insurance effective in Third World countries by means of general or bilateral agreements, particularly with European Union members. Third, Cuba has developed internationally recognized specialization in health services, such as rehabilitation. This alternative method of linking tourism does not diminish the linkage with agriculture and agro-industry. However, these activities have the national population as their primary market.

The rest of the economic sectors, assuming a dynamic insertion of the country into the Caribbean basin, would share their international orientation with those activities more directly related to tourism but on a more limited scale. This would be the case of manufacturing; transportation, including the infrastructure of harbors and airports; higher education; finance; and commerce. In all of these, the role of subregional distribution may be significant in possible future scenarios in which current economic limitations have been surpassed. In these areas, tens of thousands of jobs could be created with high average earnings as well as occupational stability in comparative terms.

The components of the alternative development path outlined above indicate a substantive change with relation to the period of 1970–94. Although, the major trends indicated that normal economic development tended to involve a relative expansion of services, the authorities emphasized the production of goods. The challenge of the Cuban government and that of the Cuban Communist Party, given their productive activities development bias, is to incorporate an economy of services into the existing socialist model.

Human Resource Development

The transition from a model of growth based on the production of goods to one emphasizing the service sector will require a reorientation of the development of current and prospective human resources. Moreover, in the next two decades, as the working-age population continues to expand, the service sector will increase more slowly, at an average rate below 0.25 percent per year. The bulk of the population that will require retraining will be those workers already employed.

This pattern of human resources development represents a radical change to professional formation before entering the labor force relative to that which prevailed until the crisis of 1989 and has continued to the present as a result of inertia. Cuba will have to develop institutions for massive professional development that include training in services, perhaps utilizing distance education. It is advantageous to conduct this retraining soon for several reasons. First, part of the labor force is presently unemployed or underemployed, which means that the real cost of training would be lower and available time for retraining would be greater. Second, the labor force will age faster in the next two decades, increasing the difficulty of reabsorbing it in productive employment, since the effectiveness of retraining declines as workers age. Third, the availability of workers with an adequate basic professional formation will make national investment and also foreign direct investment more attractive.

The success of human resources development will depend on the participants' capacity to view professional development as a continuous activity associated with a life of work. Such professional development, of course, needs to be associated with appropriate positions and reasonable remuneration, corresponding to the levels of qualification of the various groups of professionals. This motivational factor must be understood in the context of the collective mentality that has emerged from the prolonged crisis that the country has experienced and of the prevailing norm in which workers remuneration has been largely unrelated to professional qualification.

Past practices regarding formal education planning are not the most appropriate for Cuba's new era. In part, the problem will be resolved through the central role enterprises will increasingly play in determining the opportunity, mode, and content of human resource development. The situation is more acute in the systems of formal education (pre-university, professional and technical, and post-university), where the inertia of the past continues to be a burden.

Professional education will begin to reverse the tendency of labor force participation rates to decline, as occurred during the Periodo Especial, so that the current levels could be brought to the 50–60 percent levels that characterize developed nations. The achievement of this objective would make the increments of the labor force greater than those of the working-age population in the period 2000–2020, incorporating presently unemployed people for remuneration in the labor force.

However, if the Cuban government continues to refuse international conditionality regarding human rights and democracy, it would be difficult to succeed in a renegotiation of external debt thereby becoming eligible for long and medium term loans. Therefore, even if the U.S. Congress authorizes tourism from the United States, it is unlikely that the necessary volumes of investment would occur so as to create sufficient levels of high productivity and high-income employment.

Conclusion

The alternative approach presented above may be similar to the one that has been evolving since 1990 in some Caribbean basin and Central and Eastern European countries. It is evident that the current Cuban strategy is resolving the limitations of the Special Period only partially. Similarly, the strategy shaping up in neighboring countries such as the Dominican Republic, which is a product of the combination of tourism and *maquiladoras* (manufacturing enterprises), creates a reference point. This chapter has presented arguments that confirm that the Dominican Republic–type of approach would not be capable of generating sufficient economic resources to guarantee the population a standard of living similar to that of the 1980s. On the contrary, this alternative would represent a misuse of available human resources since it would be employed in a service economy of low level of income and labor productivity. As for the existing development strategy, it suffices to say that the preservation of the current prevailing conditions of the Special Period and their causes are not desired by the government, the national community, nor, fortunately, by the political and economic interests of the international community.

The development experiences of Hungary, Poland, and the Czech Republic since 1989 show that it is possible to develop strong tourist sectors while at the same time propelling agricultural and industrial sectors toward sustained improvement while intensifying economic integration with each other and in the European Union. Closer to Cuba, Mexico and Costa Rica have continued their tourist development of past decades and have established the export of health services to nonresidents, with favorable results so far. The three Central and Eastern European countries suggest a possible scenario for Cuba with its socialist heritage, a similar demographic dependence, and, consequently, a similar necessity to achieve the high levels of productivity and income. Mexico and Costa Rica also serve as a reminder to Cuba that it has competitors and that the opportunities in the new and more dynamic industries of tourism and health services could be very advantageous.

Internationally, with an increased priority given to tourism, the government has initiated projects in the past few years to explore new types of tourism and has adopted measures to control the negative tendencies (that is, crime and sex tourism) within that industry. However, the economy and important strata of the Cuban population continue to be in vulnerable conditions that are not compatible with sustained development. Moreover, the exodus of artists and professionals, key elements for the future development of the country, is continuing toward both the underground economy and the exterior. Such artists and professionals, for human rights reasons as well as for the well-being of the country, require freedom of movement so that they can achieve a level of international recognition relevant to their capacities. This does not exist at this time within the framework of the internal and external limitations of the Periodo Especial.

Notes

1. The analysis of this process, as well as the reduction of the rural population and rural employment, has been carried out in Cuba by the Center of Demographic Studies (CEDEM). In this work I employ the outputs of these studies, especially those conducted by Eramis Bueno and Beatriz Ervitti on population aging and rural employment respectively.

2. According to data provided by the State Committee of Economic Cooperation, the number of civilian workers was around 150,000 allotted in forty-five countries (Martínez 1991). With regard to the military contributions, the major and most prolonged of all those contributions was when 377,033 soldiers and 50,000 civilians were involved in the sixteen years of cooperation in Angola Castro (1991, 5).

3. During the peak of internationalism, 1975–90, the people working in the exterior were doing so by means of contract from the government and state institutions, which suggest that they are part of the labor force consigned in official statistics. Presently, the majority of those who obtain the permit to work in the exterior do so at their own risk. The permit given by the Cuban government also requires the

beneficiary to contribute part of his or her labor income to the government and in some cases to the home institution. It allows them to maintain residence, private property (housing, automobile), free entry to the country, and social benefits access (that is, health).

4. A proposal shared by the author with Cuban specialists on the island and abroad (Fernández 2000; Brundenius 2002).

References

Brundenius, Claes. 2002. "Industrial Upgrading and Human Capital in Cuba." In *Cuba: Development in Prospects: An Agenda in the Making,* edited by Pedro Monreal, 137–57. London: ILAS.

Cardoso Eliana, and Ann Helwege. 1992. *Cuba after Communism.* Cambridge, Mass.: MIT.

Castro, Raul. 1991. "El prestigio, la autoridad, el respecto de que goza Cuba en el mundo son inseparables de nuestro desempeno en Angola." Speech given at the ceremony of Cacahual. *Granma,* 28 May.

Comisión Económica de America Latina (CEPAL). 1989. *Transformación ocupacional y crisis social en América Latina.* Santiago, Chile.

______. 1998. *La economía Cubana, reformas estructurales y desempeño de los noventa.* Mexico, D.F.: Fondo de Cultura Económica.

______. 1999a. *Anuario estadístico 1998.* Santiago, Chile.

______. 1999b. *Panorama social 1998.* Santiago, Chile.

Fernández F., Marcelo. 2000. "Cuba: Recuperación económica y apertura. Nuevas reflexiones sobre 'el período especial.'" *Revista bimestre Cubana* 3, no. 12 (June): 235–49.

Ferriol Muruaga, Angela. 1993. "Política Social en el ajuste económico." Havana, Cuba: Institute of Economic Investigations.

______. 1998. "El empleo en Cuba, 1980–1986." In *Cuba: Crisis, ajuste y situación social, 1990–1996,* edited by Angela Ferriol Muruaga, Alfredo González Gutiérrez, Didio Quintana Mendoza, and Victoria Pérez Izquierdo, 21–54. Havana, Cuba: Social Sciences Editorial.

______. 2001. "Reforma económica Cubana e impactos sociales." Congress of Latin American and Caribbean Scholars, 25–29 June.

González, Alfredo. 1993. *Modelos económicos socialistas: Escenarios para Cuba en los años noventa.* Havana, Cuba: Instituto Nacional de Investigaciones Económicas.

______. 1995. "La economía sumergida en Cuba." *Cuba: Investigación económica* (Havana) 2: 77–103.

Madrid-Aris, Manuel. 1998. "Investment, Human Capital, and Technological Change: Evidence from Cuba and Its Implications for Growth Models." *Cuba in Transition* 8:465–82.

Martínez Martínez, Osvaldo. 1991. "Desarrollo humano: La experiencia cubana." In *Cuba económica* 1, no. 1:16–36.

Mesa-Lago, Carmelo. 1991. "El proceso de rectificación en Cuba: Causas, políticas y efectos económicos." *Revista de estudios políticos,* n.s., 74 (October–December): 497–530.

Rodríguez, José Luis. 2000. *Informe sobre los resultados económicos del 2000.* Havana, Cuba: Ministerio de Economía y Planificación.

Varela Pérez, Juan. 2001. "Nuestro país puede mostrar hoy una situación económica diferente." *Granma,* 21 December.

Ministerio de Economía y Planificacion. 2001. *Plan económico y social, 2001.* Havana, Cuba: MINEP.

Contributors

Luis Casacó

An information technology project manager in a state-owned firm, Luis Casacó has worked in the computer industry for more than twelve years, both as a hardware engineer and as a software consultant. For the past two years he has managed the first national business-to-business e-commerce Web site and other Web initiatives. He has also lectured at the Foreign Trade Institute in Havana on e-commerce topics. He received a B.S. in automatics engineering from the Havana Institute of Technology and an M.A. in economics from Carleton University, Ottawa. Currently, he is working at Asociación Latinoamericano de Integracíon in Montevideo, Uruguay.

Carmelo Mesa-Lago

Carmelo Mesa-Lago is Distinguished Professor Emeritus of Economics and Latin American Studies at the University of Pittsburgh and Professor and Research Scholar on International Relations and Latin America at Florida International University. The founder and editor for twenty years of *Cuban Studies,* he is the author of fifty-eight books and some two hundred articles and book chapters, half of them on the Cuban economy. His most recent major work is *Market, Socialist, and Mixed Economies: Comparative Policy and Performance—Chile, Cuba, and Costa Rica* (Johns Hopkins University Press, 2000). Mesa-Lago was regional adviser for the UN Economic Commission for Latin America and is a consultant with many international organizations. He has lectured in thirty-three countries throughout North America, Latin America, Europe, and Asia. He has been awarded the Emilio Bacardi Chair on Cuban Studies at the University of Miami, the Alexander von Humbolt Senior Prize for outstanding research, and the *Choice* award for outstanding book.

William A. Messina Jr.

Executive coordinator of the International Agricultural Trade and Development Center at the University of Florida, William A. Messina Jr. is the codirector of the center's collaborative research initiative with the University of Havana on Cuban agriculture. In 1999 Mr. Messina and project codirector Jose Alvarez were awarded the U.S. Department of Agriculture Special Honor Award by Agriculture Secretary Dan Glickman for "outstanding service to U.S. and Florida agriculture for research on the economic challenges and opportunities associated with resumption of trade with Cuba." Messina has been a consultant to the Food and Agriculture Organization of the United Nations and to a number of U.S. agricultural commodity associations. He holds a B.S. in agricultural economics from Cornell University and an M.A. in food and resource economics from the University of Florida.

Francisco Léon

A Cuban-born citizen of Chile since 2002, Francisco Léon is a graduate of the University of Havana and Louvain University. He has been an international official in the UN Economic Commission for Latin America and the Caribbean (UNECLAC) and the Instituto Latinoamericano de Planificación Económico y Social in Santiago, Chile, from 1971 to 2000. He has conducted countless missions to various countries in Latin America, advising governments on social policy issues, and has written broadly on social development issues in Latin America and the Caribbean and on development issues in Cuba.

Jorge F. Pérez-López

An international economist residing in the Washington, D.C., area, Jorge F. Pérez-López is the author of *Cuba's Second Economy: From Behind the Scenes to Center Stage* (Transaction Publishers, 1995), coeditor of *Perspectives on Cuban Economic Reforms* (Arizona State University Press, 1998), and coauthor of *Conquering Nature: The Environmental Legacy of Socialism in Cuba* (University of Pittsburgh Press, 2000). He received a Ph.D. in economics from the State University of New York at Albany in 1974.

Brian H. Pollitt

An Honorary Senior Research Fellow of the Faculty of Social Sciences at Glasgow University, Brian H. Pollitt has studied Cuban agriculture in general and the sugar economy in particular since 1963. His work is based on extensive fieldwork in field and factory, most recently in 1994, 1996, and 2002 with the support of the Carnegie Trust, the Nuffield Foundation, and Glasgow University and with the collaboration of the Cuban Ministry of Sugar (MINAZ). His publications include "The Cuban Sugar Economy in the Soviet Era and After" (with G. B. Hagelberg), *Cambridge Journal of*

Economics 18 (1994), and "The Cuban Sugar Economy: Collapse, Reform, and Prospects for Recovery," *Journal of Latin American Studies* 29 (1997).

Archibald R. M. Ritter

Arch Ritter is Professor of Economics and International Affairs at Carleton University, Ottawa, and chair of the Department of Economics. He has written on a variety of issues relating to development in a Latin American context. His works on Cuba include *The Economic Development of Revolutionary Cuba: Strategy and Performance* (Praeger, 1974) and *Cuba in the International System: Integration and Normalization* (Macmillan, 1995). He was an initiator as well as Canadian coordinator of the master's in economics program of Carleton University and the University of Havana.

Nicholas Rowe

Nicholas Rowe is former chair and current associate professor in the Department of Economics at Carleton University in Ottawa, where he is also associate dean on the faculty of Public Affairs and Management. He holds a Ph.D. in economics from the University of Western Ontario. Rowe has visited Cuba numerous times since 1993, mostly to teach macroeconomics for the economics program of Carleton University and the University of Havana. His research interests currently focus on monetary policy, with particular emphasis on the choice between fixed exchange rates and inflation targeting, and on the econometric analysis of inflation targeting regimes.

María Cristina Sabourin Jovel

María Cristina Sabourin Jovel completed undergraduate work at Karkov University in the Ukraine. She received a master's in economics through the economics program of Carleton University and the University of Havana and is completing a Ph.D. in economics at Carleton University, Ottawa. She is in the faculty of economics at the University of Havana and has taught courses on national accounting, public economics, microeconomics, and mathematical analysis. She has published a textbook in public economics, *Compendio de conferencias, economía del sector publico* (University of Havana Press, 2001).

Larry Willmore

An economist with the UN secretariat in New York City, Larry Willmore holds a bachelor's degree in history, with minors in philosophy and English, from the University of Nebraska-Lincoln; a master's degree in international affairs from Carleton University, Ottawa; and a doctorate in economics from the same institution. He has published widely in academic journals, often on aspects of Latin American industry and trade. Willmore lives with his wife, a Costa Rican anthropologist, in White Plains, New York. He and his family have lived in Chile, Brazil, Mexico, and Trinidad, where Willmore worked with the UN Economic Commission for Latin America and the Caribbean before being transferred to UN headquarters in 1994.

Ana Julia Yanes Faya

Ana Julia Yanes Faya is a Ph.D. candidate in economics at Carleton University, Ottawa. She holds an M.A. in economics from the program jointly administered by Carleton University and the University of Havana. From 1995 to 1997 she was a member of the board of directors of the Centro Félix Varela, a nongovernmental organization in Havana. She is currently working on a dissertation focused on the nonprofit sector as a supplier of economic assistance for development.

Index